Additional Praise for *Common Sense School Reform*:

"In this book, Rick Hess performs a valuable public service. His analysis of school reform is both thoughtful and provocative. His ideas on how to improve schools are welcome relief from the romantics and ideologues who dominate the national education debate."

—Tom Loveless, Senior Fellow and
Director, Brown Center on Education Policy, Brookings Institution

"Few will agree with everything that Frederick Hess asserts in this book. Many, like I, will think he is too hard on what he calls 'status quo reformers.' Nonetheless, the burden of proof is now shifted to those who would disagree with his main point: that widespread improvement in U.S. schools will remain a pipe dream without painful adjustments. An important contribution that will challenge school reformers."

—Ronald F. Ferguson, John F. Kennedy
School of Government, Harvard University

"With an insider's knowledge, and an outsider's vantage point, Hess questions old assumptions and prods the conventional wisdom on school reform. His arguments for radical change may leave some feeling uncomfortable, but you needn't agree with all of his characterizations to find his provocative observations an important contribution to the dialogue on public school improvement."

—Kim Smith, Co-Founder and
CEO of New Schools Venture Fund

Common Sense School Reform

Frederick M. Hess

palgrave
macmillan

COMMON SENSE SCHOOL REFORM
© Frederick M. Hess, 2004.

First published in 2004 by
PALGRAVE MACMILLAN™
First PALGRAVE MACMILLAN™ paperback edition: April 2006
175 Fifth Avenue, New York, N.Y. 10010 and
Houndmills, Basingstoke, Hampshire, England RG21 6XS.
Companies and representatives throughout the world.

PALGRAVE MACMILLAN is the global academic imprint of the Palgrave Macmillan division of St. Martin's Press, LLC and of Palgrave Macmillan Ltd. Macmillan® is a registered trademark in the United States, United Kingdom and other countries. Palgrave is a registered trademark in the European Union and other countries.

ISBN 1–4039–7310–5 paperback

Library of Congress Cataloging-in-Publication Data

Hess, Frederick M.
    Common sense school reform / Frederick M. Hess.
        p. cm.
    Includes bibliographical references and index.
    ISBN 1–4039–7310–5
        1. School improvement programs—United States. 2. Educational
    accountability—United States. I. Title.

LB2822.82.H49 2004
371.2—dc22   2003190057

A catalogue record for this book is available from the British Library.

Design by Newgen Imaging Systems (P) Ltd., Chennai, India.

First PALGRAVE MACMILLAN paperback edition: April 2006

10 9 8 7 6 5 4 3 2 1

Printed in the United States of America.

To Cecia, Suzanne, Joleen, and Grandma, my very
own founts of common sense

Contents

Acknowledgments

This book seeks to highlight important truths that too often get lost amid the jargon, bickering, and banalities that dominate talk about school reform. As I fear the result may ruffle a few feathers, I want to be especially careful about how I acknowledge those individuals who have been kind enough to help me out in the course of writing it.

Some of those who have shared thoughts or provided assistance will disagree with much, or all, of what I argue here. The fact that someone is thanked below in no way implies that they have endorsed any part of the argument, only that they have been generous with their time or knowledge.

I owe a debt to those friends and colleagues who have helped shape my thinking upon these questions or have provided more material assistance. In particular, I'd like to thank Steve Adamowski, Julian Betts, Mike Casserly, Chris Cross, Jacquelyn Davis, Dick Elmore, Bill Evers, Checker Finn, Steve Fleischman, Jim Fraser, John Gardner, Dan Goldhaber, Jay Greene, Jane Hannaway, Kati Haycock, Bryan Hassel, Jeff Henig, Paul Hill, David Imig, Rick Kahlenberg, Dan Katzir, Wendy Kopp, Hank Levin, Keke Liu, Tom Loveless, Kathy Madigan, Bruno Manno, Don McAdams, Sara Mead, Terry Moe, Howard Nelson, Paul Peterson, Mike Petrilli, Mike Podgursky, Diane Ravitch, Nina Rees, Michelle Rhee, Andy Rotherham, Mary Ann Schmitt, John Schnur, Kim Smith, David Steiner, Sandy Stotsky, Tom Toch, Kate Walsh, Marty West, John Witte, and Pat Wolf. I'd particularly like to thank Alan Bersin, Dennis Doyle, William Howell, Cathy Mincberg, Abby Thernstrom, Stephen Thernstrom, and Joanne Weiss for having taken the time to read earlier drafts of the manuscript and provide thoughtful feedback.

This book draws upon a variety of research and scholarship I have pursued in the past ten years. Those efforts have been generously supported by a number of funders, including the National Science Foundation, the Spencer Foundation, the Mellon Foundation, the Bradley Foundation, the Bodman

Foundation, the Broad Foundation, the Progressive Policy Institute, the Olin Foundation, and the Program on Education Policy and Governance at Harvard University's Kennedy School of Government. I have also benefited from the opportunity to present elements of the argument at various scholarly and popular forums and would like to thank the attendees at those events for their thoughts and suggestions.

I owe a debt of gratitude to Andrew Kelly, Emily Kluver, and Brett Friedman for their invaluable assistance and tireless support. I'd also like to thank Joleen Okun for her assiduous proofreading and Dave Walsh, Dave Romano, Kim Hazen, Sharon Herraty, Scott Orenstein, Heidi Sprang, Mason Mattox, Sanford Hess, Cheryl Baron, and Loren Baron for their moral support.

I'd particularly like to express my appreciation to the American Enterprise Institute for providing the warmest, most nurturing intellectual environment I could imagine.

Finally, I'd like to thank my editor at Palgrave, David Pervin, for his steadfast support and invaluable counsel. I'd also like to thank Melissa Nosal and Donna Cherry for their editorial and production work on the book.

Preface

This book was written in response to a question. The question was posed by a good friend, the superintendent of a midsized school district.

We were eating a good dinner at a local steakhouse. I'd been giving him a hard time about his school reform plan, and finally he said, "Look, you're the guy who wrote the book saying that urban reform never amounts to squat. You've got the Harvard Ph.D. You get to visit all these districts and poke around. So what you would do if you were in my shoes?"

"Well, it's tough to say," I waffled.

"Uh-uh," he smiled. "Come on. What would you do?"

"Fine," I said. "I'll tell you. But you'll be disappointed. All I've got to offer is common sense. I sure didn't need a Ph.D. to figure it out."

I told him that all the pedagogical and curricular tweaking that so concerned him was nothing but a distraction because his system itself was dysfunctional. I told him that the first steps in real improvement had little to do with instruction and a lot to do with sensible management.

I told him that the very design of his school system fostered incompetence and that no amount of new spending, professional development, or instructional refinement would change that. I told him that for all their good intentions, his civic partners, expert consultants, and site-based committee members were probably doing more harm than good. And I said these truths went overlooked year after year because reformers kept approaching school improvement as a matter of educational expertise rather than common sense.

"It's not that improving professional development or pushing for small high schools are bad ideas," I said. "It's just that you're busy tidying up the living room while the foundation is shaking and the walls are crumbling. You can do these instructional and curricular things too, but you've got to tackle first things first."

As we paid the bill that night, he said, "You should put this out there. You should write down what you just told me."

"I don't know, it's pretty bloody simple," I said.

"It is," he agreed. "I think some of it's too simple and I'm not sure about the rest of it, but it's something the folks in the community and the schools should hear. I've got a shelf of books on school reform in the office, but there's not one that says what you just did."

I thought about that for awhile and decided he was right. Palgrave Macmillan was kind enough to publish the result. I hope you find it worth your while.

*   *   *

As a former teacher and education professor, I'd prefer to spend my time talking about pedagogy and the possibilities of a new century rather than common sense management. The explosion of tools for instruction, communication, and assessment provide rich opportunities for invention. Unfortunately, as I find myself saying over and over, "We'd all like to talk about the possibilities of twenty-first century schooling, but first we need to drag our schools into the twentieth century." So that's what this book is about.

Education is so wracked by sentiment that the most inane phrases pass for wisdom. Aspirations like "every child deserves a great teacher" and "all schools should be palaces" have come to serve as comforting, meaningless talismans. These sticky banalities have smothered tough-minded reform while convincing us that school improvement is a question of soulfulness. The noble ambition of these clichés has itself served as an excuse for disappointing results.

The thing is that good intentions do not excuse incompetence. Schools exist for the kids and the kids need to learn. They need us to teach them. They don't need good intentions, fancy language, or high-minded promises.

After all, as I used to tell my university students, education is the only public service where we shape the heart and mind of our citizenry, day by day and child by child. Every other service, no matter how essential, whether health care or environmental protection, is about improving and protecting the world around us. Education is about forming the very minds that will constitute our nation.

Given the realities of public life, it can be hard for officials to step away from the legislative battles long enough to rethink the world they know. For reformers and educators caught up in the whirlwind of practice, it is easy to get preoccupied by the latest proposals and turn away from more profound challenges.

We cannot continue to avert our eyes. I write this book to prod common-sense reformers to stay focused on the real issues, to remind status quo reformers that the horse should come before the cart, and to convince you, dear reader, that there is a simple, sensible course that can help provide all of our children with the schools they deserve.

CHAPTER ONE

Introduction

Common sense is not so common.

—Voltaire

School reform is the province of utopians, apologists, and well-intentioned practitioners who inhabit a cloistered world where conviction long ago displaced competence. For too long we have permitted this phalanx of thinkers and advocates to trample common sense beneath jargon, grandiose schemes, and earnest aspirations. The result is schools in which success is often a happy accident, the notion of professional responsibility is attacked as anti-education, and the doors of opportunity are slammed on tens of millions of America's children. Those eager to advance their interests and ideologies have seized the banner of "public education" and used it to repeatedly knock aside calls for serious reform. Meanwhile, those who question school performance or the promise of new educational recipes are skewered as enemies of public education. Somehow, the public nature of schooling and its centrality to our democratic way of life have fostered the notion that reforms must pass muster with utopian education theorists. It is time, indeed, it is long past time, to recapture our nation's schools from the wide-eyed dreamers and to imbue education reform with the simple discipline of common sense.

The United States boasts the world's highest per capita income and one of the best-funded school systems, yet our children fall below international norms in graduation rates and test performance. Though born with significant advantages, U.S. students lose ground during their years in school. While our 9-year-olds score above international norms, our 13-year-olds slip below average, and our 17-year-olds avoid the bottom only by eking past nations like South Africa, Cyprus, and Lithuania.[1]

Researchers have estimated that in 2001 just 32 percent of all 18-year-olds graduated from high school with basic literacy skills and having completed the courses needed to attend a four-year college. The comparable figure was just 20 percent of all African American youth and 16 percent of Latino youth.[2] In 2001, the national high school graduation rate was just 69 percent. It was 51 percent for African Americans and 52 percent for Hispanics.[3]

The 2003 National Assessment of Educational Progress (NAEP), the only national assessment of student performance, found that just 31 percent of fourth-graders and 32 percent of eighth-graders were "proficient" in reading and that fully 37 percent of fourth-graders and 26 percent of eighth-graders scored "below basic." On the 2003 NAEP mathematics exam, just 32 percent of fourth-graders and 29 percent of eighth-graders were "proficient" in math, while 23 percent of fourth-graders and 32 percent of eighth-graders performed at a level that was "below basic."[4] While these results are troubling enough, those for minority populations and urban school systems are horrifying. Sixty percent of black fourth-graders and 56 percent of Hispanic fourth-graders failed to demonstrate even "basic" reading skills, while 46 percent of black fourth-graders and 38 percent of Hispanic fourth-graders had not mastered even "basic" math skills.[5] For 2002, six cities reported NAEP reading scores: Atlanta, Los Angeles, Washington, D.C., New York, Chicago, and Houston. In each, more than half of the fourth-graders scored at "below basic" on the reading exam. In Atlanta, the figure was 65 percent at "below basic." In Chicago, it was 66 percent; Los Angeles, 67 percent.[6] Too many students are unprepared for the world they will enter, jeopardizing their futures and undermining our shared community.

In 2002, three-quarters of employers expressed serious doubts about the basic skills of public school graduates in the areas of spelling, grammar, and writing clearly, and more than 60 percent reported that public school graduates had fair or poor math skills. Perhaps more surprising is that college professors, teaching a self-selected group of the nation's graduates, expressed similar concerns at almost identical rates.[7] These impressions are consistent with test results. Researchers have found that 25 percent of *college-bound* high schoolers can't name the ocean that separates the United States from Asia and that 80 percent don't know that India is the world's most populous democracy.[8] According to the 2001 NAEP, 65 percent of U.S. high school seniors did not know the primary subject of the Bill of Rights, and 69 percent did not know the purpose of NATO. Among eighth-graders, only 35 percent knew the meaning of Jim Crow laws and just 29 percent could provide even a partial explanation of the checks and balances in the Constitution.[9]

Of course, there are always scattered glimmers of progress amid this disturbing reality. There are many exceptional schools and school districts across the nation. Federal, state, and local officials routinely take pains to tout the progress they have made, point out this promising trend, or highlight that innovative program. Their enthusiastic promises and uplifting anecdotes are cheerful sparks that too often distract us from the dismal landscape. As Don McAdams, President of the Center for Reform of School Systems has noted, "Even the best-run school districts are still dysfunctional organizations." The truth is that our nation's schools today fail to fulfill their essential obligation and only forceful action will reverse this state of affairs.

There are a number of nonschool changes that might improve the lives of children and boost their academic success. Better child nutrition, heightened parental involvement, more stable families, cleaner air, improved health care, safer streets, expanded library service, more extensive after-school programs, or more engaged civic leadership would all help. School reformers like Monty Neill, executive director of FairTest, complain, "No one is addressing the poverty that makes it difficult for so many children to learn in school. Housing, nutrition, and medical programs are being cut at both the state and federal levels."[10] When discussion of school improvement meanders into these issues, however, it is easy to drift from tackling the education problems we can address to bewailing larger questions that schools are ill-equipped to manage. Social issues such as economic or racial inequality have a tremendous impact on children's opportunities and life chances, but it is unhelpful to allow school reform to dissipate into musings on tax policy, public housing, welfare reform, medical care, or criminal justice. We do not improve medical care by fretting that more educated adults are generally healthier. While that disparity is real, sensible efforts to improve medical care focus on what doctors, hospitals, and health policymakers can do rather than grandiose strategies to promote college attendance. While there are a number of broad social changes that would improve education outcomes, school reform cannot and should not be about a utopian agenda of "social justice." School reform should be about reinventing and improving schooling.

Among the institutions of a civilization, schools have a limited but crucial role. Churches tend to the spirit. Hospitals serve the body. Universities promote inquiry. Police maintain order. Armed forces protect the nation's borders. Courts administer justice. Schools inform and train young minds. Before all else, this means that schools must ensure that children master the essential skills of civilization: most notably literacy and numeracy, but also a broad understanding of history and the sciences and a grasp of the rights and responsibilities of citizens in their community and nation.

These are the gatekeeper skills. Mastering these ensures that children are at least minimally equipped to pursue schooling or secure employment, frame and express their thoughts, and participate in their local and national communities. Providing that opportunity is the absolute minimum a democratic nation owes its children in the twenty-first century. As one assistant superintendent grumbled to me after protestors complained that the Texas state tests didn't fully reflect what students needed to know, "Hell, if the kids couldn't pass the [state achievement] test, it meant they lacked basic skills. They couldn't read, couldn't write a sentence. Kids like that aren't going anywhere. Period." Of course, these essential skills are not the end-all and be-all of schooling. These skills are only a beginning, but they are a crucial beginning. While many high-minded reformers correctly caution that it's not enough to just teach the gatekeeping skills, each year more than a million children leave high school without mastering them. As long as that is true, educational equity and social equality will remain a distant dream.

Research tells us that schools account for only a portion of student performance, with the rest driven by home and family life. Some reformers seize upon the importance of parents and families to such an extent that they get distracted from the need to improve schooling. Steps that increase parental involvement are desirable. The task for school reformers, however, is not to pursue grandiose social engineering but to help schools do their share. Common sense dictates that if schools do their share, it is more than enough to ensure that every high school graduate is, at the very least, literate and numerate and equipped with the basic knowledge and skills needed to open the doors of opportunity. Unfortunately, too many well-meaning professional educators reject this simple dictum. Marilyn Cochran-Smith, the 2004 president of the American Educational Research Association, has declared, "Teachers alone, whether through individual or group efforts, [cannot] alter the life chances of the children they teach, particularly if the larger issues of structural and institutional racism and inequality are not addressed."[11]

Unfortunately, seduced by their own jargon and noble intentions, educational "experts" lose sight of the simple truth that schools and teachers can indeed make a difference. Influential education reform gurus like Michael Fullan, professor of education at the University of Toronto, begin with the sensible observation that student learning is influenced by broader social conditions and wind up concluding, "We are talking about the larger social agenda of creating learning societies. The focus of change must be on all agencies and their interrelationships."[12] By defining school reform this broadly, educationists let schools and educators off the hook, muddy the issue, and set the stage for lingering paralysis. These arcane conversations have permitted schooling to remain the preserve of a cloistered band of guildsmen isolated from the sharp eye of good sense. When critiquing this status quo, reformers fall into the trap of debating the guild members in their own indecipherable terms, yielding jargon-laden debates that only the experts can follow. My aim is to step back, gain the clarity of perspective, and subject schooling to the steely gaze of common sense.

When America works, which it does ridiculously well and with remarkable consistency from any historical perspective, it is almost always because we stumble into arrangements that use and cultivate the same simple virtues. Whether one considers personal computing, higher education, professional athletics, financial services, health care, cinema, or steel production, Americans have been well-served when arrangements have summoned entrepreneurial energy, opened the door to talented and motivated practitioners, spurred creative thinking, rewarded hard work, created room for innovation, and managed to select out the ill-equipped or ineffective. We have suffered, in these sectors and elsewhere, when self-indulgent monopolists, influence-peddling corporations, overreaching attorneys, or overzealous regulators have stifled the accountability, flexibility, and competition that nurture excellence.

A Culture of Incompetence

Even a glancing familiarity with our nation's schools can leave one gaping at a system seemingly designed to frustrate competence. Teachers are hired, essentially for life, through drawn-out recruiting processes that pay little attention to merit and alienate many highly qualified candidates. Little or nothing about teachers' or administrators' performance affects their career prospects or job security. Educators who propose new approaches or new efficiencies are treated with suspicion by district officials and must run a gauntlet of official and cultural resistance in order to try anything new. There is little systemic recognition for excellent educators, while pay, perks, and assignments are distributed primarily on the basis of longevity. The result is a culture of public schooling in which educators learn to keep their heads down, play defense, and avoid causing waves. It is incredibly difficult and expensive to fire a teacher, even when they use classroom Internet access to view pornography at their desk or possess drugs on campus.[13] Districts tuck failed principals into lifetime positions in the bureaucracy where they draw salaries of $70,000 or $90,000 a year to manage ineffectual training programs, supervise school safety, or tackle other jobs for which they often have no particular knack.

We have a teaching profession designed in accord with the practices of an earlier, industrial era. We treat teachers like assembly-line workers, with mandated training of little value, no rewards for excellence, and little opportunity for career advancement. Staff assignment to schools and classrooms, due to collective bargaining dictates and established norms, is routinely driven by seniority rather than suitability or merit. Teacher unions and the education schools have fought to erect stiff barriers that control who may enter the teacher workforce. The result is that we attract too many clock punchers, alienate many of our best teachers who are frustrated that their efforts are not compensated, and make it hard to either reward or punish teachers for the work they do.

School leadership has been conceived as an exercise in managed mediocrity. We select and train leaders with little attention to crucial skills, shy away from those with unconventional backgrounds, place them in a ghetto isolated from the world of management, and fail to hold them accountable. Principals have little control over who teaches in their schools and cannot compensate teachers based on their performance or the scarcity of their skills. Not only do they have little leeway to fire ineffective teachers, but standardized pay scales based entirely on experience and degrees mean that principals can't even deny raises to ineffective teachers.

Rules, procedures, and collective bargaining agreements have rendered public school systems heavy-footed and sluggish. Federal laws and court decisions governing special education, student discipline, and disadvantaged students have resulted in the creation of paper-heavy bureaucracies. State regulations on a litany of issues such as teacher hiring, class size, administrative qualifications, funding, school construction, and textbook acquisition have tied the hands of school and district leaders. Collective bargaining agreements adopt seniority-based pay scales, make it hard to fire or even reassign employees, minutely govern the workday, and wind up issuing rules on most everything that the state or federal authorities have not already regulated.

A World That Once Made Sense

Our schools look this way because the arrangements once made sense. In a world where most students went on to work in factories or other blue-collar jobs, it was enough if schools kept children occupied and educated the priv-ileged. When schools had a captive teaching force of talented women and African Americans, it made sense to limit entry to the profession and encour-age teachers to stay put for their entire careers. When it was difficult to rap-idly collect and analyze solid information on student learning, it was reasonable to compensate educators without regard to student performance and to protect them from being capriciously fired.

The world has changed. A changing economy requires that all students master skills once restricted to the elite. The assurance that talented women and minority college graduates will choose teaching due to a lack of viable options is long past. Many of these individuals who would have made ster-ling teachers in an earlier age now have the freedom to become astronauts, attorneys, accountants, and aerospace engineers. Schools compete for increasingly mobile workers in a labor market filled with tens of millions of white-collar jobs that beckon to potential teachers. Advances in technology and testing have made accountability and information available in a manner unimaginable even fifteen years ago.

Yet, while the world has changed, our schools have not. Why is that? The answer is rather simple: those who would bear the brunt of change do not desire it. Workers anywhere are products of the work culture they inhabit. If their professional world lacks clear objectives and if the tools of authoritative leadership are absent, they will romanticize ambiguity and consensus. If their world tolerates mediocrity and punishes risk-takers, the mediocre will flour-ish and the ranks of the entrepreneurial will be thinned with time. If employ-ees hold lifetime positions and are insulated from management's scrutiny or ire, the work culture they construct will come to seem an unyielding and inescapable reality of the profession. Pursuing change in this cozy world by exhorting timid, consensus-loving souls to envision a bold and uncertain tomorrow is not a winning strategy. Real reform, sensible reform, must begin by tipping this world so that authoritative leadership is possible without con-sensus, mediocrity becomes a vice, and entrepreneurship becomes a badge of honor. Reformers must remove the protections that buffer failure and, in so doing, strip away the presumption that culture is an unyielding primal force immune to determined leadership.

The task of commonsense school reform, then, is not to find villains, revisit the history of American education, or take sides in broad ideological conflicts. It is to tip the world of schooling. This is not a book about how to launch more scattered sparks of excellence. It is a book about how we fan the flames of systemic competence. It seeks to answer one simple question: *How does one build such a system?*

Two Kinds of Reformers

There are two kinds of reformers in American education: the "status quo reformers" and the "commonsense reformers." The status quo reformers have called the shots for decades.

Status Quo Reform

The "status quo reformers" believe that the nation's millions of teachers and administrators are already doing the best they can and the only way to improve America's schools is to provide more money, expertise, training, and support. Status quo reformers run the school systems, fill the schools of education, lead the professional associations, and dominate the education bureaucracies. Status quo reformers squint at our stunted system of schooling and, unable to imagine fundamentally different arrangements, allow the status quo to define the possible.

Status quo reformers are all for reform so long as it changes nothing of consequence. Status quo reformers are happy to dabble in curricular and pedagogical reforms but shy from real changes in job security, accountability, or anything else that would fundamentally change schooling. In the difficult-to-parody prose of one best-selling education reform author, "Productive educational change at its core, is not the capacity to implement the latest policy, but rather the ability to survive the vicissitudes of planned and unplanned change while growing and developing."[14] Some status quo reformers, like the unions, are guided by simple self-interest in rejecting such change. Others, like highly-touted reform gurus, seek to avoid conflict and to improve schools through painless measures that don't ruffle too many feathers, keep business humming, and allow them to rise to prominence as temperate consensus builders. Still others, like widely read education professors Michael Apple or Henry Giroux, assail efforts to make schools accountable as a racist, capitalist assault on their private world.

Though the fundamental problem is our toleration of incompetence, status quo reformers fuzz the issue by cloaking the status quo in the language of "reform." They suggest lots of "reforms," most accompanied by a demand for more spending. Their solution is to suggest more of the same. They recycle various proposals for professional development, curriculum, pedagogy, and school organization in a variety of pleasing packages while loudly explaining how *this* time they have finally latched onto the idea that will change everything. Status quo reformers imagine that we can drive widespread improvement without having to tackle structural problems if only we make schools smaller, raise teacher pay, shrink class sizes, supply new and improved professional development, develop new civic partnerships, buy more and better textbooks, address racism more forcefully, modernize school facilities, use the "right" pedagogies and curricula, buy more computers, have schools start later, give parents more say in school management, give teachers more say in school management, or adopt any other number of proposals touted by experts and advocates. It's not that any of these proposals are necessarily bad ideas. Many of the suggestions are good ones. The problem is that they too often serve as distractions from the harsh discipline of more common-sensical reforms.

Status quo reformers insist that incentives and accountability will only distract educators. "Oh, sure," status quo reformers allow, "there may be individual teachers who are ineffective. But they are the exception. The solution is to make sure that all teachers are as professional as the 99 percent who are slaving away every day." Status quo reformers assume educators are already doing all they can; improvement is just a question of tinkering with school or class size, adding a dab of this curricula, or tossing in a dash of that training. They seek to create more "rewarding" school cultures by tiptoeing around the status quo and without ever acknowledging structural problems with accountability, incentives, and management. Ultimately, all of the "reforms" touted by status quo reformers don't change anything that matters.

While status quo reformers share a common confidence that the "right" kind of tinkering will suffice to drive improvement, they routinely disagree as to just what the proper remedies are. Some status quo reformers think middle schools need to be more academic, some that they need to be less academic, others call for creating more specialty high schools, while others insist that high schoolers need a common academic experience. Status quo reformers offer various prescriptions for how we should provide for students with special needs, manage school discipline, group students, or integrate music and art into schooling. They have been offering endlessly evolving guidance on all of these matters for decades, some of it for close to a century. The primary result has been a gradual accumulation of one once-popular reform atop another, littering schools and districts with fragments of half-for-gotten initiatives and leaving educators skeptical of new proposals. Again, the problem is not necessarily with the advice itself. There are probably some schools and some students for which almost any of these conflicting recommendations make sense. The problem is that each of these remedies permits reformers to skitter away from the hard realities of a broken system, allowing them to feel productive even as they churn their way through one reform after another and avoid the unpalatable course of commonsense restructuring.

Commonsense Reform

Commonsense reformers know that school cultures and practices are critical but that cultures are not changed by wishful thinking and that no one approach is a silver bullet. Commonsense reformers recognize the merit of many status quo suggestions, but believe that these proposals hold little promise if they forestall necessary, painful reform by buying off frustrated constituents with shiny new promises and programs. They see status quo reforms as tangential to the real work at hand and too often an excuse for inaction. Commonsense reform provides a foundation upon which any number of pedagogical and instructional approaches can comfortably rest, but without which systemic excellence will prove illusory.

Commonsense reform is straightforward. It focuses on two precepts: accountability and flexibility. Centuries of experience in fields from architecture to zoology tell us that people work harder, smarter, and more efficiently when they are rewarded for doing so; that they can get lazy or distracted when left to their own devices; that people do their best work when goals are clear and they know how they'll be evaluated; and that smart, educated, motivated people will find ways to succeed. Commonsense reform sets as its guiding beacon the goal of constructing a culture of competence in schools: a culture where success is expected, excellence is rewarded, and failure is not tolerated.

The commonsense reformer assumes that educators, for better or worse, are a lot like everybody else. Some educators are passionately committed to their craft, highly skilled, and will be so regardless of rewards or guidance, but most—like most engineers and attorneys and journalists and doctors—will be more effective when held accountable for performance, when rewarded for excellence, and when given the opportunities to devise new paths to success. Commonsense reformers do not imagine that educators are motivated only, or even primarily, by material benefits. Nothing in commonsense reform suggests that intrinsic rewards are unimportant. As Thomas J. Peters and Robert Waterman noted twenty years ago in their best-selling *In Search of Excellence*, "People must believe that a task is inherently worthwhile if they really are to be committed to it."[15] Employees are most productive when they believe in the importance of their work and when the organization fosters conditions that support intrinsic motivation. Commonsense reformers do not seek to replace passion, but to reinforce it and provide new opportunities for educators to shape schools, instruct, mentor, and contribute. Commonsense reformers seek only to ensure that those who excel in these varied roles are recognized and rewarded. In the jargon of organizational reform, they seek to align intrinsic incentives with the extrinsic.

Good teachers and doctors and journalists are motivated by pride and passion and purpose. Commonsense reform cultivates these, not with empty words but by aggressively recruiting, recognizing, and rewarding them. Americans are comfortable with the notion that good doctors or mechanics can do well by doing good. Rewarding hard work, ingenuity, and excellence is sensible, not odious. In fact, treating the doctor who does not heal just like one with a gift for healing would be thought a dubious course. A commonsense reformer believes that rewarding educators for serving students is both sensible and ethical.

The commonsense reformer knows that great schools are not legislated into existence. Great schools, like any great enterprise, are the product of genius, hard work, commitment, and skill. They require nuanced leadership that forges a sense of shared purpose, rewards creative thinking, and inspires excellence. Public policy cannot mandate great schools any more than it can mandate great leadership or great teaching; it can only make it easier or harder for great schools to exist. Such schools are more likely when creative and energetic educators find it easy to build programs, recruit like-minded educators, and enjoy their work. Commonsense reformers do not imagine that any reform proposal can ensure great teaching, great leadership, or great schools. Instead, commonsense reform aims to create school systems where a culture of competence can readily flourish, always recognizing that this is but a first step in providing the schools our children deserve.

The Commonsense Prescription

The dictionary tells us that reform means to remove defects, to form again. School reform means to reinvent schools to address defects—to make schools more effective. This is not accomplished by playful dabbling with fancy new curricula, training programs, or parent advisory councils. It is not accomplished by gentle tinkering. Serious reform requires transforming the "can't do" culture that holds sway in schooling into a culture of competence. Doing this requires rethinking everything—including who should be running schools, who schools hire, how schools are staffed, how performance is recognized and rewarded, how ineffective employees are removed, how services like information management and human resources operate, and how money is spent. When status quo reformers go into schools, however, they skirt these contentious topics and focus on using professional development, new curricular suggestions, and pedagogical proposals to help current personnel improve without any painful dislocation. In fact, absent accountability for outcomes or substantial operational flexibility, educational leaders have shown a predilection to pursue a series of shallow and inconsequential innovations.

This is the flaw in the status quo approach. In any line of work, most employees will resist changes that hold them newly accountable, force them to change routines, or threaten their jobs or wages. The way we overcome this resistance is not by pleasing but by making action less painful than inaction. That is the power of accountability. Accountability rewards excellence and penalizes failure. Sustained mediocrity becomes a career killer. Hunger for security, recognition, opportunity, and the fruits of success support a steady demand for improvement.

Flexibility is the flip side of accountability. Chasing improvement requires that managers and workers have the freedom to reward excellence, remedy failure, experiment, and work creatively. Flexibility provides the tools to manage effectively, build teams, govern schools and classrooms, and reward those who take on oversized challenges or put forth exceptional efforts. Of course, there's a need for sensible oversight and regulation since, people being what they are, some may take shortcuts or shortchange their charges. However, sensible regulation doesn't require setting narrow rules as to who is permitted to seek work, how to staff schools, or how to pay employees. It doesn't mean telling professionals how many computers to buy or how many assistant principals they need. It requires only that we ensure that schools are educating effectively, serving community needs, and being fiscally responsible.

The case for accountability-backed flexibility in education is not a sentimental defense of localized control or a zealous appeal to some mythic notion of the market. Rather, it is a clear-eyed response to a century's worth of lessons in such fields as hospital administration, environmental regulation, public safety, postal reform, welfare, mass transit, higher education, and military operations. In case after case, efforts to shape more flexible and responsive policies have produced better results than have centralized and standardized rules. The commonsense approach is to embrace those simple virtues that promote a culture of competence. Commonsense reform permits those making decisions to make full use of their knowledge of the teacher, student, and school; takes advantage of goodwill and intrinsic motivation while recognizing that these are not sufficient to meet the needs of the 50 million children in our public schools; attracts motivated practitioners and problem-solvers; encourages entrepreneurship; empowers accountable educators to make informed decisions about cost-effective service provision; weeds out ineffective educators and managers; and recognizes that the world is a complex place where crude rules are often problematic. Unfortunately, blinded by their commitment to what they misleadingly term "compassionate reforms," status quo reformers frequently respond with overwrought claims that accountability and flexibility entail "scapegoating those who labor in America's schools" or "treat[ing] educators as if they were unskilled hacks."[16]

Commonsense reform is manifestly *not* about punishing educators. In fact, it rests on the same ancient and time-tested pillars as American democracy itself. One of these is pragmatic James Madison's wry admonition in the *Federalist Papers*, "If men were angels, no government would be necessary." Angels do the right thing and resist temptations because...well, because they're angels. However, while it's painful to admit, we know that everyone isn't an angel. If we can get people to do the right things for the wrong reasons, we figure that's good enough. In fact, that's not a bad adage for how our pragmatic, imperfect, frustrating nation works—a bunch of people who often do the right thing, often for the wrong reasons. A second pillar is Alexis de Tocqueville's famed observation in *Democracy in America* that the wellspring of American community and democracy is "self-interest properly understood." Tocqueville saw that the genius of the United States didn't rest on the exceptional virtue of its individual citizens, but on the young nation's ability to encourage typical people to identify their self-interest with that of the larger community and to summon the best within them by appealing to "selfishness."

The American system of checks and balances, protected liberties, and democratic government is rooted in the conviction that a free people are served best when they need not trust too much to the good intentions of public servants. The founders lodged the responsibility for writing laws in the legislative branch, for enforcing laws in the executive branch, and for interpreting the law in the judicial branch out of fear that concentrated power might pose a risk to our freedoms. Their handiwork rested on the assumption that it is not enough to trust human goodness and that it is foolhardy to trust overmuch in the imperfect virtue of man. Our democratic institutions tough-mindedly harness vices like ambition, skepticism, and greed so that these very frailties will motivate public servants to fulfill their duties. That great American tradition of tough-minded realism is the cornerstone of commonsense reform.

Look, let me be very clear. Commonsense reformers respect the romantic impulse in education. We know that schooling is the one institution of civilization where we not only shape the social arrangements in which we live but where we forge the hearts and minds that will create our shared future. Commonsense reform will not turn schools into callous factories of learning but rescue students and educators from a barren system in which excellence is a happy accident that results when fine teachers happen to cluster in pleasing environs. Because commonsense reformers embrace the sacred and democratic purposes of schooling, we believe educational excellence is too important to be left to good intentions and chance.

Becoming Intolerant of Failure

When he was chief of the U.S. Army, General Carl Vuono used to preach to the commanders of major Army units: "Poor training kills soldiers. If the American Army is not well trained, you can't blame it on Congress, you can't blame it on the media, you can't blame it on the mythical 'they.' It's your fault, your fault, your fault and my fault because we didn't do our job."[17] Where are such voices in schooling? Military leaders too would like more money. They too must make do with the available recruits, cope with political pressure, and endure public scrutiny. Yet they are expected to get the job done. Why do we accept anything less in schooling?

The unfortunate reality of the classroom is that educators work as efficiently, as thoughtfully, and as determinedly as they choose to.[18] If a teacher's child is sick and he rushes through grading a stack of essays, the students won't know, the principal won't know, and the parents won't know. If a math teacher plans poorly and, at the end of the year, winds up rushing through the most challenging units, the students can't tell, and no one else will know. In other lines of work, like journalism or engineering or law, professionals know that their work will be assessed. Historically, teachers have been largely left to their own devices, with the future of every child left utterly dependent on our unverified faith in each teacher's professionalism.

Officials shy away from necessarily harsh measures for fear of being labeled "anti-teacher" or "anti-education." This geniality has real victims—the children stuck in subpar schools. Being fair to children and to talented educators requires being firm with ineffective practitioners. This requires an unwavering commitment to excellence and not the kind of verbal gymnastics typified by the status quo education text, *No Quick Fixes*, which helpfully explains, "Failure is often viewed as the opposite of success."[19] (It's the "often" that makes the quote so much fun.)

We have too long allowed well-meaning but soft-hearted experts to define the easy road as good policy. Banalities like "We need a great teacher in every classroom" have been a distraction. They've served as placeholders while the experts keep promising that we'll turn the corner if we just follow the trail a little further. If we provide yet more money, hire more education school graduates, pay teachers more, make classes smaller still, change reading programs just one more time—if we'll just do this one thing . . . our schools will deliver. This is nonsense. Their trail has led us deeper into the forest. Every additional step we take is another we will have to retrace as we seek our way out. Good intentions aren't enough—not when they leave millions of children unprepared for life success and dependent on the goodwill of the teachers they happen to draw.

A commonsense reformer isn't arguing that teachers don't work hard enough (though some don't) or that schools need to be humiliated into performing (though some do). Commonsense reform honors educational expertise. The commonsense reformer simply believes that an effective education system rewards success, penalizes failure, and creates room for talented practice and then gets out of the way of practitioners.

Let us not delude ourselves. Commonsense reform won't do away with broken homes or stop some children from coming to school hungry. It won't put an end to student turnover that exceeds 50 percent a year in some urban schools. Commonsense reform will not perfect American society or eliminate the challenges that educators must wrestle with every day. What commonsense reform will do is ensure that schools are focused on educating all of our children. There will be many other battles to fight, but it is a disservice to our children to procrastinate on sensible measures while we debate grand philosophies of social justice or get distracted by clever new instructional methods.

Taking the Choice Out of Change

In 2002, New York City mayor Michael Bloomberg daringly announced his intention to take a personal role in transforming the city's schools. With broad political support, he recruited renowned attorney and former Clinton administration official Joel Klein to become chancellor of the New York City schools. In January 2003, Klein announced his intention to move aggressively, especially on the problem of school leadership in the city's most troubled schools. He boldly proposed inserting a clause to the new collective bargaining agreement being negotiated with the principals' union that would allow him to pay $25,000 bonuses to some of the city's best principals if they would accept reassignment to low-performing schools. His proposals won accolades from a variety of do-good groups. What happened?

By April 2003, the proposal was dead and the principals' new contract granted an 8 percent pay raise. The president of the principals' union had rejected any plan that paid some principals more than others and said it wasn't the right time to change administrative work rules. The interests of students were sacrificed to protect those of principals. Klein's eminently sensible attempt to reward excellence, create incentives, and compensate those willing to undertake particularly challenging jobs failed in the face of entrenched interests. This is tragic but not unusual.[20] Meanwhile, during the course of 2003, new initiatives included spending $43 million on parent coordinators at each school, $51 million to make schools smaller, and tens of millions of dollars on a controversial new reading initiative in the hope that enough tinkering and spending would yield excellence without ugly confrontations.

For decades, American schools have been constantly reforming without ever really changing. So long as we give veto power over change to those who like the status quo—the teachers, administrators, education schools, state bureaucrats, professors of education—we'll continue to avoid real change. The way to force wrenching change through is not by convincing these folks, but by leaving them no choice in the matter.

Like educational leaders, the heads of nonprofits and private sector firms like to avoid conflict and keep their employees happy. No executive wishes to inflict pain on her employees or stakeholders. Executives take such steps only under duress and only when self-preservation demands it. Today, success as a private sector CEO can require standing up to balky employees or making painful cuts in spending or the workforce. Why? If companies cave when they can't afford to, they get overtaken by competitors or booted by irate investors. In education today, we rarely exercise such discipline over school or school district leaders. Instead, they are buffeted by regulations, beseeched by employees, and petitioned by local interests. Undisciplined by the relentless pressure to improve performance or increase profitability, it is far too easy for leaders to simply oil the squeaky wheel, hail such moves as technically astute or efforts to "build consensus," and let the culture of incompetence drift along.

It's not a question of compelling managers or employees to work harder; it's about forcing managers and leaders to rethink systems and practices. Consider the Detroit automakers who fell upon hard times in the late 1970s. They had taken to producing oversized and poorly designed cars, had gotten lazy about quality control, had permitted costs and union contracts to spiral out of hand, and had added layer upon layer of middle management.

The emergence of fierce competition from Japanese firms and a dramatic loss of market share shocked these firms into action, as energetic new leadership rethought their product line, redesigned quality control, slashed middle management, and renegotiated contracts while cutting costs. The transformation was not about berating workers, but about requiring—not requesting, but requiring—those in charge to bite the bullet and make painful decisions and those below them to accept the changes.

The affiliates of the National Education Association (NEA) and the American Federation of Teachers (AFT) aren't unusual among their union brethren in having sought and won contracts that promote inefficiency, inflexibility, and mediocrity. Similar demands have plagued the airline industry, for instance, driving several airlines out of business or to the brink of bankruptcy. Teacher contracts are far from unique on this count—it's just that the absence of accountability has made it easier for district leaders to accept the status quo than to fight for change.

If a school district has lost students, it may be time to close some schools. If a popular reading program isn't producing results, teachers should be told to use another. If students enjoy electives but aren't mastering the essentials, popular choices may have to be cut. If a principal is well liked but the school isn't performing, she may have to be fired. In each case, the easier course is to avoid acting if at all possible. Forcing action requires making inaction unacceptable.

Status quo reformers spend their time pleading with educators to change because they imagine that appealing to the good natures of the well-intentioned is the only path to reform. They are mistaken. Accountable employees with clear goals find it suddenly much easier to forge the common purpose from which consensus naturally flows. Such environments attract committed employees and generate enthusiasm. Good organizations are marked by commitment and enthusiasm not by happy chance but because they are built to cultivate a culture of competence.

Many status quo reformers read management books authored by sports coaches, CEOs, or business school gurus and are taken by the emphasis on mind and heart and attitude. The difficulty for education reformers is that the gurus take for granted the ability of executives to hire their own people, put incentives in place, sack weak performers, and access the management tools they need. It's not that the management experts are wrong about the importance of communication, team-building, and culture; it's just that trying to mimic these without paying attention to the foundations is like trying to roof a house before the walls are in place.

The Status Quo Analysis

Status quo reformers believe that our nation's schools are basically doing okay, notwithstanding the fact that a third of fourth-graders can't read or do math at even a rudimentary level, only half of African American and Latino students graduate, and that just a third of 18-year-olds graduate high school fully prepared to attend a four-year college. Three education professors perfectly captured the status quo zeitgeist in a recent book, insisting, "Unlike many of the loud voices heard in the media, we believe that our educational system is not broken; instead, we recognize that some schools, some classrooms, and some children have complex issues that make learning difficult."[21]

Status quo reformers are certain that, if there are any problems in our schools, educators shouldn't be held responsible for them. After all, they explain, educators are already doing all they can. The blame for any "difficulties" is properly directed at a lack of money, a lack of support for teachers, a lack of parental or community involvement, or social inequities. The three professors I quoted a moment ago explain that the "complex" problems they identify can only be addressed if we are willing to make new and "significant investments of time and resources."[22] The status quo reformers claim it is unfair to expect results until schools have the resources they need, though the point of "sufficiency" somehow always recedes over the horizon.

Educators complain about "brutal" cuts whenever budgets are tightened. In early 2003, the heads of the nation's elementary and secondary principal interest groups took out a national advertisement to list the "painful" and "drastic" cuts taking place in some locales. They were aghast that, in some places, "teaching jobs are being eliminated when someone leaves," "assistant principalships are being made into part-time positions or eliminated," "guidance and behavioral counselors may be let go or be put on part-time status," "technology hardware and technology staff will be curtailed," and "field trips will be cut back or cut out... [and] bus routes will be eliminated." Trying to convey their shock, they noted, "One principal said that in 26 years as an educator this will be the first time he has to face a reduction in force in which teachers must be let go for budget reasons."[23] Only in education would layoffs be deemed revolutionary or cutbacks in hardware purchases thought unnatural.

The president of the NEA, the nation's largest teachers' union, with 2.7 million members, offered similar comments in his 2003 annual address. NEA President Reg Weaver listed "destructive" budget cutting that included bus service being discontinued for a thousand students in Oklahoma; cuts to music and arts classes in Indiana; pink slips for teachers in South Carolina; and reductions in after-school programs in California. Weaver never even entertained the thought that these cuts might be prudent or necessary, roaring that they demonstrated "that children, students and public education have yet to become our nation's priority!"[24]

While bemoaning inadequate resources and social inequities, educationists will claim to believe that all children can learn. But spend a few days at a school of education or at a professional education convention and it is clear that influential status quo reformers do not believe that all children will be able to master even basic skills until we reconstruct American society. Until the government provides every child with health care, decent housing, appropriate diets, and supportive families, only a handful of status quo reformers think it reasonable to demand that all children master essential skills.[25] Many suggest that school improvement must wait until we remake the nation's political economy through radical wealth redistribution and increased government spending. Influential status quo author Jean Anyon, a professor in the Department of Education at Rutgers University, argues in *Ghetto Schooling*, "Educational change in the inner city, to be successful, has to be part and parcel of more fundamental social change." Anyon calls for "an all-out attack on poverty and racial isolation" that requires new regulation of teachers, expanded social services, new federal and state spending on cities, a higher minimum wage, and "improved" teaching and learning. To fund all of this "school reform," she advocates cutting defense spending and agricultural subsidies, and imposing new taxes on corporations, Social Security, capital gains, and executive pay.[26] If this sounds more like a political platform than a serious proposal for school improvement, it is because many status quo reformers are ultimately more interested in social change than mundane questions like how to provide schools that promote quality teaching and learning.

More than a few status quo reformers regard schools as cudgels they can wield to expose America as a corrupt, racist, sexist, imperialist bully. The philosophy is generally a militant liberalism of the kind voiced by David Berliner, dean of the Arizona State University School of Education, who has explained, "United States [schools] will not improve in international standings until our terrible inequalities are fixed. The schools that serve our poorest children are not working well, but less criticism of those schools and more help for the neighborhoods and families they serve are in order.... Accountability programs won't change these realities at all."[27] As American Educational Research Association president Marilyn Cochran-Smith has conceded, "[Notions like] teaching for social justice, teaching for social change . . . and teaching to change the world . . . are based on the assumption that it is impossible to teach in ways that are *not* value-laden and ideological [italics in original]." Cochran-Smith forthrightly explains that she believes good teaching requires practitioners to become "activists based on political consciousness and on ideological and heart-felt commitment to diminishing the inequalities of American life."[28] The point here is not to critique the political ideology of the Anyons, Berliners, and Cochran-Smiths. They are entitled to their views. The commonsense concern, however, is that it is easy to become unserious about school performance and improvement when swept up in broader social agendas.

Not too long ago, a dean of a New Jersey school of education and new president of the American Association of Colleges of Teacher Education (the association of the nation's schools of education), explained to me: "School improvement takes time, and parents have to be patient. It may take twenty years in a troubled district like Newark."

"And in the meantime?" I asked. "What are those families to do? Are they just supposed to trust that the professionals will get it straight?"

"No, they should participate and help. But they need to be patient."

"So, they're just supposed to sit there and trust your experts to do the right thing while their children rot?" I asked.

She was shocked. "Of course not," she said. "I would never say that."

Status quo reformers carefully avoid confronting the logic of their position. It is true that some children have particularly daunting needs and that a few may be incapable of achieving even minimal standards. Status quo reformers seize this simple fact and proceed to argue that because educators do not all face identical challenges, they cannot reasonably be held responsible for the results of their work. Natural variation in student ability and unevenness in the allocation of resources become an all-purpose apologia for incompetence. The rationale for this is unclear. We don't imagine that different doctors, architects, attorneys, or accountants must confront identical challenges before we can evaluate their work or hold them accountable for it. It is no great feat to make allowances for relative levels of difficulty.

Ironically, it was Jonathan Kozol, much beloved by status quo reformers, who noted in another context "the tendency to label obvious solutions that might cost us something [as] unsophisticated." He further remarked upon the broad support for "diffuse solutions that will cost us nothing and, in any case, will not be implemented."[29] While Kozol was arguing that Americans are unwilling to pay the price tag of school improvement, we will shortly see that it is the status quo reformers who are unwilling to have educators or the education establishment bear the costs and dislocations required by commonsense reform.

Contrary to the claims of status quo reformers, the evidence suggests that well-run schools funded at today's levels can effectively educate poor children and serve as engines of social mobility. While family background is the single biggest influence on a child's educational success, there are thousands of private and public schools that enjoy great success educating low-income minority urban children and narrowing achievement gaps. It is possible to successfully educate disadvantaged populations with available resources. The respected left-leaning advocacy group Education Trust has highlighted thousands of schools that have enjoyed marked success educating disadvantaged populations.[30] The conservative Heritage Foundation has likewise documented the performance of high-poverty schools that produce impressive student results.[31] Operating on budgets equal to or less than the public school norm in their states, individual public schools like the KIPP Academies, Hi-Mount Elementary in Milwaukee, Hi Tech High in San Diego, and the Urban Academy in New York excel at educating disadvantaged populations on a daily basis.

Another example is provided by the nation's thousands of urban Catholic schools, which have enjoyed remarkable success serving poor, minority children while routinely spending no more than half as much per pupil as the local public schools. In fact, the average tuition at Catholic elementary schools is under $2,000 a year, only a fraction of what their public counterparts spend.[32] Nevertheless, working with limited resources, these schools have managed to provide orderly, effective educational environments. Despite outdated facilities, limited instructional resources, fewer support staff, and almost no educational technology, these schools have managed to graduate students and send them on to college at a much higher rate than other urban schools—*even after* taking into account student race, family background, and so on.[33]

When asked why we shouldn't demand that all schools perform like these, status quo reformers tell us we should be grateful for the scattered successes we enjoy and ought not expect more unless we're "willing to pay for it." How much do they seek? How much will be enough for them to have educators take responsibility for results? How high do they think taxes should be raised, how much more do they think they should receive at the expense of health care or homeland security or higher education? They don't say. In the professional education community's worldview, there is no "enough." And if spending rewards incompetence, pumps money into ineffective schools, or undercuts any pressure to spend wisely—what then? We only have so many public dollars to spend. Every dollar we spend on one service is a dollar we cannot spend on another. A particular irony, of course, is that status quo reformers like Anyon and Kozol are among the loudest voices demanding more money for social programs besides schooling. Like any other former teacher or education professor, I too want to provide schools with all the money they need. Yet it seems that a healthy balance must always be struck.

Gerald Bracey, author of *What You Should Know about the War against America's Public Schools*, has long maintained that we shortchange the public schools. In this recent book, he offers a few anecdotes about schools that are short of desks or chemicals for their chemistry labs, and then explodes, "As long as such conditions exist, how dare people say, 'Don't throw money at the schools?' Until poor students attend schools under conditions that middle-class students take for granted, such statements represent sheer and despicable hypocrisy. Right-wing critics have spread both the [idea that more money is not the answer] and the myth that we spend more than any other country through the popular culture."[34] In fact, every public service—from the Environmental Protection Agency to your local bus system—claims it needs more money to do its job. Such pleas do not constitute proof of need. The fact is that we spend a lot of money on K-12 education, even in the districts that Mr. Bracey regards as poor.

Mo' Money, Mo' Money, Mo' Money

The status quo reformers have been successful at getting pundits and politicians to accept as a given that our schools are woefully underfunded. Journalists skeptically raise their eyebrows when commonsense reformers suggest that America's schools already have the money they need. Governors across the nation brag of their commitment to pouring more money into schools. Courts in Nevada, Kentucky, New Jersey, New York, North Carolina, and elsewhere have ignored budgetary limits and ordered states to pour more money into schools—with little regard for how wisely the money was spent.[35]

There's one problem with this approach. By any reasonable standard, American schools are exceptionally well funded. In fact, it may surprise some to learn how U.S. education spending compares internationally—especially given that the United States tends to lag on international assessments. In 2000, the most recent year for which international comparisons are available, the Organization for Economic Cooperation and Development (OECD) calculated that the United States spent $6,995 per primary school student and $8,855 per secondary school student. This was significantly more than any other industrial democracy, including those famous for the generosity of their social programs. On a per-pupil basis, the United States spent on primary education 66 percent more than Germany, 56 percent more than France, 27 percent more than Japan, 80 percent more than the United Kingdom, 10 percent more than Sweden, 62 percent more than Belgium, 62 percent more than Finland, and 122 percent more than South Korea. At the secondary school level, on a per-pupil basis, the United States spent 30 percent more than Germany, 16 percent more than France, 41 percent more than Japan, 48 percent more than the United Kingdom, 40 percent more than Sweden, 29 percent more than Belgium, 45 percent more than Finland, and 118 percent more than South Korea. In fact, of all the world's nations, only Denmark equaled U.S.'s per-pupil spending on primary education and only Switzerland did in the case of secondary education.[36]

Even these impressive figures significantly understate real per-pupil spending in the United States. Because we typically calculate spending on the basis of claimed enrollment, rather than the number of students who actually attend our schools, official reports and news accounts tend to understate real spending by 10 to 20 percent per child. This calculation is not the only source of confusion, however.

The standards for school budgeting would bring a smile to the face of any former executive of Enron, Tyco, or WorldCom. Unlike private-sector businesses that must abide by generally accepted accounting principles (GAAP), school systems use a system of standards created for governments that allows them to exclude a number of major costs when reporting "current expenditures." The result is that reported school spending figures do not include capital outlay for property acquisition, construction, and reconstruction; debt service; community service programs; or other programs for adults or continuing education.[37] In New York City, during 2001–2002, the cost of debt service, school construction, and renovation added $2,298 to the $11,994 in reported current expenditure—meaning the district actually spent $14,292 per student. In Los Angeles, these costs added $3,185 to a reported 2001–2002 current per-pupil expenditure of $9,889—for a total of $13,074 per pupil.[38] In Ohio, analysts found that including all of the expenditures consistent with GAAP boosted the real spending figure for some districts by 30 percent or more.[39]

All told, a reasonable estimation is that the per-pupil spending figures routinely cited in the newspapers and on television represent only about 70 to 80 percent of what the United States spends on each student in our public schools. In other words, the official figures showing us at the top of the international heap in spending significantly *underestimate* our real per pupil expenditures. Harvard economist Caroline Hoxby has estimated that we actually spend more than $9,200 per pupil annually, up from an inflation-adjusted $5,900 in 1982. After inflation, spending has jumped more than 60 percent in the past two decades. Moreover, the biggest increases have been in the poorest districts, with more than 90 percent of the nation's districts now spending at least $6,500 per pupil.[40]

In recent years, state and federal education spending have both grown at a rapid clip. Nationally, after-inflation spending more than tripled between 1960 and 2000. From 1995–96 to 2000–2001 alone, spending on public elementary and secondary schools grew by 39 percent, from $287 billion to $401 billion. In California, which spent 2003 wrestling with a budget short-fall upwards of $20 billion, 13 of the state's 20 largest school districts had personnel costs exceed revenue growth between 1996–97 and 2001–2002, even though revenue increases had outstripped enrollment growth in almost every case. Sacramento had enrollment growth of 4 percent, revenue growth of 33 percent, and an increase in personnel costs of 41 percent. Oakland had no increase in enrollment, a 40 percent increase in revenue, and a 52 percent increase in personnel costs.[41] Federal spending on elementary and secondary education increased by 550 percent between 1983 and 2003, from $6.5 billion to $35.8 billion, while general federal spending grew at less than half that rate. Just between 1996 and 2003, total federal spending on education more than doubled, from $23 billion to more than $50 billion. The small cuts that many financially strapped states asked of schools in 2002, 2003, and 2004 took place against a backdrop of consistent and generous increases in school funding.[42] While defenders of the status quo have argued that the growth has been driven by spending on special education students and is therefore not available for general education, the truth is that the growth in special education accounts for less than a quarter of the growth in spending.[43]

All of this money has allowed schools to avoid cutting fat during an era when other private and public organizations have slimmed down. In 1949–50, schools employed one nonteacher (administrators, supervisors, librarians, guidance counselors, secretaries, and so on) for every 2.36 teach-ers. By 1998–99, there was a nonteacher for every 1.09 teachers—even though the number of teachers tripled in that time![44] In New York City, for instance, the public school district employs about 25,000 central district per-sonnel to manage the affairs of the district's one million students. The New York archdiocese, which manages the city's extensive network of parochial schools and enrolls about 110,000 students (about one-tenth what the New York city public schools enroll), makes do with a district staff of 22. In Los Angeles, the district has 75,000 employees, less than half of whom are classroom teachers.[45] Any sector that kept piling on nonessential personnel at the rate the public schools have would be ripe for a radical overhaul.

Since 1970, we have poured money into shrinking class sizes and reducing teacher workloads, and yet the amount of time teachers actually spend in front of students each day shrank from an average of 4.5 hours in 1980 to 3.9 hours in 1998.[46] Meanwhile, between 1960 and 2000, the ratio of teachers to students fell from one teacher for every 26.0 students to one for every 16.1 students, meaning that today's teachers instruct only about sixty percent as many students as teachers did forty years ago.[47]

We're spending a lot more to hire more non-teachers and more teachers who each spend less time teaching fewer children. Even though our total spending on teachers has zoomed, individual teachers have seen limited increases and feel underpaid. Additional personnel have soaked up dollars that could have been better spent rewarding accomplished practitioners, investing in instructional or informational resources, or providing first-rate professional development.

Dismissing such concerns, status quo reformers complain that they don't get all the money they need and therefore cannot be held responsible for helping all students to succeed. Ken Baker, principal at the Wyoming High School in Cincinnati, complained during 2003: "We're supposed to drive all the kids toward success, and we have to do it with one hand behind our backs. The fact is that there are going to be students left behind."[48] He uttered this complaint after Cincinnati spent $10,328 per attending pupil in 2001–2002. Similarly, Bernice Whelchel, the principal of Baltimore's City Springs Elementary School bluntly threatened, "Without the necessary funds per pupil, we won't be successful."[49] She said this after Baltimore County spent $8,667 per attending pupil in 2001–2002. With all due respect, if Ms. Whelchel does not believe she can educate the largely middle-class children of Baltimore County (not Baltimore City) with more than $8,600 per pupil, the problem may not be one of resources. Mr. Baker's and Ms. Whelchel's quotes do not represent a few isolated cases; the mindset they represent is pervasive. When asked about the most pressing issue facing their district, 70 percent of the nation's superintendents skip right past issues of governance, management, or teaching and report that it is "insufficient funding." In fact, 27 percent agree that "lack of funding is such a critical problem that only minimal progress can be made" in their district.[50]

A military commander who said, "If my men die, it's not my fault because Congress didn't spend enough on equipment and training," would be a pariah. A doctor who said, "Don't expect me to be able to heal my patients, because Congress hasn't adequately funded health research," would be an outcast. A police officer charged with apprehending a serial murderer who warned, "Unless we get extra funding, don't expect us to catch the killer," would be dismissed. Yet, in schooling, we are so used to this crude blackmail that it doesn't even shock us.

The unending demands for "more" seem particularly crass at a time when Americans and their leadership are wrestling with economic hardship and other pressing needs. As the 2003–2004 school year began, the nation was mired in a jobless recovery and millions of households were struggling to make ends meet. In September, the Labor Department reported that private employment had fallen by 3.3 million jobs between February 2001 and August 2003. Meanwhile, the Census Department reported in September that median household income had declined in 2002 for the third straight year and that 1.7 million people had slipped into poverty during the year. The Bureau of Labor Statistics reported that in the month of August, on the eve of the new school year, 134,000 workers had lost jobs in 1,258 mass firings. This backdrop gave the traditional complaints accompanying the beginning of the 2003–2004 school year an awkward ring. In Buffalo, Marion Canedo, the superintendent of a district spending well over $11,000 per student opined, "I don't know how to make services multiply with decreased revenues. I don't know how that's humanly possible, unless it's like the loaves and the fishes."[51] In Florida, where the state boosted school funding by 6 percent amid the economic crunch, Andy Griffiths, the president of the Florida School Boards Association complained, "Our increase is whacked out by costs we can't control."[52]

All organizations, even worthy ones, must sometimes tighten their belts. The American Red Cross announced in 2003 that it would lay off 231 of its roughly 4,000 employees, including 145 from the blood services division. The Red Cross, rocked by the challenges of 9/11 and leadership turmoil, did not moan about the necessary cuts or express indignation. The chief financial officer simply noted, "The entire fundraising environment in the country is tough." The CEO observed that the situation required that "hard choices be made."[53] That was that. TIAA-CREF, the nonprofit provider of pension plans for educators, announced in 2003 that it was cutting more than 500 positions, or 8 percent of the workforce, as it sought to "build an efficient and effective organization." While an internal assessment had found the organization to be still "dominant in the markets" it serves, a company spokeswoman reported, "There was room for improvement."[54]

Public schools are not being singled out for harsh treatment. In summer 2003, a decline in income forced San Francisco's public television station KQED to eliminate 12 percent of its 265-member staff and cut salaries and work hours for everyone else by 10 percent. During 2003, Seattle's renowned public station KCTS was forced to lay off one third of its staff. Budget pressures led Oregon to eliminate its support for public broadcasting and dozens of other states to cut their funding, forcing some localities to consider selling off public television stations.[55] Sharp cuts in state support forced community colleges to raise tuition nationally by 11.5 percent in 2003–2004 and to hunt for cost savings.[56] These kinds of cuts are a fact of life. Often, they are a healthy one.

Periodic cutbacks force public and private organizations to focus, prune back overgrown bureaucracies, purge less productive employees, wring out inefficiencies, and regain a fighting trim that can be lost when times are flush. Workers lose jobs, take pay cuts, or sacrifice important benefits. The stories are always sad and there are always individuals who seem unjustly affected. During 2003, workers enjoyed the smallest pay raises in 27 years, averaging about 3.4 percent, while most large employers made employees pay more for health coverage and many cut retirement contributions.[57] Absent painful necessity, no executive would choose such a course.

Checker Finn, former U.S. Assistant Secretary of Education, has put it succinctly, "Public schools have a terrible time coping with budgetary adversity. They put nearly all their money into salaries and benefits—80.6 percent of school operating budgets, says the Census Bureau—and they keep hiring more people and giving them across-the-board raises. Then they confer tenure and enter into contracts such that it's nearly impossible to let anyone go, much less cut their wages. Yet the regular world isn't like that. Airlines faced with the threat of bankruptcy have been renegotiating contracts, slashing salaries (from mechanics and cabin attendants up to top executives) and laying off thousands....Airlines also opt for smaller planes and lower-salaried pilots when they must. Technology replaces baggage handlers and check-in people. The Internet substitutes for reservations office and staff. Why can't public education think that way? Put some of its creativity into devising cheaper ways of doing things?"[58]

Educators can and must begin to think that way. We all live on budgets and within limits. In fact, it is the pressure of finding ways to excel with limited resources that produces useful innovation. When times are tough, public and private organizations tighten their belts, lay off employees, and ask for pay concessions. Yet, public educators seem downright offended by static funding. More importantly, they seem to have convinced public officials and business leaders that asking educators to live by the same rules as other public agencies is somehow anti-education. This is a dangerous conceit that encourages waste and gives rise to lethargy.

William Ouchi, a professor in the graduate school of management at UCLA, has looked carefully at the spending figures of school systems and concluded, "The problem is not that there isn't enough money in public schools. School districts like New York City and Los Angeles have already raised teacher pay, they've reduced class size, they've bought the latest reading books and computers, yet nothing seems to work."[59] How can this be? Quite simply, the problem is not one of insufficient money. The problem is one of insufficient accountability, flexibility, and good management. The problem is our failure to foster a culture of competence in our schools.

Neither bracing encouragement nor harsh rebukes will change this state of affairs. The truth is that no one likes becoming more efficient. Efficiency means disrupting familiar routines, displacing instructional approaches that have always been "good enough," and asking workers to accept that success requires finding ways to do more with less. Efficiency is not a choice; it is a reflexive response to the dictates of self-preservation.

What Characterizes Good Schools

One point of agreement between status quo reformers and commonsense reformers is that we know a lot about what makes for good schools. None of it is especially complicated. Good schools have focus, a clear sense of purpose, high expectations for students and educators, and a committed faculty. Two decades ago, education researchers identified several key traits that characterized successful schools. Known as the "effective schools" research, the findings were exactly what any reasonable observer might expect. Effective schools:

- are safe and orderly
- have a climate of high expectations for the success of all students
- have a clear and focused mission
- have an active and engaged principal focused on academic performance
- and make it a point to frequently monitor student progress.[60]

Nobody disagrees with any of this. Conservatives and liberals, progressive educators and traditionalists, are all pretty comfortable with this description of good schools. In short, there's a lot more agreement about what it takes to make a good school than we sometimes recognize. Further, reasonable people generally agree on what students need to know, what they need to be able to do, and what good teaching looks like. There is agreement that effective schools should have well-defined academic standards, a research-based curriculum and instructional strategy, measurable benchmarks and goals, a strong assessment system, and professional development for teachers.[61] For the most part, it's not difficult to find popular consensus as to what makes for good schools. The challenge is making it happen.

While most good schools share a number of similar traits, they can put these into practice in very different ways. I have witnessed impressive successes in progressive schools where the curriculum emphasizes philosophical inquiry and students master the basics along the way and in direct instruction schools where classes are carefully choreographed by teachers focused on having students master prescribed knowledge and tasks. Some excellent schools make the arts central to their curriculum while other excellent schools regard the fine arts as a distraction. In short, there is no one recipe for success.

Evidence from outside the United States makes the same point. For instance, a 2003 study funded by the National Science Foundation and Department of Education found that students in both Japan and Hong Kong excel on international assessments, even though the favored teaching approaches are radically different. Japanese teachers spend most of their time introducing new content and helping students solve problems, while teachers in Hong Kong spend almost all of their time lecturing students.[62] A commonsense reformer does not endorse any one model of schooling, but focuses on building a system in which all kinds of good schools can flourish.

Because great schools can excel in a variety of ways, some will inevitably emerge even in the absence of commonsense arrangements. At times, this handful can be offered as evidence that commonsense reform is not necessary. The question is not whether a handful of exemplars exist but how to create the conditions in which those few will become a multitude. Many of today's best schools are that way because talented educators selflessly throw themselves into their work. The finest public schools, charter schools, or private schools boast assemblages of such educators who feed off one another and are privileged to work in rewarding and well-regarded school climates. The mistake is to imagine that these inspiring successes provide a workable model for extending excellence everywhere. Unfortunately, there are not—and will never be—enough great educators to fill all the nation's schools, just as there are not enough all-star doctors or baseball players for every hospital to become Massachusetts General or every baseball team to be the New York Yankees. The solution is to produce excellence not by trying to turn every local hospital into Massachusetts General but by taking care to build organizations which will inspire and compel competent, hard working adults to excel.

"The Law of the Aluminum Bullet"

Efforts to replicate promising individual successes at scale have routinely and predictably foundered. Why? First, the first schools to pioneer any effort whether it be a reading program or a whole-school reform—are led by entrepreneurs who are invested in the idea, have thought it through clearly, know how it works, and have reasons for wanting to adopt it at their school. Second, these pioneers find it easy to attract motivated teachers from other schools who are eager to be part of a focused, exciting, and visible program. Third, in order to avoid parental conflict and ethical concerns about experimenting upon unwilling children, dramatic new reforms tend to be launched in schools "of choice" that families choose to attend. The result is that families are generally supportive and invested in the program. Finally, pioneering reformers tend to receive a lot of support from external sources and from the district that's not available for subsequent adopters.[63]

The resulting "law of the aluminum bullet" means that many surefire, silver bullet reforms boast promising results at a few schools only to disappoint when applied more broadly. Misleadingly, status quo reformers suggest that this is because the reforms were not handled properly and then demand more funding for implementation and training. The problem is not with the failure to properly implement each and every status quo proposal but with a culture of incompetence that can give rise to scattered successes but cannot sustain systemic improvement.

Strategies that improve a single school do not necessarily work for entire systems of schools. Individual schools may harness the personal gifts of a principal and use that to foster a culture that motivates and inspires. This isn't a very helpful approach to delivering excellence in ten schools or in a hundred. Individual schools may profit by offering a haven to teachers seeking a bastion of commitment and learning, plucking the best teachers away from other schools or communities. This will work at a few schools, but it won't go very far. Accountability and incentives can be informal and personal at a single school, but such an approach is unreliable when attempted across systems in which personnel possess uneven levels of ability, expertise, and commitment.

Resisting the Lure of Personalized Leadership

Commonsense reform is hampered by the seductive belief that good schools should be islands of tranquility free from the corrupting influence of pressure. The problem is that the absence of rewards and sanctions personalizes coercion and forces managers to rely too heavily on charm and personal pleas. When principals cannot readily fire or punish ineffective employees, they must try to cajole, guilt, and otherwise prod the reticent. Such efforts are time-consuming, tedious, and often ineffective. Personal leadership will suffice to create pockets of temporary excellence, but little more. Think of the principal's situation as analogous to that of a teacher with a student who keeps stealing lunch money from his classmates. It is possible to keep watching the student, nagging him, and explaining why this is bad behavior. All of these, however, will be more effective if the teacher can back them up with straightforward punishments—like detention. This is just common sense.

Moreover, not every potentially good principal has the skills to pull such leadership off. Many may not be well equipped to wheedle and threaten. Meanwhile, making each personnel issue a personalized ordeal makes leadership unnecessarily exhausting and burns out hard-charging leaders. The demands of personalized coercion distract leaders from mentoring and planning, leaving leaders with less energy to spend forging ties with the community or addressing classroom issues.

Personalized management is no way to build organizations for the long haul. Effective organizations institutionalize coercion, not to make the environment unpleasant but to help leaders focus on more constructive tasks. Institutional coercion allows leaders to reward effective employees with money, perks, and opportunities and to cleanly demote, fire, or reassign weak performers. With such tools, principals don't need to jawbone one teacher to transfer out of the school, cajole another into updating an aged lesson, or beg a third to participate in a collaborative effort.

It is important to note that good managers in effective private and public organizations tend to be personal, positive, and to have a light touch. Experts on management repeatedly caution executives that good management is not about firing people or intimidating employees but about cultivating focus, building strong cultures, and drawing the best work out of each employee. In no sense should commonsense reform be thought to endorse heavy-handed or authoritarian leadership. However, what it is easy for those skeptical of commonsense reform to forget is that positive leadership is most often successful when it rests on the assumption of institutional coercion. In firms where it is recognized that good employees will be rewarded and weak ones will be removed, the burdens of leadership are much lighter.

Compliance

School reform starts with making sure that schools are getting their job done. U.S. schools have traditionally done this through compliance—by providing strict rules for how schools should operate. Compliance requires the school district, state, and federal government to set and monitor rules detailing how schools and educators should operate. Officials can decree that a classroom will have no more than twenty-four students, a teacher will hold a state teaching license, new math textbooks will be bought every six years, and so on. All of this ensures a minimal level of service, though none of it ensures that students will be served especially well.

Status quo reformers heartily approve of compliance. Given their faith that student learning can't really be measured and their conviction that educators are doing the best they can, they like to focus on resources and procedures rather than results (for which they believe it isn't really fair to hold educators responsible, anyway). Commonsense reformers, on the other hand, see compliance as a choice to emphasize regulations rather than results. Compliance can make sure people do what they're told to but cannot ensure that these things do any good. Compliance rewards obedience rather than excellence.

Commonsense reform starts with refocusing educators on results rather than rules. That requires accountability. Beyond compliance, there are two possible ways to hold educators accountable. The government can hold educators accountable for producing certain results, or parents can be empowered to judge quality and make decisions based on their preferences.

Tough-Minded Accountability

Tough-minded accountability requires public officials to set clear goals for schools, explain how performance will be measured, set out consequences for success and failure, and then step back and let the educators educate. Student performance is the measure of school effectiveness. If students are performing acceptably, the educators are deemed to be effective; if students aren't, managing to follow the rules is irrelevant. Tough-minded accountability is appealing and powerful, but it poses two potential problems. First, it inevitably narrows the focus of schooling by emphasizing the knowledge and skills being measured. Second, it requires a lot of political will for elected officials to stand behind such systems when they start to pinch individual teachers and students. One way to address both problems is to harness private competition.

Competition

In a competitive system accountability results from families seeking out good schools and leaving ineffective ones. These atomized decisions hold schools accountable by increasing the attendance at good schools and emptying out the bad schools. In such a system, we trust that parents are able to make judgments in the best interests of their children and that they'll flee ineffective schools. Pure competition is largely agnostic about what constitutes a "bad" school, leaving consumers free to decide in the same way they judge whether a quiet vegetarian sandwich shop or a smoky barbecue joint is "better." While adopting a competitive model harnesses school improvement to a powerful engine of progress, it also raises concerns about social fragmentation, the possibility that some parents may be unwary or negligent, or the risk that some schools may shortchange public purposes. Fortunately, these problems can be addressed in large part through tough-minded accountability.

No matter how fervently we might wish for additional choices, once we've considered compliance, tough-minded accountability, and competition we have exhausted the available mechanisms of accountability. I remember a seminar at Harvard University's Kennedy School of Government. After I had explained the need to embrace tough-minded accountability or competition if we were to move away from compliance, an agitated member of the school of education nearly jumped out of her chair in her rush to tell me that I was "ignoring other good approaches."

"Really?" I said. "Such as . . ."

"For instance, at one school I work with, the teachers and administrators saw their state test scores weren't satisfactory so they teamed up to pursue improvement. They're doing it together, professionally. It's not driven by coercion or by markets. They're doing it for the children."

"That's nice," I said. "And if this doesn't work? Then what?"

"What do you mean?" she asked.

"So what if they go through this nice, professional effort and there's no improvement? If nothing is better after two years or four years—then what?"

"They haven't set any time frame. But they're not planning to fail. They plan to succeed."

"But what if it doesn't? Who is going to say, 'Enough'? Who is going to be personally accountable for the fact that kids aren't learning?" I asked.

I may as well have been speaking Greek. The question itself was outside her worldview. She simply assumed that educators will always do their best, that they know what they're doing, that the effort would succeed, and that they will push past any obstacles. The thought that it might be otherwise never occurred to her.

We'd like to trust that our doctors, attorneys, plumbers, and real estate agents will always do the right thing out of professionalism. However, the world is more complicated than that. People are fallible. They get tired, frustrated, exhausted, and burned out. They encounter barriers and decide it is easier to work around them than to confront them. Commonsense reformers recognize these truths, accept them, and take them into account. Status quo reformers simply deny them.

Five Steps to Schools That Work

Commonsense reform is simple. Rigorously identify success and failure, consistently reward success, and unapologetically punish failure. Constantly seek out and recruit new talent, find ways to put that talent to good use, and give professionals the flexibility to make good decisions. This requires fidelity to two simple principles, each amazingly radical and contentious in schooling: accountability and flexibility. Effective organizations, in education or elsewhere, are characterized by clear goals, rewards and sanctions linked to performance, operational flexibility, strong informational support mechanisms, intelligent use of technology, and personnel systems that recruit and develop talent. Commonsense reform is more about principles than prescriptions. Rather than championing a particular model of accountability or particular choice-based programs or specific approaches to education, commonsense reformers sketch principles to guide these efforts.

There are two distinct challenges in school reform. One is to build sensible systems for managing, motivating, staffing, and evaluating schools; the second is to provide schools with the training, expertise, and curricula to fulfill that promise. Both are critical, but the second won't matter much until we get the big picture right. Until then, we're just spinning our wheels. The first challenge is the one that confronts policy makers; the second is properly the province of the professional education community.

Commonsense reform begins with an accountability system based on student mastery of essential material. It advocates using choice and competition to provide flexibility in education, avoid straitjacketing educators, and to reward excellence. It calls for overhauling teaching to attract and reward talented practitioners and professionalize their work. It reimagines education leadership so as to eliminate barriers to sensible management, reward effective practitioners, and recruit and train talent to take advantage of broader changes. Finally, it harnesses modern information technology, contracting, and potential efficiencies to rethink how we organize schools and deliver instruction.

Tackling issues like accountability or teacher compensation in a disjointed, incoherent fashion is a practical and political mistake. Many of the technical problems plaguing the accountability or school choice or teacher reform movements exist because reformers try to address a piece of a dysfunctional system without reconfiguring the system itself. Moreover, the political viability of each reform is enhanced when they are pursued as a package. Taken individually, each raises reasonable concerns, but together these are softened as flexibility and accountability balance and complement one another. It's much like rebuilding an old, creaky, and strangely constructed house. Each time we try to replace a fixture, we find out that we need to redo the wiring, which calls for replacing the materials in the walls, which requires redirecting the pipes, and so on. You eventually get to a point where you either repair the foundation or realize that that none of the improvements are going to amount to much.

Aware that what works with some children in one school may not work as well in another, the commonsense reformer focuses on results and is open-minded about how educators pursue them. A commonsense reformer presumes that any school that accomplishes our shared goals is effective. If the school does it with techniques he rejects, he ruefully concedes that he may not have a monopoly on wisdom.

As we enact the fundamental changes that will transform the status quo into a culture of competence, it will be increasingly useful and appropriate to turn to the status quo reformers. Education experts have bushels of sophisticated proposals for how to improve teaching or refine accountability or hiring systems. Their suggestions are welcome, but they must not be allowed to stand in for old-fashioned common sense. Constructive suggestions for tweaking the status quo are a contribution, but they must not be thought— as their proponents too often do—to somehow alleviate the need for fundamental change. Once the broader changes are made, however, nuanced advice on implementing and refining them will prove invaluable.

After decades of social experimentation, Americans have rediscovered that the simple answers are frequently the best answers. Watching crime explode in our cities taught us that acceptance of disorder breeds law-breaking. Watching welfare become an intergenerational legacy taught us that tolerating dependence will encourage it. There are still some sophisticates who would like to roll the clock back on policing or welfare reform, but they are swamped by the sensible judgments of the American people. It is time we bring that same stolid judgment to education, jettison the faux-expertise of the status quo reformers, and realize that our children's future will be better secured by common sense than a reliance on the kindness of strangers.

CHAPTER TWO

Tough-Minded Accountability

Let's talk sense to the American people. Let's tell them the truth, that there are no gains without pains, that we are now on the eve of great decisions, not easy decisions.
—Adlai E. Stevenson

Great people, great firms, great organizations are focused. They are focused upon clear and ambitious goals. Goals focus the mind and combat the inevitable tendency to get distracted or to accept half-measures as "good enough." Clear goals let people say, "This is the most important thing."

Without such goals, organizations are unlikely to do a great job at any one thing. Relentless focus allows people to throw all of their energy into a task and to avoid distractions. Explicit goals allow superiors to identify effective employees and to reward and promote them, cultivating enthusiasm and setting examples for others. It similarly allows employers to identify ineffective workers and to hold them to a clear standard of performance.

We have failed to foster that kind of focus in schooling. The result is that it has not always been clear what our schools are supposed to be doing or how to gauge their success. This failure has created major problems. Here's one example of how this plays out. When I started teaching high school, I had earned a master's in education, had worked during college as a substitute teacher for a couple of years, had spent hundreds of hours observing classrooms in the course of receiving my license, and had student taught for a couple of months under the guidance of an experienced teacher. So, you'd think I'd have a pretty clear idea of what I was expected to do.

You'd be wrong. As I leafed through my aged textbooks and spoke to colleagues and read the state curricular guide, I could not find clear direction on what I was expected to teach. I had no guidance as to how much material students were expected to master, what content was deemed critical, or how important it was to teach writing skills as opposed to international geography. What did I do? I did what most teachers do. I made it up as I went along. I enjoyed myself and was pleased with my decisions, but that's not really the point, is it?

Ambiguity makes it hard to hold teachers accountable for student learning. If we don't tell a teacher what's expected, we're implicitly telling the teacher to make it up as she goes along. Teachers can throw themselves into coaching the debate team, working with an advanced placement class, or mentoring troubled students. This is all commendable work, but it is not all equally essential work. A teacher engaging in any of these roles may feel like he is making a difference and dismiss student performance on assessments as a poor measure of his real contribution. In the classroom, a middle school teacher might spend a lot of time on a class project and never ensure that all students have mastered basic computation skills, explaining, "Well, the year is short, we had a lot of good interest on what we were doing, and we just ran out of time." When everyone selects their own benchmarks, it becomes difficult to tell whether educators are effective. The lackluster can shrug off failing students, dropouts, or poor test scores by explaining, "Well, that's not an accurate measure of what I'm doing." This particularly protects lazy teachers, lousy teachers, and teachers who would rather put on class plays than correct student essays.

We don't allow a doctor to wave off malpractice concerns by telling the judge that she had a good rapport with the patient or an engineer to excuse an unsafe building by explaining that he was concerned with its façade. While we care about the "extras," we need to make sure that professionals are clear on their primary purpose.

Principals, superintendents, and state officials may want their teachers to focus on academic instruction or teaching the gateway skills but be unable to do anything about it. Unless students are assessed, principals and superintendents don't really know how well they are learning essential material. Absent meaningful assessments, all leaders can do is tell teachers what to do and try to make sure that they comply. A lack of clear goals often leads not to the flexibility or freedom that some might imagine but to laundry lists of rules detailing how classrooms should be staffed, managed, and run.

These challenges are particularly acute in troubled schools. While few will admit it, most educators expect less of disadvantaged students. This is true not just of teachers we regard as incompetent, but even some hailed as exemplary models of sensitivity and concern. For instance, even in famously sympathetic portrayals of urban schools, like James Herndon's *The Way it*

Spozed to Be or Jonathan Kozol's *Death at an Early Age*, former teachers proudly recall how they sacrificed educational content and social discipline in order to "connect" with black students. Herndon bragged about the enthusiasm students showed when he cut back on instruction so that students could list "top 40" radio songs on the blackboard. Kozol spoke proudly of his willingness to ignore instruction in order to befriend students. The difficulty with ambiguous goals and elastic criteria is that it's entirely possible for teachers to feel like they're doing a good day's work while their students learn little or nothing. While the teachers involved are often wonderful and committed people, their students wind up ill-served and unprepared for life. The answer is not to belittle these teachers but to craft schools in which both teacher and student are sure to take care of first things first.

Accountability enhances equity by forcing educators to ensure that even the most challenging students are making progress. As one superintendent explained to me, "Our accountability system caused us to focus on every child. It gave us the mechanism, the framework. Before, we'd looked at SAT scores and awards and other measures, but those were really only tracking our top 25 percent of kids. They weren't telling us whether we were taking care of the rest of the kids." Accountability works by making a lack of improvement so unpleasant for educators and local officials that they will take painful steps, like revamping work rules or firing faculty, that were previously dismissed as "unrealistic."

When we do not have clear goals, regular assessments, and consequences, it is easy for educators to shrug off disappointing outcomes. The status quo has accepted a culture in which educators excuse failure by protesting that (1) some students are excelling, (2) some students come to school with significant disadvantages and educators are not miracle workers, and (3) educators need more money and resources to make a difference. The relentlessness of tough-minded accountability puts an end to this state of affairs. It forces educators to find a way to make things better.

The problem is that the status quo reformers want to reject any useful measure of performance and instead to define success in terms of their values and social ends. Michael Apple, a professor of education at the University of Wisconsin and influential status quo reformer, has explained that we should not gauge school improvement on the basis of student achievement. Rather, "We need constantly to ask what reforms do to schools as a whole and to each of their participants, including teachers, students, administrators, community members, local activists, and so on."[1] Apple and his peers are ultimately far more interested in sociology, ethnography, and community activism than in whether students master mundane skills like reading, writing, or computation. Commonsense reformers must maintain a patient focus on student learning—even when such a focus is deemed "simpleminded" or "superficial" by education's intellectual class.

For teachers to be respected as professionals, they must assume a professional's responsibility for the service they provide to their charges. The only way to know that all children are being adequately served is to determine what students absolutely must know and to make sure they learn it. The flip side is that we need to tell educators what they're supposed to teach, and they need to ensure that all students are learning.

The Principles of Accountability

Accountability is not a complicated concept. It is founded on three simple truths. The first is that what you measure is what you get. The second is that the more things you measure, the less attention anyone pays to any one thing that you are measuring. The third is that if you do not measure results, you won't be able to tell the difference between success and failure.

Consider a simple example. Imagine you manage a public counseling clinic and want to improve the quality of service. You sit down with your staff and tell them that your clients would like a more personal touch. Your staff reminds you that they are evaluated primarily on how many clients they see a day, encouraging conscientious workers to whip through their appointments. The more they focus on improving their evaluation, the less energy they will devote to addressing individual needs.

This is a problem. The commonsense solution is to tell employees that they'll now be evaluated 50 percent on number of clients seen and 50 percent on client satisfaction. This will increase attention to service, though likely at the cost of reducing the number of clients they see.

The next week a state consultant visits and tells you that there's a problem because your paperwork is not as complete as it needs to be. So you meet with the staff and indicate that they'll need to become more careful about documenting client status and the substance of each session and that the quality of this information will be factored into their performance evaluation.

The resulting system bases personnel evaluations upon the speed of their service, the quality of service, and the thoroughness of their documentation. This seems reasonable. Employees are now encouraged to focus in equal part on all three elements of their job.

However, adopting too many criteria is a lot like having no criteria—employees realize that superiors can't really sort out all the conflicting information. After a certain point, employees figure that they will do well on some indices and poorly on others and that there are so many moving pieces that they can't affect the outcome. Consequently they ignore the accountability system. For instance, I was teaching down in Louisiana when the state instituted a teacher evaluation system that included more than 130 discrete teacher behaviors and attributes. Realistically, no one was going to pay too much attention to any one of these because they'd properly figure that no evaluator will be able to focus on the performance on any one indicator. If student achievement gains are just one performance measure considered alongside a series of others, then even holding teachers or schools responsible for student learning won't matter much. If you measure everything, you may as well measure nothing. This is a hard point for educators, because they want to say, "We do a lot of stuff that matters, and you should measure it all." The reality is, we can't do that.

In well-run publicly-owned companies, large shareholders keep a jealous eye on performance. They make sure that money is being spent sensibly, that executives aren't making shortsighted decisions and aren't giving away the store in contract negotiations. Unfortunately, in the public sector, efficiency often suffers as public officials avoid painful choices that will anger constituents. Instead they opt for half-measures and window dressing. Wishing for more disciplined leadership will not change the status quo; injecting cold-eyed incentives into the equation will.

Given a healthy skepticism about relying on strangers, commonsense reformers feel better about sending a loved one to a doctor's office when that doctor's livelihood and professional reputation depend on the care she provides. It's not that a commonsense reformer distrusts doctors or thinks them irresponsible. It's just that self-interest provides a reliable safeguard beyond good intentions and professional ethics. For this reason, commonsense reformers are puzzled by status quo reformers who claim that taking account of student learning when evaluating teachers is "anti-teacher." Is it anti-attorney to suggest that lawyers who keep losing cases should face the consequences or that those who run up great records should be promoted and rewarded? Is it anti-accountant to suggest the same for a CPA who botches financial statements or one who does timely and exemplary work?

Setting Common Goals

Accountability begins by making clear what it is that children are expected to know and be able to do. We have sensibly chosen to tackle this at the state level. In the past decade, we have made great progress at clarifying what students are expected to learn and what schools are expected to teach.

The truth is that a vast majority of Americans agree about the essentials that children should learn in school. At a minimum, we want children in elementary school to read, write, and perform mathematics with reasonable proficiency. In secondary schooling, we want students to master basic algebra, vocabulary, and expressive thought at a more advanced level. In addition, we would like children to be familiar with the sweep of American and world history, to master the basic principles of the biological and chemical sciences, and to be disciplined and responsible citizens. Quite frankly, you have to push pretty far into the ideological thickets on the left or the right to find much disagreement on these counts.

Commonsense standards and required assessments should focus on essential content and skills. We lose sight of the centrality of the gatekeeping skills when we start insisting on testing students at the completion of every high school course or in every subject area. As Tony Wagner, Co-Director of the Change Leadership Group at the Harvard University Graduate School of Education, has wisely noted, "One of the great mistakes of the high-stakes testing movement . . . is the attempt to test an ever-increasing number of subject areas as if they all mattered equally."[2] Let me be clear. I, like any other former teacher, want students to enjoy as many experiences and learning opportunities as possible. Nothing in this discussion is intended to suggest that commonsense reform implies anything else. We must always remember, however, to ensure that schools focus first on their core mission.

Clarifying what it is that schools are supposed to do is essential because we have traditionally asked schools to do lots of things, ranging from oral health instruction to providing information on organ donation to running antibullying workshops, and then gauged performance by determining whether schools provided all the required services. The result has been a system that does a lot of things poorly and one where large portions of the school day are consumed by trivia. Over the past fifteen years, a series of surveys by the National Center for Education Statistics found that teachers report spending only 68 percent of their classroom time on instruction related to core academic subjects. The rest of their time was consumed by tasks like disaster preparedness, fund-raising activities, socialization, holidays, and assemblies.[3] A commonsense reformer finds it incongruous that educators devote a third of their time to such activities when millions of students have not even mastered basic reading or math skills. Tough-minded accountability establishes priorities. It is not that other activities are unimportant but that successful institutions should take care of their core business first. Though it is wonderful when police departments run holiday teddy bear drives for local children, we wouldn't excuse poor law enforcement on the grounds that the local police run an exceptional gift drive. In fact, if we worried that the teddy bear drive was distracting the department from its essential duties, we might ask it to cut back even on a beloved and exemplary holiday program.

Critics worry that teachers will "teach to the test" as if that were a self-evident problem. Of course, if the test evaluates core competencies, we want teachers to teach the skills and content they'll be testing. In computer science classes at MIT or English classes at Yale, professors "teach to the test"—they test on material they think important and are sure to teach that material. Any other approach would seem peculiar.

Opposition to accountability is rooted among individuals who don't believe that all students can or need to master these essentials. Casual observers often don't realize how ideological the opponents of accountability really are.[4] The leader of a group that seeks to dismantle Virginia's nationally acclaimed accountability system has explicitly rejected the value of assessments and urges parents to "tak[e] back their schools from the testing mania that pervades our children's education."[5]

Former *New York Times* education columnist Richard Rothstein dismissed the results from the authoritative Third International Mathematics and Science Study as unimportant, even though they showed that "our 8th graders scored below their peers in almost every other industrial nation that took part." Why? Because when asked "if they liked math and science...in the United States, 35 percent felt positively about math and 32 about science, more than in almost every other industrial nation."[6]

Prominent anti-accountability crusaders like Susan Ohanian even argue that it's not necessary that all students master basic skills like math or reading. Ohanian declares, "Neither our children nor our society is well served by hyping mathematics as the ticket to fame and fortune."[7] She approvingly cites fellow status quo reformer Gerald Bracey's attack on the "algebra scam"—readers may be surprised to learn that efforts to require every child to learn algebra before graduating high school are thought in some quarters to be an insidious corporate conspiracy. In fact, Ohanian argues that, "A significant number of our students are never intended to reach the celestial standards held out by the corporate/political sleight-of-hand artists."[8] Her apparent belief that many children cannot master "celestial standards" entailing literacy, mathematical skills, and basic content knowledge illustrates the tension between the expectations of some status quo reformers and the commonsense reformers. After all, many status quo reformers pay homage to Paulo Freire, a Latin American revolutionary who argued in his *Pedagogy of the Oppressed* that having teachers "deposit" information in students was nothing short of oppressive and who urged teachers to remember that "education is always political."[9]

Fortunately, even many status quo reformers shrink from the effort to deemphasize the gatekeeping skills. After all, common sense tells us that high school graduates need to master reading, writing, math, and basic content. This is why more than two-thirds of Americans routinely support graduation testing, with even stronger support when they are told that students will receive multiple chances to pass. In fact, Americans strongly support test-based accountability in general. A 2003 report by the respected polling organization Public Agenda found that just 12 percent of Americans thought children take too many standardized tests, that 79 percent thought the tests ask fair questions, and that 87 percent of teachers think students should pass a standardized assessment before being promoted.[10]

A particular point of contention in setting standards is disagreement about what literature children should read or which historic personages should be included in history curricula. These disputes, however, tend to miss the mark. Student proficiency in writing, reading, math, history, and the sciences can be assessed by determining that students can understand a written passage, write a competent essay, and identify major concepts and events. It is not necessary to narrowly dictate what students must read or which historical figures they need to know. While some curricular experts suggest that it is vital to include certain readings or historical personages in accountability systems, from a commonsense perspective such questions are secondary.

Common sense accountability systems should also collect information on school quality that extends beyond student performance on essential material. States should collect systematic information on the rates at which students take college-level advanced placement courses and how they fare on the nationally administered exams, enrollment rates and student performance in the International Baccalaureate program, enrollment in and accomplishments of arts and music programs, school safety, attendance rates, and graduation rates and college attendance when appropriate. This additional information can help to provide a full picture of school performance.

Public Schooling is the Public's Business

Educators have their own views of accountability, and there is nothing wrong with this so long as we remember that what serves educators doesn't necessarily serve their students. Not surprisingly, educators tend to think that schooling is served by policies that make their lives more pleasant. Consequently, when teachers complain about "stress" and "intense pressure," status quo reformers view this as proof that tough-minded accountability is misguided. When educators voice their concerns, however, parents and public officials should view them not as neutral experts but as advocates with personal preferences.

Testing critics, especially professors in schools of education who have exquisitely elaborate theories of human development, think accountability is an imposition on professional educators. They vilify accountability advocates, accusing them of "abandon[ing] the interest of public school teachers and schools... [and] driv[ing] the best teachers out of schools... in the name of high standards."[11] Status quo reformers explain that professional educators view "standards" as a "vision of teaching and learning in which students are engaged in high-level conceptual learning," while they see public officials and accountability advocates as mindlessly preoccupied with a lowbrow concern for "basic skills."[12] As one Washington, D.C.-based teacher advocate confided to me, "We get sick and tired of these bozos trying to come into the schools and tell us our jobs. We're the experts. We know what works. I wish all these noneducators would just shut up, take care of their own jobs, and let us take care of ours."

A wonderful illustration of this mentality was provided by Andy Baumgartner, the 2000 National Teacher of the Year, in an embittered column he authored for the National Education Association. Mr. Baumgartner wrote: "When the discussion turns to how to improve education, politicians relegate teachers to the back of the class. My home state of Georgia, for example, had a 66-person commission on school reform, but, amazingly, less than 5 percent of them were practicing teachers.... When I used a recognition ceremony in the Georgia State Senate to express my disagreement with the commission's recommendations, especially those that would undermine the teaching profession, I apparently crossed some line meant to keep teachers in their place."[13]

Such complaints are undemocratic nonsense. Schools are paid for by public monies and filled with the public's children. Schools are not the playthings of teachers and students are not lab rats for the theories of education experts. Public educators are public employees. If the public chooses to set clear expectations, that is its right.

In fact, the presumption that teachers ought to police themselves, set education goals, dictate school management, or be able to veto reforms is a radical one in a democratic nation. It suggests that teachers—unlike public health officials, police officers, or other public servants—are entitled to regard public institutions, public resources, and the public's children as a private preserve. The public has the right and the obligation to provide educators with standards and to ensure that they are met.

In fields like police work or national defense, as in education, we recognize the value of experience and expertise. We honor police officers and soldiers.

However, respect doesn't mean we allow them to craft our laws or set foreign policy. While we generally defer to the professionals' expertise in the course of their daily work, we do not imagine that their desires should guide policy decisions about the death penalty, criminal sentencing, or U.S. involvement abroad. We certainly don't worry that we're crimping professional self-expression by expecting police or soldiers to take public direction.

The same is true in public health, environmental protection, transportation, child welfare, and so on—in each case we value input from the professionals, but don't imagine that their preferences should shape laws or public policy. In fact, careful deference to democratic control is regarded as a badge of honor in professions like the military and public safety. It is the public's country and our taxes, and we expect public employees to accept that.

However well intentioned practitioners and experts may be, they have interests distinct from those of the public. The public has the right to reject the preferences and opinions of its employees, no matter how ardently they insist on their expertise. For instance, police officers are often able to identify likely suspects based on various indicators. These indicators frequently flag young black men. Police believe that this "profiling" helps them focus on likely suspects, helping them more effectively fight crime and safeguard community members. Nonetheless, for reasons of racial justice, a number of states and communities have explicitly prohibited profiling in spite of the arguments made by the police. Even if police believe that racial profiling will save lives, if the public deems it unacceptable, police are expected to accept that and abide by it.

It is peculiar that educators, who speak so often of democracy and social responsibility, would be so resistant to this principle. Educators are employees in the public's schools. Status quo reformers would be better off embracing that role rather than complaining about it.

Where We are Now

After decades of futile hopes that enough rules, regulations, and good intentions would finally produce quality schools, commonsense reformers understand that tough-minded accountability must be the cornerstone of meaningful reform. There is no viable alternative. Compliance with regulations will only ensure that rules are being obeyed; it won't make sure that all students are learning. As for competition, the American public is leery except when it is accompanied by accountability and additional precautions.[14]

Accountability systems of varying seriousness were adopted across the nation during the 1990s. State programs featured grade-level standards and periodic assessment of students at specified grades in core subjects. By the late 1990s, more than two dozen states were at various stages of implementing accountability systems. These systems were uneven, with many adopting poorly designed tests and failing to impose real consequences for student or teacher performance.

In 2002, the federal government gave an ambitious push to these state efforts when President George Bush signed the No Child Left Behind Act. The No Child Left Behind Act required that each state annually test students in grades 3–8 and that schools demonstrate that their students, after taking selected high school courses, are making steady progress in reading, math, and writing. If schools or districts fail to demonstrate improvement, states are to impose a variety of penalties. The accountability provisions can be readily critiqued as flawed, overly mechanical, and hampered by political compromise, but they also provide a framework that is a significant improvement over the status quo.

Tough-minded accountability increases the degree to which educators will focus upon required curricula. It increases their attention to essential chores of teaching, like checking homework and working with low-performing students, and also helps shape their lesson planning and instructional decisions. It provides a common set of goals, enhances curricular coordination within schools and across the schools in a system, increases the emphasis on material deemed central, and helps to ensure that all students are being educated to a specified level. Eight in ten teachers in high-stakes states report spending more time on tested subjects, 60 percent use results to plan instruction, and 50 percent use them to select instructional materials.[15] Of course, as with anything else, the benefits of accountability are never wholly without cost. In asking that educators ensure that every student at least master gateway knowledge and skills, tough-minded accountability can marginalize some desirable programs and material. On balance, the commonsense reformer recognizes these costs but deems them well worth paying.

Common sense tells us that accountability will produce improved results, and the best research, not surprisingly, suggests this is true. Using data from 54 nations collected in the Third International Mathematics and Science Study, Ludger Woessman of Germany's Institute for Economic Research analyzed cross-national differences based on whether countries use high stakes tests. Woessman concluded, "student performance in math and science is substantially higher in school systems with central exams than in those without central exams, and this is true for students from all performance quartiles and family backgrounds. Parents, administrators, schools, teachers, and students all appear to respond to the changed incentive environment created by central exams by placing additional emphasis on educational achievement."[16]

In the most complete and carefully conducted examination of how accountability systems affect student performance in the United States, Stanford University economists Margaret Raymond and Eric Hanushek found that student performance in strong accountability states has consistently outdistanced that in weak accountability states. In their analysis of student performance across the United States during 1992–2000, Raymond and Hanushek found that the mathematics performance of fourth- and eighth-grade students in states with high-stakes accountability systems improved on the National Assessment of Educational Progress at more than twice the rate of students in states with no accountability system. The scores of fourth-graders in high-accountability states increased from 1992 to 2000 by 9.2 points, while the scores of fourth-graders in no-accountability states increased by 3.8 points. At the eighth-grade level, scores for students in high-accountability states increased by 8.8 points, those of students in no-accountability states by 4.0 points.[17]

The other authoritative study on the effects of accountability in the United States, conducted by a second pair of Stanford economists, used a different methodology but also found that eighth-grade math scores improved at a significantly higher rate than those in low-accountability states between 1996 and 2000. The researchers, Martin Carnoy and Susanna Loeb, found the gains accrued to black, white, and Latino students.[18] While ideologically-driven critiques have tried to argue that accountability in education, unlike, oh, everywhere else, is ineffective, the research that seeks to make this case fails to meet even reasonable norms of scientific rigor.[19]

None of this is intended to suggest that accountability is easy, automatic, or costless. After all, tough-minded accountability works precisely because it makes mediocrity painful. As scholars like Gary Orfield and Mindy Kornhaber are quick to remind us, the impact on students, teachers, and schools will be uneven, slow, and sometimes unpleasant.[20] Simply imposing tests will not itself yield productive change, for the same reason that stomping on the gas won't make a stalled car go. Translating accountability into improvement requires the flexibility, leadership, targeted services, and remedial opportunities that will help educators adjust and students to master the skills they need.

Tough-Minded Accountability in Practice

If we establish clear goals—mastery of math, writing, reading, and a foundational understanding of history and science—we need to make sure that students master this knowledge and that schools are teaching it. The only sure way to do this is by measuring what students know and by making sure educators are held accountable for the results. This process of monitoring and then rewarding or remedying educator performance is tough-minded accountability.

Students

While students come to school with different resources and different needs, a commonsense reformer starts from the premise that schools must help every student to master the gatekeeping skills. As I said in chapter one, schools don't have the time or money to do everything. A commonsense reformer isn't asking them to. He asks only that they ensure that, at an absolute minimum, every student is equipped for life beyond high school. The commonsense reformer has no patience for those misguided souls who excuse the inability of graduates to read or write at a minimally acceptable level but would march them into the world regardless.

Measuring allows us to ensure that students learn what the community has deemed essential. By measuring every year, we can catch students who are struggling before the problem becomes too daunting. By identifying students whose math or reading skills are not where they need to be, measuring helps educators target resources and instruction to a student's weak spots.

Assessing student performance helps guard against students slipping through the system or the possibility of graduating students who lack essential life skills. No one desires to delay students' progress through school, much less their departure from school. Sometimes, however, it is a disservice to children to promote them. We do students no favors by giving them diplomas without ever having taught them to read or to perform basic math. When Californians for Justice, a statewide advocacy group, claims that requiring graduating students to pass the California exit exam "punishes students for the failures of the state," a commonsense reformer is puzzled by the claim that it is a "punishment" to ensure that students master essential skills before graduating.[21] To the contrary, ensuring that students are equipped to face the world seems the primary obligation of public schools. Withholding a diploma until students have mastered essential skills and knowledge helps protect students from being shoved into the larger world before they are prepared to face it. Sensible people know that rewarding good behavior produces more of it. If we recognize, reward, and promote students who master their studies, a commonsense reformer trusts that we'll encourage kids to spend more time studying and less time playing *Grand Theft Auto*. Not too surprisingly, the research shows that setting high standards and rewarding academic success promote student achievement.[22] For instance, 75 percent of teachers, 85 percent of parents, and 61 percent of high school students agree that students work harder if required to pass a test for graduation.[23]

While it may seem hard to believe, status quo critics like Alfie Kohn, author of *The Case Against Standardized Testing*, reject the commonsense benefits of ensuring student competence and argue that setting goals for student learning or measuring student achievement is "unfair," "pointless," "cruel," and the "educational equivalent of an ethnic cleansing." Because not all students have equal familial and community resources, Kohn deems it "naïve and callous" to suggest that students facing barriers like "racism, poverty, fear of crime...and language barriers" be expected to master standards and instead suggests that "anyone who is serious about addressing the inequities of American education...investigate differences in available resources." In the meantime, Kohn is apparently convinced that these pitiable poor, minority children cannot learn and that it is unfair to expect them to do so. In a less enlightened age, a less restrained critic might be moved to question Kohn's fundamental commitment to equality and dignity of poor and minority children.[24]

Aside from the case of high school graduation, ensuring student competence does not necessarily require that educators hold back those students who have not mastered essential skills. While some educators believe students are served by holding them back a grade if their skills are not up to speed, some critics of grade retention argue that holding students back does more harm than good. In some locales and for some children retention is probably the right move, at other times it may make more sense to promote them and provide counseling, summer preparation, targeted instruction, and intense remediation. A commonsense reformer recognizes merit in both positions and is agnostic on this debate, so long as students don't graduate until they demonstrate essential mastery.

Educators

Measuring student learning also enables us to track the performance of schools and educators. We want to know which schools and which teachers are doing the best job of helping students learn. We judge performance not by looking at which teachers or schools have the highest-achieving students, but which helped students to make the most progress during the school year.

This distinction can be a little confusing, so let's make sure we get it right. Take the case of medicine. To judge the quality of doctors, you don't want to just measure the health of their patients. Why? If the doctor serves a young, healthy clientele, the overall results may appear very impressive even if they don't do much. Another doctor who serves an older, sicker population may have higher mortality rates even though she does a better job. What we really care about is how well each doctor serves his or her patients. The ideal way to gauge performance is to judge how much each *improves* the health of patients. We'd like to know how healthy each patient was before and after the doctor's care, and then compare the "value added by each doctor." This measurement is hard to take in some fields, like journalism, and easier in others—like sales or manufacturing. Education falls somewhere in between. On the one hand, learning is a complicated process, and basic assessments don't fully reflect what students learn; on the other, schooling does produce concrete results of critical import. We also care about the level of performance, however. A teacher or a school that consistently takes in high-performing students and then keeps them at that level is clearly doing good work, even if the students have limited room to improve.

Merely tracking the performance of teachers and schools is not enough. This information, on its own, does little good. It permits educators to assess the job they have done, identify weaknesses, and make appropriate adjustments to the material they teach or to their teaching style. However, this doesn't ensure that any hard change will occur. If a third-grade teacher likes reading aloud in class, but the performance results show that students aren't mastering reading skills, there's nothing to make that teacher cut back on reading. If an algebra teacher's students are not keeping pace with their peers in other people's classes, there's nothing to compel the teacher to shorten his summer and enroll in long hours of extra training.

Performance information is meaningful only when it is backed by real incentives; when principals and superintendents use it to reward or penalize teachers based on how well they are serving their students. This single stroke provides the foundation for forging a culture of competence. Sensible accountability begins not by using student achievement to mechanically assess teachers but by holding leaders accountable for student learning so that they will use both systematic data and professional judgment to evaluate personnel.

Principals must be evaluated and recognized on the basis of how well their students are doing. Like any manager, principals will have reason to identify and reward their best performers, find ways to make the skills of those available to other faculty, support and provide enhanced training for teachers, redirect resources from frills to core subjects, assist low performers, and remove those low performers who do not improve with assistance.

Educators will focus on making sure all students master essential content and skills. Teachers may respond by adopting new approaches when their old ones are ineffective, seeking assistance from colleagues or supervisors, redoubling their efforts, focusing upon struggling students, or shifting time and energy away from more marginal content and skills.

Accountability and Management

By subjecting ineffective schools and educators to automatic penalties, tough-minded accountability frees supervisors from nagging their poor performers into a sense of urgency. Supervisors can become constructive partners who work with their personnel to remedy problems and fend off unpleasant consequences.

Managing without Accountability

Picture a typical low-performing urban elementary school in a district that lacks an accountability system. The school is staffed with a mix of inexperienced novices and world-weary veterans who have been there for ten or fifteen years. Faced with students reading two or three grades below reading level, a new principal starts her first faculty meeting by stating, "We're going to turn this around. I intend to have all students reading at grade level in three years, and I expect us to get one-third of the way this coming year." On their way out of the meeting, the veterans grumble to one another about the principal's inexperience, uncooperative parents, a lack of resources, and the basic skills that the students lack. Some teachers, especially among the newer hires, enthusiastically accept the challenge. The principal circulates memos reiterating the goals, implores teachers to cooperate, makes extra professional development available, sits down with new teachers and willing veterans, holds pep talks to build faculty morale, takes pains to highlight effective faculty members, and appeals to professional pride. Most of the teachers toss the memos into the wastebasket, ignore the principal's pleas, and calmly explain that they're doing the best they can in difficult circumstances.

At the end of the year the principal anxiously awaits word of the school's achievement gains, only to see little improvement. A few teachers showed real improvement, but most of the faculty showed results nearly identical to the previous year's. What is the principal to do now? Sure, she can provide more training and support for the teachers who will use them. Her real concern, however, are the teachers who didn't play along. She can try more charm or more pep talks, but if faculty think they're already doing the best they can, there's not much she can say. Depending on what the teacher contract allows, she can frequent classes, haunt the teacher lounge, ask teachers to routinely turn in lesson plans for inspection, and require teachers to call parents on a regular basis. She can also nag teachers about test scores, watch the parking lot to see who is arriving late or departing early, and otherwise pester recalcitrant teachers into cooperating. She knows this will make her the nagging parent, create a constant state of low-energy conflict with much of her faculty, and may not have that much impact, but there's nothing else she can do.

Managing with Accountability

Accountability can radically alter the principal's role. Whether or not the principal does a thing, tough-minded accountability means that poor performance is going to disrupt the lives of teachers. It may result in individuals' being denied bonuses or losing their jobs, or even in closure of the school. The principal no longer needs to work so hard to convince teachers that they have to do better. The teachers who were already cooperative will be joined by others now aware that what they thought was their "best" may not suffice. Rather than mock the principal for a failure to understand their difficulties, poorly performing teachers may be moved to rethink their resistance to change. They may suddenly be eager for assistance, mentoring, creative approaches, or proven strategies. Kim Marshall, former principal and now mentor to urban principals, has recalled that he had limited success promoting schoolwide change "until Massachusetts introduced its high-stakes test in 1998. When we heard that 800-pound gorilla knocking on our door, the turnaround happened with amazing speed. As our fourth-graders took the first round of . . . tests, one of our most effective teachers burst into tears at a staff meeting and proclaimed, 'No more Lone Ranger!' "[25] After a decade of fruitless efforts to foster teamwork and end faculty isolation, Marshall's job was suddenly a lot easier. Not surprisingly, academic improvement that had been elusive suddenly came much more readily. Savvy administrators embrace tough-minded accountability precisely because, by forcing their hand, it allows them to take difficult steps without appearing to be the bad gu

Shifting intimidation from the shoulders of the principal and onto the impersonal machinery of accountability means the principal is no longer forced to beg and bluster. Just as in the most effective companies, the principal will focus on coaching, setting goals, assessing performance, and fostering a sense of teamwork. In those companies, employees know they are being evaluated and that the evaluations matter, causing them to discipline themselves. When all workers are intent on meeting specified goals, executives are free to focus on positive leadership.

Shared expectations make it easier for teachers to figure out what they're supposed to do and enable them to get feedback regarding their performance. As a result, even though teachers can feel initially threatened by accountability, there is evidence that teachers come to welcome the changed environment.[26]

Focusing on outcomes allows superintendents to stop micromanaging schools and principals to stop micromanaging classrooms. Outcome-based accountability permits educators to operate as professionals. As a principal operating under the Texas accountability system once explained, "Look, our math teachers had some concerns and decided they wanted to buy math manipulatives. While we checked what they were doing during building walk-throughs, we didn't spend a lot of time micromanaging them, because the real assessment was student test performance." So far, accountability has rarely delivered these benefits because too many principals and district officials lack the necessary management tools or managerial skills.[27] Finding and developing skilled, entrepreneurial managers who use information to empower employees and reward effective practitioners will be addressed in chapter five.

Making Accountability Work

Transforming nice accountability, in which tests are introduced but neither rewards nor sanctions are tied to their results, into tough-minded accountability requires making performance matter for students, teachers, principals, and district staff. Students ought to be required to master essential skills and knowledge in the core areas before being promoted to middle school or high school and before being permitted to graduate. In other words, students need to be expected to master a set level of competence. Passing students on without such mastery does them no favors and makes it too easy for ᵈucators to keep passing on hard-to-serve children.

　　ᵗ educators, however, we're less concerned with levels of competence
than `ᴸ student gains. As the status quo crowd properly points out,

students come to school with very different backgrounds. Educators are responsible for how well their students learn, not for where they start. Accountability for educators needs to focus on making sure that their students are making reasonable gains. Though "reasonable" is an imprecise word, a rough measure is possible: educators should be expected to have their students gaining at least as rapidly as similar students elsewhere in the state and the nation.

Educators Should be Evaluated on What Students Learn

Educators who help students learn should be rewarded and those whose students consistently fail to make expected gains ought to be identified for appropriate redress. One troubling recommendation posed with worrisome frequency by would-be commonsense reformers is the notion that, in the words of one national champion of accountability, "Between value-added measures and advanced testing systems, we have a scientific basis for managing and paying teachers." This is wrong, dangerously so. It threatens to resurrect the mistakes of Frederick Taylor and the "scientific management" revolution at the dawn of the twentieth century and recreate the problems they bequeathed.

Taylor and his colleagues argued that all productive human activity could be reduced to measurable processes and activities and that effective management meant narrowly measuring the work of each employee to ensure that they were performing optimally. The approach yielded a tradition of micromanagement, routinization, and myopic management that retarded fresh thinking and undermined teamwork. Rather than revisit a legacy of rigidity that management gurus have spent decades helping America unlearn, we need sensible systems that utilize the information provided by value-added measurement while recognizing that educators can contribute by counseling students, mentoring colleagues, providing advanced instruction, or other activities that may not show up in simple performance measures. The commonsense course recognizes that we can place due weight on value-added results without imagining that we can effectively reduce educators to automatons.

Incentives should not be algebraically linked to student performance, but should allow supervisors to take other factors into account. Improvement in student performance should constitute a significant part, roughly half of a teacher's job evaluation, but not the entire thing. Some overly enthusiastic states have tied teacher bonuses directly to student test scores. This is a problem because tests are an imperfect measure of student learning and don't reflect everything we care about. Rather than simpleminded schemes, accountability should provide a framework to support employee evaluations.

Consider how accountability functions in a well-run medical practice. The practice cares about how many patients a doctor sees and how they fare, but also care about patient satisfaction and the doctor's collaborative contributions. A doctor who mentors colleagues or has very satisfied patients might receive more generous treatment than a colleague who schedules more appointments. Productivity figures are not the final word, but provide the basis for sensible decisions that take other factors into account.

Smooth Out the Bumps

Accountability systems should be designed so as to focus on big-picture performance and overall trends. It's a mistake to make too much of small differences or small changes. Performance measures are imperfect. For this reason, they should be used to determine whether teachers or principals are performing at exceptional, high, acceptable, or poor levels rather than to make fine-grained distinctions. Because researchers have found a lot of random movement in assessment results, it's important not to put too much emphasis on any one result. This is especially true for individual classes or smaller schools, where the small number of students taking the tests, combined with possible extraneous factors including the entry or exit of students, can skew the results of statistical analysis. However inconvenient for the true believers, this recommends against mechanically linking test outcomes to teacher compensation.[28]

Rather than making too big a deal out of a one-year jump in performance, we should concentrate on rewarding sustained excellence. The goal is not to find a way to produce a year of impressive test scores but to forge schools and classrooms where students learn and grow year after year. In journalism, a reporter is judged not simply upon how many stories she writes in a year, but also the depth of her work, its quality, her contribution in the newsroom, and her ability to sustain these. Accountability systems should be developed with equal thoughtfulness.

Accountability for More than Test Results

Those critics who highlight the flaws of accountability systems that rely upon one measure or poorly designed tests are absolutely correct. Building entire accountability systems around a single test result will distort teaching and poses the risk that schools will engage in questionable activities in order to boost test results. Similarly, thoughtless or heavy-handed use of a crude instrument can create new problems. Consequently, sensible accountability systems take into account a few important contextual factors. Some educators work in advantaged communities where students tend to master the gatekeeping skills at an early age and it can be difficult for them to produce sizable improvement. In these schools, the *level* of student performance is relevant. So long as a school continues to perform at a consistently high level, this ought to be accorded more weight than student improvement.

There is also the problem that a few educators, despite massive quantities of treacly testimonials to their unmatched goodwill and selflessness, have shown a decidedly human tendency to game accountability systems. (We shall not dwell on what this fact says about status quo claims that teachers will not respond to incentives.) There is evidence from Chicago and Houston, for instance, that school districts may have held students back or obscured the number of dropouts in order to register larger gains. Of course, any accountability system will sometimes tempt some adults to try to cheat or cut corners. The answer is not to throw up our hands but to design accountability systems that are difficult to game and to sensibly monitor assessments and reporting. In general, the key to defeating unscrupulous behavior is to collect data beyond merely those on student performance, to make the information readily available, and to focus on multiyear trends.

Information beyond student achievement that is worth collecting includes attendance rates, graduation rates, promotion rates, disciplinary record, enrollment in advanced courses, and student performance on Advanced Placement assessments or diagnostic tests.[29]

All Students are Not the Same

Absent accountability, it is easy for teachers to focus on those students they find most sympathetic or interesting. In some classrooms, this means that advanced students are overlooked while teachers focus on assisting those with the greatest needs. More typically, however, the teacher either focuses on the students in the middle of the pack or delights in challenging the high achievers, leaving those in need to their own devices. Accountability has the power to change that, but only if it encourages educators to focus on these children. Accountability measures that are too focused upon aggregate scores or overall passing rates can wind up marginalizing troubled students or those with special needs.

One way to keep an eye on this is to ensure that schools are making gains across ethnic groups, with both boys and girls, with students for whom English is a second language, with students with special needs, and with poor children. Another way to handle this is to make sure that performance is improving for high-scoring, mid-scoring, and low-scoring students. These kinds of breakouts ensure that educators working with disadvantaged students get due credit for their efforts.

Rewards Should be Significant

The rewards for performance need to be large, ongoing, and tied to individual performance. In any line of work, offering a three percent bonus for new chores or onerous demands is unlikely to produce much of a change in behavior. If collecting that bonus means teachers have to work some extra Saturdays, stay at work until 6 P.M., or change their lesson plans, teachers are likely to complain, "I'm already doing the best I can."

Second, performance-based compensation should lead to something more permanent than a one-time award. One-time payouts given to a handful of schools or teachers that have posted one year of impressive test results, as under the California bonus system which offers $25,000 to teachers at a handful of fortunate schools, tend to be regarded as a sideshow or a crapshoot. This is not an unreasonable critique, given the natural variability in student gains and the fine distinctions that states wind up drawing between the schools that win awards and those that do not. Performance-based recognition should not be a one-time "bonus" but an integrated element of the career structure and compensation of educators.

Third, it's important that rewards be offered largely on an individualized basis, even if it is also useful to provide some bonuses on a school-by-school basis. Why? Rewards that are given only on a schoolwide basis risk making it unlikely Mrs. Smith's efforts will have much effect on the school's aggregate performance, ensuring that she will continue to work more or less as she always has. The undesired result of each individual teacher making the same rational calculation is the failure to improve education. At the most basic level, individual self-interest must be harnessed and rewarded, or penalized, to bring about communally desired outcomes.

At the same time, schools are cooperative communities and we don't want incentives to undermine that. Fortunately, the solution is straightforward.

Thousands of firms and nonprofits provide incentives for group perform-ance, but lay these atop systems based on individual performance. Schoolwide incentives for performance are good and can build a sense of team effort, so long as these supplement a system that recognizes individual productivity. Small bonuses (say, equal to about 5 percent of salary) can have a positive effect on group unity and can be used in conjunction with incentives keyed to individual performance.

Close Down Long-Term Failures

What happens at schools where accountability and incentives don't make a difference? What happens when the principal and the faculty continue to produce unacceptable improvement? We cannot afford to keep sending chil-dren to a school where the leadership is so weak, the faculty so ineffective, or the culture so troubled that even flagging it for low performance hasn't made a difference. When this happens, state accountability laws need to provide ways to shut the school down and start it up with a new team of educators. State law should require that this step be taken after three to five years of unsatisfactory improvement.

It is vital that the new faculty be assembled from scratch. New leadership needs to be brought into the shuttered school and given a free to hand to hire faculty. An appropriate amount of money should be provided to the new school in its first year to help get the program running.

This "death penalty" provision does three things. It puts additional mus-cle into the accountability system by forcing faculty in low-performing schools to worry about how well the entire school is serving students. It cre-ates an end point for those schools in a death spiral where good educators are trying to flee to other schools and no one is able to make the school work. Finally, it ensures that states are periodically flushing the worst schools out of the system while creating fresh opportunities for new talent.

The Status Quo Response: "Nice" Accountability

Reasonable status quo reformers generally can't bring themselves to deny the benefits of accountability, so they try to offer an alternative that secures those without having to bear the costs of being tough minded. They wind up being for "nice accountability."[30]

With accountability, as with just about any commonsense reform, the status quo reformers have a toothless version that they endorse. Status quo reformers support guidelines as to what content will be taught, because these encourage teacher collaboration and better enable teachers to work with students who switch schools. Status quo reformers are for "authentic" assessments that try to capture everything a student should know. They support using these assessments to help teachers diagnose student needs. They talk about the need to use assessment to help teachers "talk with one another about how their students are doing," "stay focused on teaching well and meeting student needs," and "pay close attention to [curricular] alignment."[31] In the words of Stanford education professor Linda Darling-Hammond, status quo reformers embrace a "model for standards-based reform...that rests on professional accountability and the use of standards and assessments as information for professional development and curricular reform rather than as punishments for schools and students."[32] In other words, status quo reformers are for standards and assessment so long as these are controlled by educators and don't demand performance from them or their students. They're for accountability so long as nothing changes.

Their gentle approach is intended to improve schools by helping teachers better understand student needs, increasing coordination across schools and classrooms, and prompting low performers to find ways to improve. Status quo accountability can produce benefits, but these depend on the ability and inclination of teachers. "Nice accountability" is well and good and helpful, and everyone is for it, but it will make a difference only if all that's slowing down schools is a lack of information on how students are doing. If we need to motivate students and force educators to become more efficient and effective, it won't make a difference.

Status quo reformers are conflicted over accountability. On the one hand, they want every child to learn, and they claim that they want to make sure educators are doing their job. On the other hand, they believe that students and educators are already doing all they can and that failure is attributable to forces beyond their control. One Texas principal and Harvard University alumnus beautifully captured the ambivalence that status quo reformers feel about accountability, saying, "Do I believe in rigorous standards for student learning and the need to put pressure on schools to improve instruction?" She answered herself, "I do, but I question whether high-stakes testing... will, in the end, serve the best interests of all students. Last year I had to tell a student that she didn't pass the 'last chance' TAAS (Texas Assessment of Academic Skills) exam administered in May of her senior year; I do not even want to imagine the heartbreak that she and her family felt. I've only had to do this once, but it was one time too many, and I don't know that I have it in me to do it again."[33]

That's sweet, but it's just not an acceptable mind-set for a responsible educator. In the words of the blunt-spoken and savvy Massachusetts Commissioner of Education David Driscoll, "There are times when you have to say no, and kids get angry. You have to say no because it's the right thing to do. The bottom line is a high school diploma has to mean something."[34]

Nice accountability doesn't help decision makers do the kind of tough cutting or reengineering that tough-minded accountability makes possible. With tough-minded accountability, the fact that failure makes painful consequences an impersonal and automatic response can help make tough, preemptive steps seem much more palatable. Harsh measures like closing schools, eliminating programs, terminating employees, or mandating new professional development regimes can be regarded as sensible where before they seemed punitive.

Some educators fret that accountability based on essential skills will prove too constricting. They worry that the need to make sure that students master reading, writing, arithmetic, and so on will unduly crimp their ability to offer innovative curricula. Linda McNeil, an anti-accountability crusader who has been featured on *60 Minutes*, has written about magnet school teachers who feared that preparing students for the new Texas achievement standards would "rob their students of experience with the curricula and the learning activities the teachers had been creating."[35] The common-sense reformer views such a complaint as ludicrous. If exemplary lesson plans fail to help students master even basic reading, writing, or math skills, a commonsense reformer has to wonder how exemplary they really are.

Status quo complaints gain validity when accountability systems extend beyond the gatekeeper skills into a sprawling laundry list of requirements. While it is essential that every student achieve a clear competence in writing, reading, and math, for instance, it is not useful to have the state mandating that every single student demonstrate a specified mastery in Spanish, chemistry, or music. When assessment is carried to that extreme, it will homogenize schools and interfere with curricular focus to no obvious end. Clearly, there is a balance that must be struck. However, recognize that any educator who complains about requiring all students to be proficient in numeracy or literacy is baldly declaring that not all students can or should master these skills. That stance is deeply troubling to a commonsense reformer.

Making Tough-Minded Accountability Work

There are obvious and even unavoidable downsides to accountability. Of course, the same can be said of accountability in medicine, manufacturing, police work, or higher education. Practitioners will inevitably fret that accountability is impinging upon their freedom or that it "distracts" them from what they see as more important. In some cases, this is true. Some schools and some teachers are so effective in unconventional ways that pushing them to focus on teaching essential skills might be disruptive.

There are three points to keep in mind. First, heightened accountability must be accompanied by increased flexibility. So long as these educators or schools are teaching essential content, commonsense reform should result in their having more freedom to operate. Second, if their students aren't performing adequately on math, reading, or history tests, then it is not clear that these schools or teachers are effective. Third, tough-minded accountability is not intended to encourage expansive excellence but rather to ensure that schools are helping all students to master essential skills. It is market-based accountability that offers a mechanism for recognizing and rewarding more diverse kinds of excellence.

Accountability can be critically compromised when goals or assessments are wrong-headed. For instance, if doctors are evaluated on how many patients he sees a day and not on the quality of care, practitioners will have incentives to process patients rapidly and to skimp on the attention they provide. American business suffered from this problem on a grand scale in the late 1990s, when professional investors started to fixate on the ability of companies to beat their expected earnings target each quarter. What had started as a sensible way to get executives focused on improving efficiency and cutting corporate fat became an exercise in excess. Companies felt increasing pressure to be sure that their per-share earnings figure released each ninety days beat the "whisper number" (the expected earnings) bandied about by the experts. In *The Number: How the Drive for Quarterly Earnings Corrupted Wall Street and Corporate America*, Alex Berenson explains how the obsession with a single, easily manipulated statistic fostered chicanery and encouraged the corporate collapses that marked 2001 and 2002.[36] This dishonesty highlights the need to focus on a system that is simple, sensible, and balanced.

The Cost of Testing

One objection offered against testing is the expense. In fact, the costs of testing are quite small, especially given the commonsense necessity of accountability.

Testing costs only a few dollars per student. This amounts to a tiny fraction of 1 percent of what our schools spend each year, or far less than any well-run private firm spends on quality control. In fact, it's not even one-tenth of what schools spend each year on buses and transportation.

In spring 2003, the U.S. Government Accounting Office priced three options for providing the tests required by No Child Left Behind for all of 2002–2008. For the entire period, the GAO estimated that high-end, gold-plated tests would cost $5.3 billion. In other words, providing sophisticated tests in every state to some high schoolers and every student in grades 3 through 8 would amount to a rounding error in the more than $3 trillion we'll spend on K-12 education. Captains of any other industry would consider it a show-stopping bargain if they could obtain critical quality control data for less than two-tenths of 1 percent of their annual revenue. The professional education crowd saw even these minimal costs, however, as a reason to complain. The executive director of the National Association of State Boards of Education said, "The bottom line is that high-quality, aligned state assessments are expensive."[37]

The reality is that we should invest significantly more in good assessments than we do. In Britain, for instance, test development and administration for tests recognized as world class cost about $50 or $60 (USD) a year per student per subject. That still amounts to only about $200 a child per year, or less than three percent of spending. Even that figure dramatically overstates the real cost of accountability, however. In a study of leading accountability states conducted using fiscal 2001 data, Harvard economics professor Caroline Hoxby found that only in one state did the entire accountability system wind up costing as much as $30 per public school pupil. The nation's most widely imitated accountability systems—in places like California, Kentucky, and Texas—cost between $18 and $21 per public school pupil. Those figures were not just for the tests, but included all of the costs related to assessment—from consultant time to web maintenance. In fact, Hoxby found that assessment in the United States consumed only about six-hundredths of 1 percent of school spending.[38] Complaints about the cost of accountability are little more than another status quo fiction.

Avoiding Overly Ambitious Standards

One problem is a tendency to get grandiose in devising standards, since no one wants to be seen as publicly calling for "dumbed down" curricula. For example, the Virginia history Standards of Learning gained national acclaim for their rigor and clarity. However, upon close consideration, such programs often prove to be imposing on paper but hollow in practice. To take one example, Virginia's tenth-grade standards called for students to be able to analyze the regional development of Africa, Asia, the Middle East, Latin America, and the Caribbean in terms of physical, cultural, and economic characteristics and historical developments from 1000 A.D. to the present. While an admirable goal, few of Virginia's social studies teachers—or professors of history, for that matter—could meet the plain meaning of such standards. The upshot is that the standards wind up being meaningless and providing little concrete guidance.

The answer is not to throw up our hands in frustration, but to remember the purpose of standards. They are a way to make sure that educators are pressed to bring all children by the age of 18 to a level of knowledge and skill that we think necessary to be a responsible and productive citizen. In the case of writing, math, and reading, this leads to pretty straightforward judgments. In science, social studies, and literature these criteria are more complex, but it's probably not essential that every graduate be able to provide a cultural analysis of twelfth-century Caribbean or Latin American history. This doesn't mean that we shouldn't aspire to such things, but that a commonsense reformer distinguishes the critical from the desirable.

What About Cheating?

Holding educators responsible for student learning poses the risk that some unscrupulous souls may try to game the system. This is a subject that demands attention. Fortunately, researchers have found that no more than 3 to 6 percent of classrooms experience situations where teachers or administrators try to doctor exams even when the results have serious professional consequences. Of course, even this rate is unacceptably high and raises grave questions about the suitability of some educators currently in the schools. More promisingly, researchers like Harvard University professor Brian Jacob and University of Chicago professor Stephen Levitt have started to devise statistical analysis strategies that can flag the vast majority of incidents and deter future cheating. While such efforts are a critical part of making accountability work, any problems that result from unethical educator behavior ought to measure against the risk of allowing these same educators to operate without anyone keeping any eye on their work. Finally, Jacob and Levitt reassure us that, "While evidence of cheating is sometimes used to impugn high-stakes testing programs, our results actually show that explicit cheating by school personnel is not likely to be a serious enough problem by itself to call into question high-stakes testing, both because the most egregious forms of cheating are relatively rare and, more important, because cheating can be virtually eliminated at a relatively low cost through the implementation of proper safeguards."[39]

Going Wobbly

During the prelude to the first Gulf War against Iraq, there was a short period after Saddam Hussein had occupied Kuwait that we were uncertain how we'd respond. During that period, President George H. W. Bush met with Prime Minister Margaret Thatcher of England. Fearful that Bush might be tempted to lapse into niceness or the pleasingly gentle route of diplomatic conversation, Thatcher memorably advised, "Don't go wobbly now, George." That advice is worth recalling, especially when the conciliatory route is popular, pleasant, and widely embraced.

Legislators, state officials, and district leaders tend to go wobbly when it comes to making tough-minded accountability work. Establishing meaningful performance standards means that some students, teachers, and schools will fail to meet those standards. Politically, this poses a big challenge because the low performers have powerful incentives to challenge the system. Accountability enthusiasts usually respond by trying to meet critics halfway. They try to tweak the accountability system to placate its critics, producing compromises that delay the start dates of accountability, lower required passing scores, break any link between student performance and teacher evaluation, or otherwise undercut accountability. By 2002, more than twenty-five states had adopted mandatory graduation exams, and more than twenty states offered school incentives linked to test scores.[40] However, phase-in periods and delays in implementation meant that the graduation requirements and the test-based incentives and sanctions for educators took effect in only a handful of states.

In practice, most accountability systems begin with at least a symbolic commitment to tough-minded accountability. Because critics rarely oppose accountability in principle, they are able to win a series of compromises that quietly hollow it out. Such critics implicitly agree that they will support tough-minded accountability if only... it wobbles into nice accountability.[41]

Conclusion

Commonsense accountability requires that student performance be annually assessed in the essential subjects, that results be made widely available along with other relevant data, and that results must count for students and teachers. Teachers whose students fare well should be recognized, while those whose students fare poorly should be identified and their performance addressed. Students who have not mastered essential knowledge or skills should not be carelessly handed along, and students who have not mastered a high school education should not be given a high school diploma.

When debating high-stakes testing, proponents tout the requisite tests as clear, scientifically defensible, manageable, and concise while critics attack them as unreliable, simplistic, overly focused on trivia, or lacking the necessary curricular and pedagogical support. A commonsense reformer recognizes that both sides are right—but knows also that imperfect accountability is better than none at all.

Proponents have difficulty standing firm on the details of any particular accountability system in large part because essential components relating to content, assessment, and sanctions are judgment calls. Determining standards for what students need to know, when they need to know it, and how well they need to know it is a useful artifice. No one can "prove" that specified content ought to be taught at particular grade levels. Such decisions are imperfect, publicly rendered judgments about the needs and capacities of children. Without such decisions, though, we leave each child to the tender mercies of a given teacher. Moreover, despite its imperfections, academic testing is now at least as reliable as the metrics used to evaluate adult job performance in other professions—from accounting to consulting to journalism. University of North Carolina psychometrician Greg Cizek, author of *Detecting and Preventing Classroom Cheating: Promoting Integrity in Assessment*, has now concluded, "High-stakes tests have evolved to a point where they are: highly reliable; free from bias; relevant and age appropriate; higher order; tightly related to important, public goals; time and cost efficient; and yielding remarkably consistent decisions."[42]

While tough-minded accountability draws fierce opposition, public sentiment often reverses once it is in place long enough to become part of the "grammar of schooling."[43] It permits educators to demonstrate that they're adding value and can strengthen their claim on public support and resources. Hardworking educators are tired of being treated exactly like their least effective peers. Making judgments about performance requires using some assessment, and given growing public pressure for such judgments, assessments based upon measured results at least provide an impersonal barometer against which to measure personal determinations.

This all makes good sense. It only works, however, when we find the leaders and teachers to make it work and equip them with the tools they need. Accountability alone is only a start in creating a culture of competence. In the words of legendary American Federation of Teachers founder Al Shanker: "Unless you start with a very heavy emphasis on accountability, not end with it, you'll never get a system with all the other pieces falling into place. As long as there are no consequences if kids or adults don't perform, as long as the discussion is not about education and student outcomes, then we're playing a game as to who has power."[44] Accountability works only when used fully to motivate and manage. Today, education leaders generally lack the requisite tools, while too many are hesitant to use the tools they do possess.

Something very much like this is at the core of local frustration with the federal No Child Left Behind Act. Under this law, Washington instructed states to evaluate schools and school districts on the basis of test results, yet neither the federal nor state governments have increased the freedom of the superintendents or principals they expect to tackle this challenge. Contract language limits principals in their ability to assign teachers to the students who need them most and constrains superintendents from transferring principals or teachers to schools where they will do the most good. State laws regulating class size prevent principals from creating classrooms where some students might receive intensive instruction in small groups, since that would require that other classes exceed the permitted size. Contracts make it difficult to reward good teachers or remove ineffective ones.

At the same time, accountability provides critical safeguards on the use of newfound freedoms. If nontraditional teachers are allowed more readily into classrooms, measuring performance ensures that only effective teachers remain in classroom. As we give principals and superintendents more flexibility to govern personnel, accountability can help identify capricious decision makers who use their freedom to pursue personal agendas.

CHAPTER THREE

Competition

I trust a good deal to common fame, as we all must. If a man...can make better chairs or knives, crucibles or church organs, than anybody else, you will find a broad hard-beaten road to his house, though it be in the woods.

—Ralph Waldo Emerson

Tough-minded accountability substitutes self-interest for the airy promise of good intentions. In doing so, it clarifies agreement on essential purposes, safeguards common interests, and provides parents and policymakers with a reliable way to monitor the performance of schools and school systems. Because schooling is a public good as well a private one, such public direction and oversight is critical. However, tough-minded accountability is a crude instrument that can unduly narrow the scope of teaching and squeeze valuable material out of the curriculum.

Competition complements tough-minded accountability by requiring schools to compete for students, with those schools that fail to attract enough students forced to shrink their size or shut their doors. Where tough-minded accountability requires state government to set goals and hold educators responsible for them, competitive accountability allows schools to satisfy varied demands. Where tough-minded accountability encourages sameness in essentials, competition encourages a complementary emphasis on an array of higher-order academic and cultural offerings.

Tough-minded accountability assumes that there are common purposes we wish schools to pursue and common skills and knowledge that all schools must teach. Competitive accountability presumes that children will have particular strengths and interests. One family may be extremely concerned about school safety or finding advanced math instruction for their child, while another may seek out a quality arts program.

Tough-minded accountability is a powerful tool for ensuring that all schools effectively teach essential knowledge and skills, but is a poor device for pushing schools to excel at teaching advanced material, content outside of the core disciplines, or the performing arts. The truth is that no school can excel at everything and that some offerings are more useful for some students than others. Parental choice allows schools to thoughtfully target resources. Mandating that every high school provide a symphony, an art studio, and a language lab ensures that few schools do any of these well and that many schools simply become furtive lawbreakers. Rather than vaguely insisting that all schools provide a long menu of options, choice arrangements permit schools to excel at particular services and empower families to select the school that's a good match for their child.

Ultimately, competition can do four things that tough-minded accountability cannot. First, competition protects against the excessive homogenization of tough-minded accountability. Because families and students have varied interests and needs, educators always confront multiple demands. Today, public schools have responded by becoming "shopping malls" that provide a smorgasbord of offerings. Allowing families to choose among different schools reduces the pressures on any given school to be everything to everybody and makes it easier to achieve a common purpose and build a faculty culture committed to that purpose. Instead of promoting fragmentation within each school, choice enables educators to address particular needs and concerns by differentiating between schools.

Second, competition provides quality control that extends beyond the powerful but basic accountability afforded by coercion. Families can switch their children from schools that offer undesirable or ineffective programs to those that are more appealing. Obviously, in making such choices, families will be steered by the data produced by tough-minded accountability. However, when choosing among adequately performing schools, families will also choose based upon things like school culture, programs, faculty, and the other students. If children flood out of a school, that's a powerful signal that the school is not performing adequately, whatever its test results. If the money that pays for those departing students follows them when they leave that school, it forces the faculty to suffer through potentially painful retrenching.

Commonsense reform is premised on the expectation that most parents can and will make reasonable decisions about what their child needs and about the suitability and the relative effectiveness of a given school. The assumption is that choosing a good school doesn't require deep expertise in pedagogy or an advanced degree. Commonsense reformers believe that finding a good school for a child is a relatively straightforward process of deciding: (1) Is this school safe? (2) Does it teach the essentials? (3) Does it meet my child's particular needs? Of course, some parents are uninformed, uninterested, abusive, or otherwise irresponsible when it comes to their child's education. However, the commonsense reformer believes these to be only a handful and that accountability and the discipline extended by the mass of parents making sensible judgments will better serve even the children of irresponsible parents than does the status quo.

Third, choice-based competition encourages flexibility and creativity by enabling entrepreneurial educators to challenge existing schools and the reigning orthodoxies. More than a decade ago, scholars John Chubb and Terry Moe made a compelling case that principals in traditional public schools find that their freedom to manage and staff schools is limited by political and bureaucratic pressures.[1] District officials charged with developing uniform policies for dozens of schools wind up placating competing familial and neighborhood concerns by subjecting all schools to standard issue rules. It is often hard for free-thinking educators to punch through the ranks of school bureaucracy and win a fair hearing for their ideas. Managers of large organizations have little time for mavericks and tend to have a strong preference for workers who stay in the lines and don't cause headaches. Unconventional teachers and principals are often regarded as troublemakers and ostracized by cautious district officials.

While traditional school districts are good at fiddling about with changes in curricula and teacher training, they are terribly resistant to changes in how schools are staffed, managed, or run. By opening the system up to entrepreneurs, competition creates new opportunities for schools that hire nontraditional teachers, harness technology in new ways, pay faculty based on performance, and make other unconventional moves. Especially in locales where poor management renders accountability stifling, competition allows innovators to put new ideas forward without having to beg permission from the system leadership. Competition does not imply that central control is always undesirable. There are areas like reading instruction or professional development where school systems can reap significant benefits by cultivating focused and consistent approaches to teaching and learning. So long as it's effective, such centralization makes good sense. The commonsense view is only that it's sensible to *permit* other schooling options to emerge if some families find them desirable or if communities of educators believe they can be effective using alternative methods.

Finally, competition permits effective schools to multiply and grow without having to wait on political processes or resistant district leadership.

Traditionally, school improvement proceeds as districts try to nudge and wrestle poor schools forward. This leaves children in those schools dependent on the ability of district officials and their trusted experts to find ways to improve these ineffective schools. Decades of such efforts have produced generally disappointing results. A more efficacious way to address troubled schools is to simply bypass them. We can do this by permitting parental choice to steer students away from the worst schools and towards successful schools. *If* the system features sensible incentives, the resulting pressures will help to shutter poor schools and encourage effective schools and school systems to expand. A competitive environment that makes it easier for successful schools to emerge and displace less effective schools is a commonsense route to systemic improvement.

Readers may be puzzled by the lack of attention devoted here to the research examining how school choice benefits participants.[2] However, while this question has drawn a lot of media attention and helps inform parents, policymakers, and educators about small-scale programs, from the commonsense perspective this debate is largely peripheral. The commonsense reformer is agnostic about the merits of any given "school of choice" and is less interested in whether students at these private schools fared better than they would have at those public schools than in how to build a system where excellence, whatever its location, is recognized, touted, and rewarded. The commonsense challenge is to drive systemwide improvement, foster schools receptive to the culture of competence, and create new opportunities for excellence.

The Principle of Competition

In theory, competition rewards excellence and raps mediocrity. It does this through thousands of individual decisions and without requiring any coordinator to intervene or render judgments on school performance. Like tough-minded accountability, competition rests on the principle that radical improvement is possible only when inaction becomes so painful that distasteful activity finally becomes easier than inactivity. Typically, education leaders find it easier to quietly work around mediocrity than to uproot it. When poor performance becomes a matter of self-preservation, however, hardworking educators who would previously have frowned at aggressive leadership as intrusive or threatening will suddenly find it much less so. In fact, imminent competition can give leaders the freedom to take steps that would previously have been deemed too radical. As one school board member from Milwaukee confided, "It would have been almost impossible to get the central administrators to embrace the [decentralization plan]. But when we packaged it as a way to show the community that we're responsive to their concerns, suddenly they were on board."

Competition requires that schools which attract students gain resources that permit the schools to reward and support their faculty. Meanwhile, faculty at schools that lose students must bear a price in terms of salary reductions or layoffs. Principals will find it much easier to suggest reducing faculty slots, cutting pay, covering more classes, or extending parental outreach when these moves are seen as a last resort intended to protect the faculty and the school.[3]

To be blunt, competition works when it hurts. Markets work precisely because they are neither gentle nor forgiving. They are impersonal mechanisms that gain their power by harnessing self-interest, drawing on desire and fear. Failure can upend lives, consume careers, and destroy fortunes. Success can bring wealth, power, and opportunities for creativity, philanthropy, or debauchery. The power of the market lurks in the knowledge that even winners may be only one innovation away from being thrown over. The entrepreneurs who take the chances that drive innovation and growth will reap rewards, modeling successful new approaches and inspiring kindred spirits.

The number of these entrepreneurs is small, because most people are hesitant risk-takers. Psychological studies tell us that people fear losses much more highly than they value potential gains. The consequence is that markets lead most investors, executives, and employees to live in constant low-level fear of losing their jobs or investments. They respond accordingly. There is nothing voluntary or particularly good-hearted about these responses. In fact, the middle manager at a large firm knows that her efforts are unlikely to significantly affect the firm's bottom line. This manager is not motivated by a vague hope that rewards for her efforts will trickle down. Instead, she is concerned with how her work will be evaluated and the effects that will have on her security, salary, and future. If individuals do good work, producers will compete for their services. If they are underpaid, they can make themselves available to competitors who will fully value their skills. If individuals don't do good work, employers will look elsewhere. Organizations inattentive to quality are soon left behind.

This "creative destruction" supports a steady shift of people and resources from weaker organizations to stronger ones while creating room for new and more effective schools and practitioners. Rather than forcing new ideas or entrepreneurs to win approval from large and balky organizations, competition creates space to pioneer radical new efficiencies and for individuals who may not have meshed with the powers that be. By firing unproductive workers, firms become more efficient; poor performers are weeded out and the rest are reminded of the cost for slacking off. Meanwhile, as ineffective organizations are shuttered or slimmed down, room and resources are freed up for new and more productive producers. This cycle keeps everyone sharp and directs resources to the people and organizations that are doing the best work. Some individuals will make gains and some will suffer losses. This cheerful macro picture of general benefit, however, cannot obscure the fact that this process requires that many individuals suffer painful, if temporary, dislocations and losses over the course of time.

Most people prefer to insulate themselves from uncertainty. Investors and executives lobby for government protections, hoping they can put to rest concerns about hungry competitors stealing customers or undercutting their prices. Unions seek to protect their membership by curtailing layoffs, requiring that firms hire union members, linking salary or benefits to seniority, and limiting the monitoring of workers.

In the private sector, when competition is threatening enough—as when American automakers and electronic manufacturers were almost wiped out by Japanese competitors in the 1980s—it can overwhelm these protective mechanisms. When the threat looms large enough, firms either reinvent themselves or are replaced by more productive competitors. Unions make painful concessions to help keep their employers competitive or watch jobs vanish. Competition forces the hand of managers and union leaders alike.

The absence of competition means that public agencies, like public schools, don't have this discipline. No matter how inefficient the public agency or level of pay, it need not worry that customers will be driven away by poor service or high prices. Subjecting public agencies to real competition puts an end to that. One of the more familiar cases occurred in the 1970s when Federal Express was permitted to compete head-to-head with the U.S. Postal Service on express deliveries. Federal Express stripped away so much business in such short order that the U.S. Postal Service employees eventually accepted automation, downsizing, and new work rules that they had long rejected but were now necessary for self-preservation.

However, even when public organizations are subjected to competition, it's not always clear that individual employees are pushed to become more productive. If schools are faced with the threat of lost enrollment but teachers and administrators are insulated from any consequences by job protections or the fact that faculty turnover outstrips student departures, then "competition" will have little impact.[4] The consequences due to student flight cannot be vague or theoretical if they are to be effective. Rather, they must be experienced in the working world of schools and classrooms.

The point of competition is not to have lots of families make lots of choices or to have students shuffle around. Rather, it is to focus schools fiercely on meeting the needs of their families and students. In truth, if educators are sufficiently sensitized, it is possible for competition to produce the desired results without more than a small number of families changing schools. Competition is not primarily about giving parents more choices but about inducing leaders to make decisions they would rather avoid.

Getting Serious About Competition

Imagine if a store manager for a national chain were told that losing customers would have no impact on her salary or job security, though if the company lost enough customers across the nation it might be forced to hire more slowly at some stores.

Assume further that the managers were told that great success in attracting customers would require them to erect trailers in the parking lot to handle the overflow. This would require that the manager assign employees to the trailers, ensuring complaints from both customers and workers. Neither the manager nor the employees would be compensated, rewarded, or promoted for successfully attracting clients. The only real change, aside from the store being more crowded and employees working harder, is that the manager might be expected to hire more employees, creating more responsibilities and potential headaches.

Such a scenario is obviously ridiculous. No one would care much about "competing." In such a world, the commonsense manager's preference would be for a stable customer population though, truth be told, she'd probably rather lose customers than gain them. If Wal-Mart or Starbucks or Coach operated this way, their most entrepreneurial managers would flee and customer growth would screech to a halt.

Nevertheless, this is exactly how we operate traditional public schools—and even most "choice" schools. Imagine the principal of "Greenlake Elementary," a school built to house 400 students that currently enrolls 375 students. What happens if the principal loses 75 students? Three retiring teachers are not replaced or are transferred to another school, three classrooms are freed up, and the small amount of discretionary money that flowed to the school to support those students doesn't come in. Given the natural rate of teacher turnover, the likelihood is that no teachers will even need to be transferred and that the principal will simply be spared the need to hire replacements. In short, the principal's job gets a little easier. She has fewer teachers to lead, fewer students to monitor, and a less crowded school.

Take the same school and assume that the principal reacts powerfully and effectively to the incitement to increase enrollment, prompting the school to add 75 students. What happens? The principal takes on responsibility for three new teachers, must squeeze students into the last available classroom, adds two trailers out back to hold two additional classrooms, and crowds the school's cafeteria and corridors. The principal now must live with two teachers who are most assuredly not happy about teaching all day in a trailer and 50 families that feel the same way about their child learning in one. In return for these headaches, the principal receives—what? At best, a small pool of discretionary monies, typically amounting to less than $50 or $100 a student.

The "successful" principal is rewarded with more responsibilities, dissatisfied constituents, and a handful of loose change. For this, she receives no more pay, no better treatment, and no more recognition than the "unsuccessful" principal. Why would we expect the typical principal to compete avidly for students? Quite simply, we wouldn't. The same is true for superintendents and board members, except in those rare occasions when the public fallout from student departures becomes severe enough to prompt political action.

Most choice-based reforms in American education, from the choice-based provisions of No Child Left Behind to most charter school laws, do little more than create hollow, Greenlake-style "competition." Schools that lose or gain students inevitably lose or gain less than the full amount of funding attached to that student, easing the blow to unpopular schools and giving those schools in demand little incentive to attract students. The rules governing employee compensation mean that neither principals nor teachers have much of a personal stake riding on whether their school attracts or repels students. Members of the professional education community often recognize this reality more clearly than many choice enthusiasts, precisely because they are not blinded by their own enthusiasm.

Making Schools Compete

Is this to suggest that educators will never respond aggressively to competition? No. It is a caution that they will not necessarily be inclined to do so. Merely giving families choices does not necessarily mean that schools will compete to attract students. Harnessing competition requires giving educators reason to compete even when it requires uncomfortable decisions or unpleasant exertions. How does one do that?

Envision Greenlake again, but imagine that a principal's pay and her future in the district are linked to her school's enrollment. Principals would then have incentives linked to student enrollment. For instance, a principal might receive a bonus for each additional student who enrolls in her school or annual evaluations might take enrollment into account. Suddenly, the many concerns that keep principals from worrying about enrollment and all the obstacles that prevent them from addressing enrollment would appear far more manageable. Since some principals obviously are dealt a stronger hand than others, whether in terms of being in higher income areas or having an existing staff that is highly effective, and some principals are asked to take over unpopular schools, sensible adjustments for such considerations are obviously appropriate.

If they were motivated to pursue students, principals would have less patience for faculty excuses and would be under more pressure to tackle persistent problems. All of these activities will not necessarily be educationally productive. Principals would devote more attention to public relations, advertising, beautifying school buildings, and launching services like after-school day care. While such changes would be positive and increase community investment in schooling, they would also divert some resources from instruction. Nonetheless, schools and school systems have such a dismal track record on public outreach that there is currently little risk of their investing too much energy in these activities. As for the future, such concerns can be addressed through sensible oversight.

If this feels a bit callous, that's to be expected. Reflect for a moment, though. Don't we believe that principals should want to attract students? A commonsense reformer believes that educators should be proud that students want to attend their school. If so, so long as we're also keeping a close eye on bottom-line measures of student achievement, why would we shrink from rewarding schools that succeed at attracting students? Don't we routinely reward doctors for attracting patients and journalists for attracting readers without destroying professional codes of conduct or provoking widespread malfeasance?

What if principals will only want to work in schools where it's easy to boost enrollment? High-quality principals who take on challenging assignments should have that factored into professional evaluations and be paid significantly more than their peers, more than making up for any forgone enrollment bonuses. The fundamental lesson is that "choice" alone is not a remedy for systemic improvement. For instance, Moscow shoppers could choose from scores of grocery stores in the 1970s, during the height of Communist reign in the old Soviet Union. Nonetheless, no one would suggest that the Muscovite grocery market was competitive or had benefited from competition. Why? Mostly because wherever customers decided to shop, the employment and working conditions of the employees at all the various groceries remained essentially unchanged. Consequently, employees didn't care about attracting customers or fear losing them. Transforming "choice" into competition requires making the consequences matter for individual educators.

Where We are Now

Merely allowing families to choose schools is clearly not enough to produce competition; American schooling has long featured a good deal of choice but little competition. While heated debates about choice-based reforms like school vouchers or charter schooling give the impression that allowing parents to choose a child's school is new or radical, nothing could be further from the truth. As the National Working Commission on Choice in K-12 Education observed in its 2003 report, "Although 'choice' is often discussed as something novel in public education, a variety of options have long existed in American schools."[5] In fact, if one totals the 36 percent of parents who report that their choice of residence was influenced by school considerations, the 17 percent who reported choosing their public school through some kind of choice program, and the 15 percent who reported selecting a private school, 68 percent of families actively select their child's school.[6]

The most widely utilized form of choice is "residential choice." When purchasing a home, parents typically pay attention to the quality of the local schools. Because our school districts are based on geography, children are normally assigned to a particular school on the basis of where they live. For decades, this arrangement has allowed most middle- and upper-class families to choose their child's school. Of course, this means that any competition takes place among new homebuyers, because once a family buys a home the child is planted in a school. The savviest of these families have excelled at lobbying school boards or school principals in order to get their children assigned to special programs or particular teachers. This kind of choice has been going on for decades, advantaging wealthy and politically astute families at the expense of families who aren't equipped to play these games.

Today, roughly six million students are enrolled in K-12 private schools, accounting for about 11 percent of the total K-12 school population. Catholic parochial schools are the most common type of private school, enrolling 44 percent of the total private school population. Nationally, Catholic schools enroll more than three-quarters of their students in grades K-8 and have a student population that is 24 percent minority.[7] While these schools tend to spend considerably less than nearby public schools, the academic performance of their students is generally equal to or better than that of similar public school students. Researchers have suggested that the relative success of private schools, especially Catholic schools serving poor and minority students, is due to their discipline, focus on academic instruction for all students, and commitment to ensuring that all children learn.[8]

The use of "home schooling," in which parents teach their children, has grown rapidly over the past two decades. Experts estimate that at least 850,000 students, or close to 2 percent of the American K-12 population, are now being homeschooled.[9] Across the country, families utilize web-based lessons, tutoring, and other resources.

In the past three decades, public schools have made it their business to offer a menu of choices to families. They do this with programs like magnet schooling, intradistrict public school choice, and interdistrict public choice. Each provides a limited number of school choices to families that take advantage of them. Many districts offer "magnet" schools that provide a special emphasis on a subject, such as science or the arts. These schools were pioneered in the late 1960s, with the goal of promoting desegregation by enticing white students to attend predominantly black schools. Students from all over the school district apply for a seat in magnets, with one-third of magnets selecting students based on ability and others using lottery systems to admit students. Today, there are more than 1,700 magnet schools enrolling about 1.4 million students.[10]

Some districts permit students to apply for a slot in one of several district schools (this is "intradistrict" choice), while some states have allowed children to transfer to schools outside of their district if the school had vacancies (this is "interdistrict" choice). In 2003, about 500,000 students were enrolled in schools outside of their home district. All of these options have become much more complex in light of the federal No Child Left Behind Act, which requires that school districts create alternatives for students at "failing" or unsafe schools. These alternatives can include charter schools, other public schools, or private schools. States are to identify such schools based on measures of student performance or student safety and are required to help ensure that students in these schools have other schooling options, whether in other district schools, traditional district schools outside the district, charter schools, or private schools.

None of these options addresses the three most radical kinds of school choice: charter schooling, school vouchers, and tuition tax credits. By 2003, more than 3,000 charter schools enrolled more than 600,000 students in 40 states, though the total charter enrollment still amounted to less than

2 percent of the public K-12 population. Just six states (Florida, Ohio, Wisconsin, Colorado, Maine, and Vermont) operate school voucher programs and those programs generally are restricted to certain cities, certain schools, or to children with special needs. There are also scores of private voucher programs operating in roughly 40 states through which philanthropists or charitable organizations fund scholarships to help low-income children attend private schools. These private programs operate by promising a set amount of money to help poor children afford tuition at a private school of their choice. To encourage those private efforts, six states, including Arizona, Florida, and Pennsylvania, have adopted tuition tax credits that offer a significant tax break for contributing to such "tuition scholarship" funds.[11]

Pure voucher systems entail issuing families an annual "voucher" for the cost of their child's education. Families are free to spend the voucher at any eligible school. Vouchers permit a wide array of schools to spring up, give families new options, and require educators to compete for students. Tuition tax credit programs help the state provide school vouchers by encouraging taxpayers to contribute to private funds that distribute vouchers to low-income students.

Charter schooling is a process by which the state permits a variety of individuals to open state funded schools. Unlike traditional public schools, which are managed by school districts responsible for all schools in a given geographic area, charter schools are chartered by a state-approved entity. In various states, charter authorizers have included school districts, state school boards, museums, city governments, universities, and others. Because their existence depends on this grant from the state, charter schools are regarded as public schools subject to conventional regulations and constraints. Therefore, unlike private schools, charter schools must abide by the same restrictions on religion as public schools, cannot charge tuition, cannot selectively admit students, and are potentially subject to a host of regulations on matters ranging from curriculum to teacher salaries.

A charter is a contract between the charter school and the state-approved authorizer and sets out how the charter school will operate. The contract also sets out performance requirements that charter schools are expected to meet if they are to keep their charter. While charter schools are generally required to abide by the state regulations that apply to other public schools, their charters can free them from many of the regulations, requirements, and teacher contract restrictions that districts impose on local schools. Charter schools are eligible for some initial federal and state money in order to get started, but fund their operations primarily out of the state money that follows students who choose to attend the school. In most states, the percentage of student funding that follows students to the charter school is about three-quarters of what district schools spend on each child. Setting the figure at less than 100 percent recognizes that traditional public schools do not save the entire cost of a departing student because the school system must still pay for buildings, transportation, and so on.[12]

In theory, by permitting students to attend the widest possible array of public and private schools, vouchers create more choice and competition than charters. In practice, publicly funded voucher programs include a number of restrictions on participating students and schools. Programs typically limit vouchers to low-income students, only make vouchers worth a small portion of local public per-pupil spending, limit the total number of available vouchers to a small percentage of local students, impose heavy legal or regulatory burdens on private schools, require that schools accepting voucher students not selectively admit applicants, and so on. Meanwhile, the public and policymakers have been more willing to let charter schools grow and expand. In states like Michigan, California, and Arizona, hundreds of charter schools have opened their doors. In cities like Washington, D.C., Philadelphia, and Dayton, Ohio, charter schools have enrolled 15 percent or more of local students.

Policymakers are more willing to allow charter schooling to expand because they remain under the direct supervision of the public school bureaucracy. Because charter school programs enjoy relatively stable political support and have solid long term prospects, for-profit firms like National Heritage Academies or Edison Schools are more eager to launch and run charter schools than voucher schools.

"Nice" Choice and Tough-Minded Choice

It can be tempting to extol the obvious virtues of choice but then casually retreat from mean-spirited competition as "too much," unnecessarily conflictual, or otherwise undesirable. This mirrors exactly the temptation that nice accountability presented last chapter. Proponents of choice can too easily settle upon "nice" choice arrangements, giving families new choices while rejecting harsh consequences for market losers and the accompanying unpleasantness of tough-minded choice.

Nice choice soft-pedals the harsh language of competition and sells school vouchers and charter schooling primarily as nonthreatening ways to provide new opportunities. Nice choice imagines that the benefits of competition can be harnessed through rhetoric alone, even as the programs do little or nothing to harness self-interest, threaten jobs, risk dislocation, promote the emergence of new schools, or otherwise upset the status quo. Famously, back in 1986, the National Governors Conference endorsed public school choice as a means to "unlock the values of competition in the marketplace."[13] In a widely discussed *New Republic* article, David Osborne, a guru of the reinventing government movement, asserted in 1999 that "those who invented charter schools...wanted to improve all 88,000 public schools in the country by creating enough competition for money and students to force school systems to improve" and went on to enthusiastically claim that "empirical studies have demonstrated that, indeed, competition works just as the reformers predicted."[14] The NGA, Osborne, and others made these heroic claims on behalf of programs that sharply capped the number of participating schools, the dollar amounts involved, and the likelihood that familial choices would cost any educator either a job or a raise. One need not disagree with the promise of competition to conclude, like ardent voucher advocate John Merrifield has, that the kinds of gentle arrangements touted by many advocates do not create enough incentives and opportunities "to create much competitive behavior."[15]

Nice choice is especially tempting because the American public is dubious about whether competition will improve schools. In fact, in a 1999 Public Agenda survey, 47 percent of adults surveyed said that they did not think teachers or administrators would "try harder to do a good job if they see they are losing more and more kids to private schools."[16] This reflects the depth of the attachment to the status quo notion that educators are so spiritual in their motivation and already working so efficiently that competition would be pointless.

Nice choice does have virtues. It permits families and educators to sort themselves in ways that make for more efficient schools. The evidence shows that parents and students who choose their school are happier with it and more invested in it, at least in the first few years. By permitting faculty and families with common interests to forge unified school communities, nice choice allows like-minded faculty members to work together and students to trade one-size-fits-all schools for campuses that match their needs. These changes will likely make for some incremental improvement, but they ultimately still rely on the good intentions and aptitudes of educators.

What We Have is "Nice" Choice

The nation's most ambitious and widely debated school choice experiment has been that in Milwaukee, where a voucher program was introduced in

1990 and where nearly two dozen charter schools now operate. By 2003, the voucher program alone enrolled more than 10,000 students in various private schools. From the beginning critics feared that money would be drained from the Milwaukee Public Schools and choice proponents thumped their chests about the competitive pressures they had unleashed. In fact, after school vouchers came to Milwaukee, the school district's student enrollment, total funding, and per-pupil funding all grew steadily. Between 1990 and 2003, enrollment climbed from slightly under 93,000 students to more than 105,000. Total school spending grew from just over $580 million in 1990–91 to more than $1 billion in 2002–2003 and per-pupil spending grew from about $6,200 to more than $10,200 in current dollars. In other words, despite losing more than 10,000 potential students, the district's budget and payroll expanded at a steady clip. What exactly would spur public school officials to painful action? In fact, given challenges of growing enrollment and outdated buildings during much of that period, many public educators in Milwaukee viewed choice programs as a useful "safety valve."[17]

In Milwaukee, and in states like Arizona or Michigan where charter schools are multiplying quickly, it would be inaccurate to say that school choice has not produced mildly positive competitive effects. It certainly has. In fact, some would argue that competition in Milwaukee has produced greater benefits than I suggest.[18] Some public schools have started advertising in movie theaters, distributing leaflets, or adding all-day kindergarten or a year of preschool. District officials and even teacher union leaders have been more amenable to permitting mavericks to operate within the system and to relaxing some regulations regarding teacher assignment.

In cities like Philadelphia and Dayton, Ohio, the exodus of students to charter schools has prompted renewed attention to schooling, engaged serious people in tackling education problems, and improved the status quo. Districts have responded by providing families with more choices, initiating services that the community had been demanding, and taking steps to improve internal accountability. The changes are healthy, but they are ponderous, constrained by existing regulations, and lacking any sense of urgency. These limited, incremental choice plans are simply not designed to produce the kind of relentless pressure that choice enthusiasts imagine or commonsense reformers demand. The places where competition has come closest to producing rapid change is in small school districts, like those in Arizona, where the opening of a charter school has suddenly deprived the district of 25 percent or more of its students in one fell swoop. Some of these districts have taken immediate steps to offer new programs, overhaul curricula, advertise aggressively, and find new leadership—though even these districts have generally failed to rethink their management routines or organization.[19]

Though many of these developments are welcome, the changes should not be overstated. Choice advocates can too eagerly regard the add-ons, rhetoric, and ad campaigns as having "transformed" education—in much the same way that status quo reformers imagine occasionally successful fiddling as a dramatic breakthrough. The steps taken are almost all additions that can be superimposed atop existing inefficient systems. They don't force all employees to change or tackle any unpleasant responsibilities. The primary purpose of competition is not to spur schools to do some additional things, but to compel principals and superintendents to find ways to do the essential things better.

The Temptations of Nice Choice

Choice enthusiasts are too often unwilling to countenance the hard and unpleasant steps necessary to transform nice choice into competition. After all, nice choice does yield real benefits. Nice choice helps some children escape bad schools, allows some families to find pedagogical or curricular models they like, fosters coherent learning communities, grants schools more ability to govern themselves, and so on. Even education school professors and teacher union leaders who flatly reject competition have frequently endorsed public choice plans on the strength of nice choice. Nice choice is well and good. Its benefits, however, are not rooted in the logic of commonsense reform. Allowing some families to utilize new options and providing more opportunities for individual educators is a strategy entirely dependent on goodwill and good intentions.

Tough-minded reformers must resist the temptation to stop at nice choice or imagine that it will suffice to drive systemic change. The challenge is to recognize that conditions vital to effective competition in schooling cannot simply be assumed but must be established. For instance, in the private sector, executives and investors generally seek to maximize the return on their investment; executives can readily collect information on performance, managers are free to hire and fire, and so on. Competition without these elements is likely to continue to prove thin and disappointing gruel.

Nonetheless, many choice proponents try to wish away this reality. As one confided to me, "I'm 100 percent for school choice, and I'm behind competition, but I'm not for this profit motive. Schools should compete, but they should be competing to help kids—not to chase dollars. . . . I have real qualms about folks making a profit off of children and schools. It just doesn't feel right."

We can have the sentimental, status quo rejection of self-interest or we can have real competition. The commonsense reformer knows that, no matter how much we wish it were otherwise, we can't have both.

Commonsense Competition

Competition can be a powerful lever for good, but it must be designed sensibly. Competition is neither a mystical force for good nor a rapacious bogeyman; it is a mechanism for harnessing the self-interest of educators and the sensible judgment of parents and using these to drive school improvement. This only works as intended if parents are equipped to make commonsense judgments and if educators are rewarded for meeting students' needs. Otherwise, "competition" unaccompanied by sensible incentives or ground rules can yield debacles like the manipulation and larceny that have struck industries like mutual funds and energy in the last couple of years. Using competition to drive school improvement requires more than merely enacting charter school legislation or setting up a pilot voucher program. It requires designing school choice to foster competition. What does that mean in practice?

Money Has to Follow the Child

Competition works only when it hurts to lose a customer. Schools will adopt onerous measures to pursue students only when lost enrollment becomes sufficiently painful, either because it is politically embarrassing or because the adults in the system feel the impact of lost resources. Because political embarrassment is an iffy proposition, it is vital that lost enrollment produce a commensurate loss of funding. That is typically not the case, however. Concerned about unfairly punishing the students who remain at schools with declining enrollments, policymakers have routinely designed choice plans to insulate schools from the consequences of attrition. For instance, most charter school laws specify that charter schools receive only about four-fifths of the per-pupil funding that conventional schools receive, with the student's old school district typically pocketing the difference.[20] New York is considering creating a fund for the sole purpose of cushioning school districts from enrollment lost to charters. When the reform school board took power in Milwaukee in

1999, the Wisconsin legislature quickly moved to reduce the amount of money the district lost when students used a voucher.

In addition, most states have funding systems that phase in any losses over several years. While understandable, the impulse to cushion the impact of lost enrollment is a recipe for sustained mediocrity. Real competition requires having the actual funding for each student follow that student to a new school as rapidly and completely as possible. The Working Commission on Choice in K-12 Education has pointed out, "Low-income, handicapped, and non-English speaking students typically cost more to educate, and unless funding reflects this reality, schools would have an incentive to avoid such students."[21]

It is important that the money following each child should accurately reflect the real cost of educating that child. If a child is disadvantaged, has special needs, or learned English as a second language, that child will probably cost more to educate than the typical student. Similarly, more advantaged students are often less expensive to educate than the typical student. If choice programs provide a flat rate of per-pupil funding without regard to these considerations, they will reward schools that attract inexpensive students and penalize those schools serving harder-to-teach students. The simple answer to this is to weight per-pupil funding to reflect basic levels of student need. Many states have used some version of this approach for years in apportioning local aid. School districts like Seattle, Cincinnati, and Houston have developed relatively sophisticated systems for determining real per-pupil costs.

The Limits of Failure-Based Choice

To alleviate status quo concerns that choice-based reform is intended to benefit privileged families, many choice proposals restrict school choice to children in low-performing schools. Most notably, the federal No Child Left Behind Act requires states to offer choice only to those children in schools that are identified as unsafe or that fail to meet accountability benchmarks.

In a system like this, competition is not an integral component of schooling but an escape offered only to those students stuck in truly dreadful schools. Because the competition in these systems is driven entirely by how schools perform on simple measures of student performance, schools will relentlessly focus their energies on boosting test scores. While such pressure can play a useful role, as in Florida, where Governor Jeb Bush has credited the tiny voucher provision in the state's A+ accountability plan with helping to jump-start school improvement, it doesn't add the broader benefits of competition. In such systems, competition will help reinforce the impact of tough-minded accountability but will not foster diverse learning environments, push schools to provide programs and instruction that extend pass the essentials, or really kick-start entrepreneurial activity. This kind of school choice does not counter the tendency of tough-minded accountability to narrow the curriculum to the essentials.

Letting Families Choose

Competition rests on the assumption that parents are able to make reasonable educational choices on behalf of their kids. This assumption stirs great anxiety among critics who worry about children with irresponsible parents or guardians. What's ironic about that concern is that American education has always given parents a large say in where children go to schools. Parents have always determined their child's school by their choice of where to live, whether to utilize private options, or whether to lean on school officials for particular treatment. Generally speaking, the research suggests that parents seek out safe and academically successful schools and that only a small number are inclined to choose schools on the basis of religion or ideology.[22] In fact, while many choice critics fear that America's parents would primarily use increased freedom to pursue racially or religiously homogenous schools, parents report that they regard diverse school environments as a plus. For instance, when asked in a national survey if they would prefer to send their own child to a "good, diverse school" or to an "outstanding, homogenous school," 67 percent of all public school parents and 62 percent of whites said they would prefer the diverse school. Just 26 percent of all public school parents and 29 percent of whites said they would prefer the "outstanding, homogenous school."[23]

As I have discussed in previous research, familial choices may be hobbled by the difficulty of accurately gauging school quality.[24] Of course, this is precisely the kind of problem that tough-minded accountability helps to address. By helping families gauge how much a school helps children learn and grow, rather than merely whether the school attracts high-performing students, the choice process can be dramatically simplified.

In chapter 2, I argued that tough-minded accountability should be largely restricted to the gatekeeper skills even though those measures are imperfect reflections of school quality. In order to help families make good choices, states should also collect systematic information on a variety of measures beyond student achievement gains including school safety, attendance rates, graduation rates, college attendance rates, and other appropriate measures. While it would be a mistake to use all of this information in a tough-minded accountability system, such information can be invaluable in helping families make educated comparisons of schools. If families value these criteria, and the evidence suggests that they do, competition will ensure that schools compete on dimensions that stretch well beyond core academic competency.[25]

Families are unlikely to take advantage of this information unless it is available in a straightforward and easily utilized format. If the information is too complex or is hard to obtain, families will take reasonable shortcuts—most likely, they will rely upon the easy-to-interpret evaluations of tough-minded accountability. States should use the Internet and other means to make systematic information available on all of the enumerated dimensions of school performance. A variety of intermediaries, whether foundations or school districts or PTAs or entrepreneurial schools, will be free to use this information to produce guides or ratings that compare schools in whatever manner they wish. Schools might be compared in terms of arts, advanced courses, school safety, or by using some kind of weighted formula. Self-interested actors should be free to present and interpret the data however they wish. The state's role is not to monitor how others use its data, but to serve as an impartial referee and reliable source in collecting and issuing the data.

Competition doesn't require that every family make outstanding choices, only that enough make solid choices. In fact, as three scholars note in their authoritative volume *Choosing Schools*, "Looking for encyclopedic knowledge on the part of parents may be a futile, unnecessary, and even harmful endeavor, setting the bar higher than necessary and then faulting parents for not being able to clear it."[26] All competition requires is for enough parents to make reasonable decisions and for schools to compete for their business. This scenario is not a stretch. In fact, it is the status quo reformers who frequently remind us that schools are eager to attract students from these families. Less savvy families benefit from this competition because self-interest will push educators to respond to the parents who are more sophisticated about school quality. How does this work? For example, only a limited number of consumers scrupulously study automobile safety ratings or gas mileage when purchasing a new car. However, these savvy consumers are enough of a market force that auto manufacturers compete for them by seeking to improve quality and safety. The benefits of this competition incidentally spill over to even the uninformed or apathetic consumer. Lethargic consumers are also able to cut corners by mimicking the behavior of the savvier consumers or by using cheat-sheets like *Consumer Reports* that spring up to exploit the need for easy-to-use information.

Which Choices Will Promote Competition?

Though the relative independence of voucher schools can make voucher programs attractive to proponents of competition, the limited political prospects of vouchers, and the small size and heavily regulated nature of existing programs make them an uncertain mechanism for promoting competition. The willingness of private school operators to open new schools or expand in response to voucher programs is not yet established, and will depend on how stable they judge the program in any community to be.

Tuition tax credits and privately funded vouchers enjoy broad appeal among choice proponents because they bypass the political challenges posed by more direct efforts to win state funding for choice-based reforms. However, these measures are relatively ineffective ways to promote competition. Privately funded vouchers only indirectly affect the schools that lose students, since state funding formulas mean that districts typically lose much less than the cost of each departing student. Because tax credit and private voucher programs are limited in size, district officials find it easy to believe that losses will be limited. In fact, in many urban districts struggling with a lack of classroom space, private scholarship programs are quietly regarded by district officials as a useful "safety valve." Because tuition tax credits or tuition "scholarship" programs are funded through tax breaks, they show up simply as overall reductions in state revenue. They do not hurt the local district. Tuition tax credit programs affect only those districts where parents elect to use credits or scholarships to remove their child from the public schools, in which case, again, the effect is the muted one of reduced enrollment.

Despite the fact that charter schooling is seemingly less radical than school vouchers, its brighter political prospects and the current acceptance of higher per-pupil payouts mean that charter schools may provide a better means to promote competition. This conclusion, however, depends on charter proponents resisting regulations that cripple the autonomy and competitive impulse of the schools. If charter proponents accept such conditions then, in the words of one economist, we may find charter schools to be "a detour, and a devastatingly bad one."[27]

Schools Must be Allowed to Fail

Competition works in two ways at once: by pushing the best to get better and by putting the worst out of business. Closing down the worst performers and cycling their people, resources, and clients into more productive endeavors is essential. Without that safeguard, competition may serve to extend the performance of the very best schools while permitting the very worst schools to fester in sustained mediocrity. It is crucial that schools not only be shuttered when they continually fail to meet accountability benchmarks but that they fail when enough families flee.

Existing public choice programs offer families a selection of schools. However, once a desired school is filled up, the systems routinely assign children to whatever schools have space available. Popular schools are not eager to take on overflow students, for reasons I have already discussed. The result is that these districts keep unappealing schools in business. These schools should be permitted to fail.

The concern that quality-conscious families will flee low-performing schools and leave the worst-off students even more isolated is valid but becomes manageable if we weed out failing schools and replace them with carefully groomed replacements.

Who Authorizes New Schools?

If new schools are to be independent of the traditional school district, it is important to consider how these new entrants will be approved for state funding—whether as part of a voucher or a charter program. In the case of school vouchers, a reasonable option is the accreditation model favored by private schools, in which schools are approved by one of the many accreditation agencies throughout the nation. For charter schools, the existing strategy of "authorization" is a sensible one. Authorizers are explicitly charged with approving a contract that sets performance goals for each school, monitoring performance, and deciding whether to renew the school's charter. To date, the overall performance of authorizers has been acceptable but not particularly impressive.[28]

Authorizers have done a fair job of gauging the quality of would-be charter operators and have been effective at shutting down schools for reasons of financial or professional malfeasance. They have been less effective at monitoring ongoing school activities or at shutting down schools for reasons of mediocre academic performance. It would be sensible to extend the range of existent authorizers—which tend to be school boards, state boards, or universities—to other nonprofit and for-profit entities that may have greater investment in individual schools. In fact, it makes sense to expand our conception of traditional districts, instead thinking of them as "charter districts" that are free to operate their schools under the same rules as charter authorizers.[29]

Choice Doesn't Always Equal Flexibility

Choice-based reform is a vital element of commonsense reform, but it is not a panacea in and of itself. School choice can enhance competition and accountability, create flexibility, and facilitate broader reforms, but must not be an excuse to forsake these broader concerns. Among the dozens of states that have adopted charter school laws, most have retained various restrictions on who is permitted to teach in these schools, how they may compensate employees, the ability of for-profit entities to operate them, how these schools may promote themselves, and so on. Voucher programs in Milwaukee, Cleveland, and Florida have imposed a variety of restrictions on which children are eligible for vouchers, what kinds of private schools may enroll voucher students, how schools with voucher students must accommodate students with special needs, how these schools must modify their moral or religious instruction, and so on. California legislators and voters have enacted a slew of rules to make charter schools look more like regular district schools, including requiring charter schools to use facilities "reasonably equivalent" to those of district schools and granting the state board of education extensive authority to regulate nontraditional or computer-assisted instruction.[30] Stanford professor Terry Moe, a staunch school choice advocate, has pointed out that the American public is uncomfortable with unregulated schools and demands some regulation as a condition for any radical expansion of choice.[31] In other words, choice can promote flexibility, but it doesn't necessarily do so. Flexibility needs to be pursued in its own right.

The Status Quo Critique

Real competition exerts a harsh discipline. A commonsense reformer is cognizant that this discipline is accompanied by real costs. The commonsense reformer does not claim that competition is costless, only that—when sensibly monitored and paired with tough-minded accountability—its benefits will significantly outweigh its costs. Unsurprisingly, status quo reformers regard the very notion of educational competition as mean-spirited.

Status quo reformers are appalled by school vouchers and tuition tax credits; are willing to tolerate toothless charter school laws; and are frequently big fans of the kinds of public school choice that allow students to shuffle among conventional schools. As Michael Engel, an ardent critic of choice-based reform has argued, "Market-oriented school choice programs—that is, all but most intradistrict programs restricted to the public sector . . . destroy the concept of public education as a community enterprise."[32]

The common thread for the status quo'ers is an utter rejection of competition as useful or desirable, since they insist that educators are already doing the best they can. They believe that, unlike everyone else, educators won't find ways to be any more creative, efficient, or motivated when faced with competition. Instead, status quo reformers imagine that these good-hearted souls will dispiritedly file out the door seeking work where skilled workers are miraculously untroubled by performance review or competition. The presumption that public schools are running at peak efficiency and that any lost money will require sawing into sinew is why critics say choice-based reform will "drain money from the public schools." This complaint reflects a fundamental confusion about the purpose of public schools. The purpose of public funding is not to support adults in their current schools but to educate students. If students are changing schools, it's peculiar to speak of "harm" when the money the public is paying to educate them is simply following them to their new school. Competition is supposed to steer money away from ineffective districts, schools, and classrooms. If the departure of students from a poor school forces the school to shrink its staff, that's not a problem. Effective teachers and administrators will find work elsewhere.

The status quo reformers are probably right when they suggest that some educators will abandon the schools if they are required to demonstrate their worth. Most of these departures will be good news, and the commonsense reformer is happy to lose teachers who imagine they are above scrutiny. Commonsense reformers are happy to see these folks leave the profession for one where the costs of their potential ineffectiveness are not so devastating. In the case of those teachers who may be effective in the classroom but constitutionally averse to oversight, a competitive system will actually help to create room for them. If a group of such teachers wished to form a cooperative, pay themselves based on a traditional scale, ignore internal measures of performance, and refuse to promote themselves, they would be free to do so.

Such resolutely noncompetitive boutique businesses flourish today in private schooling, day care, and higher education, as well as in businesses ranging from psychotherapy practices to grocery stores. Such is the case of the Minnesota New Country School, which is governed by a collegial teacher cooperative that runs the entire school without a traditional full-time administrator. In other words, so long as students are learning, a competitive environment can *increase* the ability of teachers to forge schools and classrooms they find appealing.

Some critics worry that choice schools may permit families to self-segregate on the basis of race or class and leave the children of uninformed parents trapped in poor schools. Viewing education as an incredibly complex process, others question whether most parents understand their child's needs or are equipped to make reasonable judgments about school quality.[33] Yet, most parents focus on commonsense criteria like teacher quality, school safety, and student performance when choosing a school.[34] Moreover, since it is minority and low-income parents who are trapped in the worst schools, providing choice options can actually reduce segregation by allowing students to escape from neighborhood schools. One result is that private school classrooms are arguably more racially heterogeneous than those in public schools.[35] Similarly, charter schools enroll highly diverse populations, with SRI International reporting in 2002 that just over half of charter students are members of minority groups, 12 percent received special education services and 6 percent were English language learners. None of this should be surprising, given that the SRI study found that 79 percent of charter schools were focused on serving low-performing students and 75 percent on teaching students from low-income communities.[36] In *Choice With Equity*, University of Washington professor Paul Hill assessed the risks of choice-driven segregation and concluded, "Given the radical forms of 'sorting' prevalent in existing public school systems, it is hard to see how choice could produce worse segregation, resource inequity, denial of access to excellent programs, or assignment to opportunity-limiting programs than the current system."[37]

Ironically, while fretting that choice will transform our "public schools" into a two-tiered school system, critics routinely offer up as exemplars of public education elite magnet schools and exam schools that are free to reject children based on their musical ability, grades, exam scores, teacher recommendations, or other criteria. Unable to offer a framework for systemic excellence, status quo reformers content themselves by observing that schools that collect together hand-picked teachers and students are able to excel. That's not good enough.

Finally, while we look to our schools to help forge a common culture and to promote our shared values, there is no evidence that traditional public schools do a better job than do private schools or charter schools of inculcating shared values like civic participation or volunteerism. In fact, preliminary research in this area suggests that private schools do a better job than public schools of encouraging children to volunteer, forge interracial friendships, and become civically engaged. More fundamentally, given their ability to promote a coherent focus and their greater freedom to discipline students, it should not be at all surprising if these schools do a better job of teaching civic values.[38]

Making Competition Work

What can a commonsense reformer do to make competition work as intended? There are three issues that merit special attention.

Making it Pinch

Competition works through fear and hope, yet most choice programs have been crafted to minimize the losses for public districts that lose students or rewards for schools that gain students. To promote meaningful competition, the actual cost of educating a given student should follow that child when she changes schools. It is important that the size of choice programs not be capped or otherwise restricted.

One way to promote competition-enhancing fear is through the threat of job losses. However, the urban areas targeted by choice-based reforms typically scramble to replace 10 to 15 percent of their teachers every year, meaning that even significant enrollment declines are unlikely to cost jobs. On the other hand, in wealthy suburban areas where there is intense demand for teaching jobs, educators may prove far more sensitive to the possibility of job losses. Creating a similar sense of urgency in urban communities requires expanding the pool of potential teachers so that districts have the ability to replace unsatisfactory personnel.

When principals and district officials try to monitor and motivate their employees, they are hindered by regulations, professional norms, and contract language. In the private sector, employees who ignore directives suffer financially and professionally, even in fields where workers are protected by strong contracts. Principals and superintendents need to be able to hire, fire, promote, and reward employees.

Finally, contemporary educators are unprepared to respond effectively to competition. Schools of education offer administrators little or no formal preparation in management or business practices, concentrating almost entirely on procedural routines, legal concerns, and "leadership." In the private sector, firms generally have access to personnel skilled in areas such as market analysis or advertising. School and district leaders rarely have even a glancing familiarity with such concerns.

Encouraging Entrepreneurship

Competition must be threatening to be effective. Educators concerned about losing their jobs, desirable assignments, or material rewards will be much more likely to cooperate with efforts to respond to a competitive threat. This means increasing the number of choice schools, the size of these schools, or the financial hit that public schools suffer when they lose enrollment. This will require more than just lifting the enrollment caps on charter or voucher programs; it requires nurturing new competitors.

Generating competition will require a substantial increase in either the size or number of new schools. Though the number of charter schools is expanding rapidly, their size is so small that founders would have to open 2,000 such schools a year through 2015 for charter enrollment to approach 10 percent of the public school population.

Many barriers, formal and informal, have slowed the growth of choice options. The educators who traditionally open charter schools or run private schools are unlikely to drive significant expansion. Why? Most charter school and private school administrators, for instance, like the idea of running a small, familial school and are not interested in maximizing enrollment or running multiple schools. They have no interest in managing a large, bureaucratic operation that separates them from the students. The way to address this problem is by offering enough rewards—money, prestige, perks—to tempt entrepreneurs to trade the freedom and fun of their small enterprise for the headaches of expansion.

Small choice schools face the same challenges that make operating a small business in any field extraordinarily difficult. As George Whalin, a California retail consultant has noted, "If you're Federated Department Stores...they have hundreds and hundreds of stores and the financial wherewithal to ride through [big] problems. The small store just doesn't have that cushion."[39] New charter schools typically receive federally funded start-up grants of $10,000 to $150,000 for one to three years but can expect no other public funding until the day they open. Small operators often lack the resources to ride out the bumps in the road, especially when they are former educators without much business savvy.

Entrepreneurs face barriers that tilt the scales heavily against risk-taking. Salary schedules based on seniority and pension plans based on continuous service penalize longtime educators who leave their position for a new opportunity.

The fastest and most effective source of growth may be for-profit schooling. Opening a school requires an extensive initial investment, one that it is often easier for profit-seeking than for nonprofit ventures to raise. School managers motivated by profitability are more likely to open big schools and chains of schools because they are attracted to the potential return. Encouraging for-profit operators will dramatically increase the pool of capital available to open and expand schools and lessen reliance upon philanthropic and government resources.

For all their imagined and occasional excesses, for-profit firms are focused and accountable in a way that nonprofits and government agencies are not. Public providers are led by public officials, whose number one rule is to not make any organized interest too angry. This translates to cautious leadership, the kind that's afraid to tackle established routines or sweep away procedural barriers. Nonprofit providers are free from many of the constraints on public providers, but their very sense of mission and public-spiritedness can limit their willingness to pursue efficiencies. For-profits have cause to continuously seek ways to improve effectiveness and efficiency because their investors self-interestedly demand it. If these firms fail to serve students and generate cost savings, as many will, they will fold. Meanwhile, they will have the incentive and freedom to pilot radically different arrangements—some of which may result in new benchmarks for efficiency or effectiveness. As Stanford economist Eric Hanushek observed a decade ago, "The most obvious way to introduce cost control pressures is through choice programs that institute competition among schools. If schools compete in part on the basis of their costs, more schools might find it in their interest to use alternative technologies to control costs."[40] In fact, research on charter schooling in ten states suggests that charter schools run by for-profit education management organizations may produce bigger achievement gains than nonprofit charter schools.[41]

Providing Good Information

Making competition work requires that families have reasonable information on schools. However, while most parents are concerned with school quality and wish to get their child into a good school, they lead busy lives and most don't have the time or the inclination to extensively research purchases or decisions. Schools, for their part, rarely mount informational efforts that encompass much more than brochures, press releases, parent–teacher nights, a promotional newsletter, and the occasional video.

The kind of information that's readily available to families is crucial if competition is to make a difference. If the only readily available information is on test scores, then those will largely drive decisions. If information is readily available on advanced courses, fine arts programs, school safety, or after-school services, those offerings will prove much more influential. This is hardly a novel challenge. Researchers have considered similar issues in areas ranging from medical care to food regulation and learned much about the importance of mandatory reporting, standardized information, and information availability.[42]

Merely making information available, however, is not enough. We live in a world of sensory clutter. If information is available only in pamphlets available at schools or in kiosks in local libraries, most of it will be tuned out. Competition requires moving beyond these passive dissemination strategies and adopting aggressive strategies that use mailings, television, print media, Internet, and radio to push information. On the rare occasions when public schools have tried their hand at marketing, they have done so half-heartedly and reflexively. Promisingly, in cities like Milwaukee and Philadelphia, groups like the Black Alliance for Educational Options are launching sophisticated, sustained, multimedia efforts to inform parents about school performance and school options.

The Comforts of Tough-Minded Accountability

In theory, choice proponents can make a reasonable argument that you don't need tough-minded accountability if you have effective competition. Market-driven accountability can be a powerful tool for monitoring quality. However, given the public dimension of schooling, there is a legitimate concern that some parents may not place as much emphasis on the essentials as the community would like or may make otherwise questionable choices. Tough-minded accountability helps address this concern.

Because not all children are equally easy to teach, there is also the concern that schools may attempt to "cherry pick" easy-to-educate or otherwise desirable students and deter those most in need.[43] Rating schools on value-added accountability measures helps to minimize this temptation by encouraging families to focus on what the school is doing rather than who the school may attract. Since schools will be gauged largely on student gains, it's not clear that they would benefit by attracting students who have done well to date rather than those who have much room for improvement.

By shuttering ineffective schools, highlighting effective ones, and providing useful information, tough-minded accountability minimizes the potential problems with choice-based reform. It's ironic that many critics of tough-minded accountability also oppose choice-based reform, since choice skirts the perils of standardized testing. In opposing both competition and centralized control, these status quo critics either embrace procedural compliance or, more often, they simply insist that educators be trusted, like clergy or medieval royalty, to police themselves.

Conclusion

Imagine a market in which organizational success is linked only loosely to customer satisfaction; competitive pressures are readily trumped by government support; companies have only sparse information on the performance of personnel and can rarely fire or demote employees; and competitors must overcome hostile political and legal forces. Why would we expect competition to rattle established firms in such a market? The answer: we wouldn't. Making competition work for students requires that we address these conditions.

A commonsense reformer regards choice as an important tool for promoting accountability and flexibility. However, school vouchers or charter schooling are not the silver bullets imagined by some would-be commonsense reformers. When touting school choice, choice enthusiasts often make the status quo reformer error of viewing choice-based reform as a simple way to slice the Gordion knot of educational change and turn away from uncomfortable but essential measures. In doing so, they mistakenly foster the impression that choice-based reforms alone will necessarily spur entrepreneurship, reward excellence, enhance workforce flexibility, reduce procedural oversight, and harness competition.

In fact, when choice enthusiasts like Peter Brimelow or Andrew Coulson romanticize choice-based solutions as a silver bullet—by proclaiming that "vouchers are the Kryptonite of the Teacher Trust" or advocating that we "phas[e] out state schools in favor of a for-profit educational market"—they can hinder or complicate broader efforts to promote commonsense reform.[44] Given that schools play both a "public" and a "private" role, serving the needs of the student and also shared societal purposes, the state will always play a crucial role in funding, accountability, information dissemination, and oversight. Imagining that choice-based reform can be debated in isolation from other elements of schooling is a grave mistake.[45] The international experience with choice-based reform and our own national experience with deregulation in various industries make it clear that the public will insist that the state play a significant role in any kind of choice-based system. Finally, a commonsense reformer recognizes the perils of an unmonitored and unregulated "market" system and the need for appropriate oversight. In fact, competition is most promising in tandem with tough-minded accountability, as it presses schools to stretch beyond their minimal obligations while it is buttressed by the assurance that even irresponsible parents will be constrained in their decisions.

In truth, many choice advocates themselves have been ambivalent about competition. Many charter proponents support innovation and freedom but, as one national leader muttered to me during a conference, "I don't like all this talk about charter schools as a tool for 'making' public schools better. Charters are valuable as innovators. I don't like seeing them set up as a competitor to district schools. We're all educators trying to serve children." Talking to proponents of nice choice is often a lot like talking to status quo reformers; there is the same sense that wishing will make it so.

While school choice gives options to families, especially those who are currently the worst-served, it does not automatically produce competition or operational flexibility. If policymakers adopt choice plans but proceed to tie the hands of new entrants or old schools with restrictions on hiring, compensation, curricula, management, and service provision, then familial choice will not fundamentally alter schooling. Charter schools have more flexibility than typical public schools and private schools have more freedom than traditional public schools, but there is *absolutely nothing* to stop states from imposing new regulations on even relatively unfettered private or charter schools as they move to expand school choice.

Choice-based competition is an important arrow in the quiver of commonsense reform, but it is only one arrow in that quiver. Expanded parental choice alone will not necessarily invite new talent into the schools, reward excellence, produce new opportunities, or encourage more effective use of resources. Choice-based reform can certainly promote such change, but only if restrictions governing the operation, staffing, and management of schools are loosened. In fact, these measures must be pursued whether or not choice-based reforms are adopted. It is to these that we now turn.

CHAPTER FOUR

The Teaching Force

Nothing astonishes men so much as common sense and plain dealing.
—Ralph Waldo Emerson

The mantra of the commonsense reformer is accountability *and* flexibility. If we tie the hands of teachers and principals, we ignore the fact that they know their students and school far better than any distant official. The most important decision that educational leaders make is determining who should teach. Teachers are the most important factor in determining school quality.

The commonsense charge is straightforward. We must make it easier to recruit and hire promising candidates, reward excellent teachers and those willing to take on particularly daunting challenges, design staff positions that are professionally rewarding and that make full use of faculty skills, and identify and remove ineffective teachers.

Of course, the effectiveness of a given educator is rarely transparent, especially since teachers benefit to some degree from the cooperative effort of many people. In this, schooling is similar to many endeavors, such as publishing a newspaper. The problem is that it's not clear what it means to hold the entire school faculty or newsroom staff accountable for results. In fact, if everyone is equally responsible, the practical outcome is that no one is responsible. The solution is to give editors and principals leeway to make sensible distinctions based on individual contributions and performance. The ability of executives to flexibly reward individual excellence and punish individual failure is crucial to the success of commonsense reform.

A Profession Designed for Mediocrity

Since the nineteenth century, teaching has been a generally feminized profession. When other professions were closed to women, the schools enjoyed a captive pool of talented female applicants. Although classroom teaching was designed as a dead-end profession with little opportunity for career growth or merit-based promotion, classrooms were primarily staffed by talented women who had few alternatives. Beginning in the 1920s, and accelerating in the 1950s, a push for professional solidarity among teachers fed efforts to equalize the pay between teachers regardless of position or grade. By the 1960s, the resulting pay scales were rigidly based on teaching experience, formal education, and extra college credits accumulated while teaching. Today, teachers have grown up with these scales, so that veteran teachers are accustomed to them and fiercely resist any proposals to change the rules now that they are benefiting from the arrangement. The result is that the most influential teachers are those with the greatest stake in keeping the salary schedule as it is. Districts also developed generous industrial-model pension systems that rewarded teachers for staying in place for 25 or 30 years. Since most teachers were married women who stayed in one place, this was a satisfactory agreement both for the teachers and school districts desiring stability.

Meanwhile, the states have given control over who would enter teaching to schools of education and teacher training programs at colleges and universities. Except in unusual circumstances, those who wished to teach had to graduate from a state-approved teacher training program. Intended to ensure quality, this arrangement gave educators professors a chokehold over who would enter the teaching profession and protected schools of education from any outside competition.

In recent years, trends have challenged these staid arrangements. By the 1970s, as professional barriers to women started to fall away, schools could no longer depend on a steady stream of brilliant young women. The same women who once had entered teaching were now entering engineering, medicine, law, and business. Workers became more mobile, making licenses and industrial-era benefit plans less attractive to the most accomplished individuals. In the 1980s, states began to adopt "alternative certification" systems that made it possible for some candidates to become teachers without completing a traditional education school program. Today, though 10 to 15 percent of teachers enter the profession through such routes, three-quarters of these "alternative" programs are run by traditional teacher preparation institutions.

In too many locales, especially our most troubled districts, today's teaching force is not equal to the challenges our schools face. Even veteran teachers and teacher educators have concluded, "The number of good classroom teachers, and therefore the quality of teaching itself, is in perilous decline and will continue to worsen."[1] Academically stronger students tend to shun the teaching profession. Undergraduate education majors typically have SAT and ACT scores lower than those of other students and those teachers who have the lowest scores are the most likely to remain in the profession. The lower the quality of the undergraduate institution a person attends, the more likely they are to wind up in the teaching profession.[2] From 1982 to 2000, the percentage of teachers who had earned a master's degree in their subject area fell from 17 percent to 5 percent.[3] Professional licensing exams are so simple and the standards for passage so low that even the Education Trust concluded they exclude only the "weakest of the weak" from classrooms.[4] While none of these data points is damning, together they paint a troubling picture.

We need to open the doors of the profession, provide for more sensible hiring, reward teachers who are effective and who take on challenging roles, make it much easier to eliminate poor performers, create a more professional and flexible career structure, and rethink the way the job of individual teachers is organized. A commonsense reformer doesn't have a silver bullet to propose, but a set of principles that can guide improvement.

The Mo' Money Answer

Not surprisingly, the "mo' money" crowd always wants to begin and end the conversation about teacher quality by demanding more money. The status quo reformers attack as "anti-teacher" any who question their demands. One of the results is that almost everyone "knows," in the words of *Washington Post* national columnist Richard Cohen, that, "Teachers make lousy money."[5] Because the "mo' money" folks have been successful at cowing skeptics and convincing the general public that money is the problem, let's start by talking a bit about teacher pay.

The case that teachers are underpaid is a weak one. Teacher pay is actually quite reasonable when considered in context. The average teacher salary in 2001 was $43,300, compared to the average full-time worker salary of $40,100.[6] While a starting salary of $30,000 may seem shockingly low to the typical *New York Times* reader, it's actually higher than what many Ivy League graduates earn when starting in the policy world, advertising, or similar nontechnical jobs. For instance, those 2002 graduates of journalism and mass-communication programs who landed jobs earned a median salary of $26,000 if they had a B.A. and $32,000 if they had an M.A.[7]

Economist Richard Vedder has observed that the Bureau of Labor Statistics' National Compensation Survey shows that teachers earn "more per hour than architects, civil engineers, mechanical engineers, statisticians, biological and life scientists, atmospheric and space scientists, registered nurses, physical therapists, university-level foreign-language teachers, [and] librarians."[8] In fact, the Bureau of Labor Statistics reported that the average pay per hour for all workers in the "professional specialty" category in 2001 was $27.49, while public secondary school teachers earned $30.48 and elementary teachers $30.52—or about 10 percent *more* than the typical professional.[9]

How can this be? Don't we *know* that teachers are woefully underpaid? Let's consider the facts. Most Americans work about 47 weeks a year (with about three weeks of vacation and two weeks of assorted holidays). Teachers, on the other hand, work about 38 weeks a year (teaching for 180 days and working additional professional days). In other words, after accounting for vacation, most Americans work about 25 percent more than the typical teacher. This doesn't even factor in the fact that, according to the U.S. Department of Education, during 1999–2000 (the most recent year for which data are available) about 5.2 percent of teachers were absent on a given day—a rate much higher than the 1.7 percent absentee rate reported by the Bureau of Labor Statistics for all forms of managerial and professional employment.[10] The availability of substitute teachers makes teaching very different from professions like medicine, sales, law, or journalism where there is often no one to stand in for a worker in the event of an unscheduled absence. That translates into the average teacher missing an additional nine days during each 180-day school year. So, technically, the truth is that the typical teacher works 36—not 38—weeks a year. While some teachers might prefer more money and less time off, this is a lifestyle choice that teachers make when choosing a career. Teaching, for instance, with its summer breaks, regular schedule, and lack of travel is particularly family friendly. Now some teachers would prefer to work more and earn more or work in less conventional positions. As we will see, commonsense flexibility can help to create such opportunities.

Public educators also receive generous benefits, including "defined-benefit" pensions that do not require any contribution from the teacher. A career teacher, without ever having to contribute a nickel, can normally retire at age fifty-five and receive close to 70 percent of his salary for life. There are hundreds of thousands of retired teachers drawing annual pensions of $40,000 or more—many young enough to begin second careers. About half of teachers also pay nothing for personal medical coverage, compared to just one-quarter of private-sector professional and technical workers.[11] Public school teachers receive benefit packages worth about 26 percent of their salaries whereas the typical private-sector worker's package is worth 17 percent of theirs.[12]

Teacher advocates protest that none of these considerations factor in the long hours that teachers put in at home. After all, according to the *Schools and Staffing Survey*, teachers claim to work slightly more than 49 hours a week during the school year, including 38 hours in school, three hours with students, and almost nine hours at home.[13] There are a couple of problems with claiming that this represents an extraordinary workload. First, when people are asked how hard they work, they tend to overestimate the actual figure. So, that 49-hour figure is really more of an upper limit than an unbiased estimate. Second, the typical workday for nonprofessional workers often stretches from 8:30 to 5:30, or 45 hours a week, and is even longer for many professionals. It is not unusual for journalists, accountants, engineers, technology workers, or other college educated professionals to routinely work 50 hours or more a week and to take work home at night or engage in professional travel. Of course, these work days often include a lunch break, and a worker who is at the office for nine hours with an hour-long lunch is said to work a 40-hour week, not a 45-hour week.

On the other hand, it is apparent that teachers are counting every minute they are at school in reporting their workweek. Since teachers report working 38 hours a week at school during the school day and most district contracts specify that teachers' entire school day runs about seven and a half hours, or about 37 to 38 hours a week, it is clear that the reported working day includes lunch breaks and preparation periods. If teachers use much of their lunch break and preparation period to relax, eat lunch, and socialize, which is the norm in my experience, just as it is in most any line of work, they are actually teaching, planning, and grading about six and a half hours a day in school, or about 33 hours a week. Accepting teacher self-reports about their workload at home and with students after school at face value, the typical teacher is working about 45 hours a week, all told. This is perfectly respectable but hardly unusual.

Let me be clear. While, on the whole, teachers are not underpaid, good teachers, those working in tough circumstances, and those with critical skills are often wildly underpaid. The flip side is that mediocre teachers are overpaid, sometimes substantially. In the past few years, the notion of the "$100,000 teacher" has come into vogue. In books like *The Two-Percent*

Solution and *The $100,000 Teacher*, authors like Matthew Miller and Brian Crosby have called for paying good teachers $100,000 or more. A common-sense reformer knows that Miller and Crosby are right. If we are serious about attracting and retaining the energetic and talented practitioners we want, we need to pay our best, hardest-working teachers that kind of money. However, overlooked in these discussions is that a number of teachers are already extremely well compensated. The most recent systematic data, collected five years ago by the U.S. Department of Education's 1999–2000 *Schools and Staffing Survey*, estimated that over 5,500 teachers were earning more than $100,000 a year. Between 1999 and 2004 teacher salaries have steadily increased, to the point that one can reasonably estimate that today at least 15,000 to 20,000 teachers earn more than $100,000 a year for their teaching duties.

In 2000–2001, for instance, the median teacher salary was above $70,000 in more than one-third of New York school districts. This means that half of the teachers in those districts earned at least that much. In Scarsdale, New York, half of all teachers earned more than $91,000 during 2000–2001.[14] Nonetheless, mo' money claimants like New York gubernatorial candidate H. Carl McCall argued that the state was only spending enough to provide students with "an eighth-grade education" and that it "is not enough."[15]

The commonsense problem is not the total amount paid to teachers but the fact that basing teacher pay on experience and credentials rather than performance means that the money isn't necessarily going to those teachers who deserve it. Highly paid teachers earn their salaries not because they are exceptional teachers or have tackled tough assignments but because they are have accumulated seniority in wealthy school systems where pay is based upon longevity. Providing raises in such a system is enormously expensive because so much of the spending is soaked up by the undeserving. While there is a need to pay good teachers more, the commonsense solution is to spend selectively.

I'll offer one final caveat on salary. Some experts urge us to pay teachers more but simultaneously argue that money doesn't really motivate teachers. (Presumably, we're supposed to pay out the money so that we'll feel good about ourselves.) Scholars like Harvard University professor Susan Moore Johnson point out that private school teachers earn less than public school teachers but are generally happier because staff morale is high at their school, they feel valued, and they enjoy parental support.[16] Of course, all of this is true and the commonsense reformer is working hard to create a world where such workplace environments thrive. None of this, however, should distract us from the merits of commonsense compensation, including its ability to help focus teachers on serving students.[17] While money may not be the only way or even the best way to attract the teachers we need, it is a useful tool and one we can readily wield. Rather than suggest that teachers are uninterested in money or propose more tinkering in lieu of real change, we should spend wisely while pursuing other sensible efforts.

Licensing and Hiring of Teachers

The first challenge confronting the commonsense reformer is the need to get more good teachers into the schools. Two obstacles currently hobble efforts to improve teacher quality. Training programs exert little quality control over incoming teachers, provide little training of value, and serve to deter lots of individuals who we'd like to have in the applicant pool. Meanwhile, school districts do a horrible job of recruiting.

Licensing

Though teacher "certification" varies from state to state and is punctuated by an array of exceptions and loopholes, the current system generally requires that teachers get certified. Teachers are typically certified by completing a licensure program at one of the nation's 1,300 preparation programs and passing an embarrassingly easy test of basic skills.

Professional licensure makes sense when the required training is a necessity if one is to be a competent professional or when it weeds out unsuitable applicants. Teacher licensure, unfortunately, does neither of these. The evidence shows that teacher preparation programs are neither teaching essential content nor screening out unsuitable candidates. In fact, in 2003 Boston University Professor of Education David Steiner conducted the most comprehensive study to date of what is taught in the nation's elite teacher education programs at schools like Harvard, Stanford, UCLA, the University of Wisconsin, Michigan State University, and the University of Virginia. Steiner regretfully concluded that they are "neither preparing teachers adequately to use the concrete findings of the best research in education nor are they providing their students with a thoughtful and academically rich background of what it means to be an outstanding educator." Instead, he found that they were primarily "trying to teach an ideology to teachers" that evinced a "profound suspicion for [accountability and content-rich curricula]."[18] Similarly, a 2003 analysis of 120 undergraduate and graduate teacher preparation programs found that the *graduate* preparation programs reported admitting about 78 percent of applicants, that program officials were ambivalent about their obligation to prevent ineffective candidates from becoming licensed, and that programs weeded out only about *2 percent* of all teacher candidates during their student teaching trial period.[19]

What these data tell a commonsense reformer is that teacher licensure systems neither teach important skills nor keep unsuitable candidates from reaching the classroom. Certification is most effective when the licensing body ensures that aspiring professionals have mastered essential skills or knowledge and denies a license to inadequate performers. Licensure is not an assurance that professionals are talented practitioners, only that they have demonstrated an established degree of professional knowledge. If we agree that lawyers need to know a certain body of law or that civil engineers need to know how to calculate stress tolerance for a bridge, then it becomes straightforward to judge whether the aspirant is competent.

The biggest challenge for teacher licensure is that we know that teachers matter a great deal but we are not sure how they matter. Professional educators explain that teaching is a "contextual" and "adaptive" profession but fail to explain what kind of training or preparation is necessary to be a competent professional. In fact, researchers have estimated that we can explain only about *3 percent* of the variation in student learning from one teacher to the next through conventional measures like experience and training.[20] The only teacher characteristics found to have a strong and consistent relationship to student learning are the teacher's content knowledge and intellectual acuity (typically measured in terms of verbal ability).[21] None of this is especially surprising. Most sensible people would expect that people who are smart or have communication skills will make better teachers. More generally, we know that some teachers are consistently better than others but we have a hard time identifying these teachers before they start. It is for just this reason that we typically hesitate to prohibit some individuals from practicing a profession if clear standards of professional competence do not exist.

Even in professions with clear knowledge- or performance-based benchmarks for certification, like law or medicine, a license is not imagined to ensure competence in ambiguous, subtle skills like comforting a patient or swaying a jury. The skills that teacher educators deem most important—listening, caring, motivating—are not susceptible to standardized quality control. Nor is it necessary to go through teacher training to have such skills.

To make teaching certification more akin to certification in law or medicine, it would be necessary to determine a core of essential mastery. The obvious core is the content knowledge of aspiring licensees. While few believe that encyclopedic knowledge alone makes someone a good teacher—just as knowledge of case law alone does not make one a good attorney—it is an essential ingredient. Listening, caring, and motivating are of little use if knowledge, skills, and competence are not thereby conveyed.

The traditional system of certification simply presumes that even dynamic college mathematics professors, for instance, cannot be considered to teach even basic courses in schools desperate for math teachers. It presumes that even a former attorney who now directs an urban literacy program cannot be considered for a position as a second-grade teacher. A commonsense reformer would have everyone remember that allowing these individuals to apply for a position does not mean they will be given a job. It merely means they can be considered alongside the other possible candidates. By preventing nontraditional candidates from even applying, licensure presumes the need to protect students from the possibility that a principal will mistakenly hire an ill-suited candidate in a moment of weakness. After all, unless principals are incompetent or unconcerned with teacher quality, they would seem well suited to hire the best candidate. The situation is even more troubling than it appears. Many large school systems have classrooms filled with uncertified teachers and long-term substitutes who are hired at the last minute, when the systems—having discouraged or turned away a slew of promising candidates—are desperate for bodies.

Especially frustrating to commonsense reformers is the reality that the most talented and hardest working potential candidates have the most options and will be the most reluctant to tolerate certification. They are the least likely to forgo work for a year, sit through poorly regarded courses, and endure procedural hurdles. The barriers are especially imposing for potential career changers who have children or mortgages and can't afford a year without pay, are unwilling to devote days to tracking down the paperwork required to pursue alternative certification, and lack the time to sit through the required coursework.[22]

Clearly, some sort of screening process for aspiring teachers is essential; parents expect appropriate safeguards. In order to be able to apply for a teaching job, candidates should be required to hold a college degree, pass an examination of essential skills and content knowledge that would vary by grade level and subject, and pass a criminal background check. Now, while there is no systematic way to ensure that teachers are sufficiently caring or compassionate, it is indeed possible to develop a competency exam that would ensure teachers have a grasp of essential clinical skills. The National Board of Medical Examiners and the Federation of State Medical Boards, for instance, will be instituting a test of basic communication and diagnostic skills in 2005. Screening candidates for such commonsense qualifications is entirely consistent with a commonsense reform strategy.

Beyond the criteria outlined above, it is obviously desirable that candidates pursue additional preparation and training, just as in other professions like journalism or consulting in which subtle interpersonal skills are essential to effective performance. However, how and when this training should be provided ought to be dictated not by regulations but by accountable employers. The commonsense course is in no way an attack on teacher preparation. Trained candidates will have a leg up in the hiring process, just as trained journalists have a leg up when competing for a position. Aspiring teachers will flock to good training programs while schools will look to respected programs first when hiring. Commonsense reform will not dissuade individuals from pursuing training, it will merely allow other potentially effective candidates to apply for jobs and force preparation programs to demonstrate the value of their training.

In recent years, most states have moved to reform their licensure requirements in a commonsense fashion. Forty-four states and Washington, D.C. offer some kind of alternative certification. States including New Jersey, Texas, and California hire at least 10 percent of their teachers through alternative routes. While these routes remain strewn with procedural obstacles, are often inconvenient, and can be difficult to use, they represent tentative steps toward welcoming talent into the schools.

Remember that teachers, unlike psychologists or doctors, are not empowered to independently set up shop. Instead, they work in schools where they are monitored by managers who are themselves accountable for school performance. If and when schools are reinvented such that teachers are self-employed professionals rather than members of a faculty, it will be time to reexamine a more extensive licensure system.

Status quo reformers claim that certification doesn't dissuade potential teachers who would be good hires or that we need only to persuade current teachers to stay longer. They say this with a straight face even as the vast majority of the 200,000 new teachers we train each year graduate from mediocre institutions that accept every applicant, while alternative programs recruit accomplished mid-careerists and new graduates. The degree to which traditional practices squeeze out new talent is illustrated by organizations like Teach for America (TFA), which provides a streamlined route for new graduates to enter the teaching profession. In 2003, for instance, TFA had about 18,000 applications for less than 2,000 spots—the majority from students at elite colleges and universities. In fact, in 2002, 25 percent of the Yale graduating class applied to TFA. In 2003, the New Teacher Project (NTP), a TFA spin-off, reported more than 19,000 applicants for 2,000 slots in its New York City Teaching Fellows Program, more than 1,300 for 100 vacancies in its Washington, D.C. program, more than 8,000 for 412 slots in Los Angeles, more than 800 for 75 slots in Baltimore, and more than 2,100 applicants for 30 slots in Atlanta. In Washington, D.C., Atlanta, and Los Angeles, over half of the applicants were minorities. In all five cities, the college GPA of the applicant pool was over 3.0, roughly a quarter of applicants held graduate degrees, and at least 40 percent of applicants were eligible to teach math, science, or other areas that districts identified as "high need." While programs like TFA and NTP are not silver bullets, they are healthy improvements on the status quo. The applicant pool they are drawing illustrates that current barriers are not only failing to weed out poor candidates or teach essential skills, but are also deterring talented candidates deserving of consideration.

Hiring

After graduating with distinction from the University of Michigan's School of Education, Scott Cochran found a comfortable teaching job at a middle school in Charlevoix, Michigan. When he decided to seek a new position, he contacted the Detroit school system and asked them to mail him an application. They refused to mail it that time and the next four times he called, each time telling him he would have to drive five hours to the personnel office if he wanted one.[23] Cochran's experience is not unusual.

While observers fret about the desperate shortage of good teachers in urban schools, the most troubled districts themselves show a penchant for destructive personnel practices. Roughly one-third to one-half of the applicants to urban districts withdraw due to frustration with the hiring process, often to accept jobs with districts or schools that are more timely about making job offers. "Highly qualified candidates" who are eager to teach even in tough districts start bailing out in May and 40 percent have withdrawn by the end of June. Poor-performing districts do not pursue talent, pay little attention to recruiting talented personnel, routinely lose the best prospects, and find themselves forced to fill vacancies with weaker candidates who have no other attractive options.[24]

As a deputy superintendent in one large district confided to me, "Our hiring practices are unbelievable. I'll walk into personnel and see twenty people squatting on a tile floor, writing on their knees and on the ground. We won't let people apply online.... We've got boxes of applications just stacked around down there [and]... I think we've figured that we actually, physically, lose something like five or ten percent of the applications we get. This is no way to recruit professionals. . . . If someone tried to describe this to me and I hadn't seen it, I don't think I'd believe them." Unlike their counterparts throughout the public and private sector, human resources departments in school districts have not been pushed to abandon preoccupation with procedures and regulations. As a result, they are too often careless about when they hire teachers, who they hire, or how they assign them to schools. Applications are lost or misplaced. Job candidates who inquire about positions in January or February will routinely hear nothing for six or eight months and then receive hurried offers of employment in late August, long after the most desirable applicants have moved on.

Districts have been hobbled by collective bargaining provisions and outdated regulations governing teacher employment. Teacher assignment is typically based on seniority, meaning that districts have to assign new hires to schools where there are openings—rather than where they will be effective. New teachers can't be hired or assigned until the status of all veterans is cleared up, so that districts frequently don't start hiring actively until July or August. Because schools have to scramble to hire teachers during the month before school begins, barely one-quarter of new teachers observe the school in action before being hired and less than one in ten sit down with current faculty.[25] Though large districts routinely have hundreds of teacher openings, many refuse to begin hiring a single prospect until they have confirmed the exact number of new hires needed. Although the New Teacher Project had 600 high-caliber teacher recruits cleared and ready for hiring at one site by May 2002, not a single one was offered a contract until mid-August.

Researchers have found that in Florida and California, one-third of all new teachers are hired after the start of the school year, and more than 60 percent of teachers are hired less than thirty days before the school year begins.[26] If superintendents made it an imperative not to let talented candidates slip by, they might lean on their human resources department to be more proactive. In the absence of such pressure, human resources personnel are content to serve as what Vice President Al Gore once termed "reactive processors of paperwork"—whatever the cost in the quality of candidates.[27]

While districts with appealing positions and money to burn can get away with these practices because so many talented teachers are eager to work for them, low-performing systems pay a huge price in terms of teacher quality. District officials have many excuses for the way they operate. They explain that they have trouble knowing precise enrollments until school begins, the state budget procedures can handcuff them, and union regulations can prohibit districts from ascertaining whether teachers are returning until the beginning of the new school year. As one Michigan principal wearily related, "I'm absolutely not allowed to ask a teacher if she'll be back next year, even if it affects hiring or planning. I've actually had teachers near retirement taunt me on this, saying things like, 'It won't affect anything if I decide to come back now?' " Status quo reformers accept these explanations at face value and treat the constraints as given. Commonsense reformers do not.

The answer is not exhorting district officials to "try harder" but to use tough-minded accountability and incentives to compel leaders to tackle the painful chores of revising outdated policies, standing firm on new contract language, firing unimaginative human resources personnel, and giving principals and instructional leaders more control over the recruiting and hiring process. Those doing the hiring, whether human resource personnel or principals, must care enough about quality to take on the headaches of accelerating time schedules, pursuing waivers, and abandoning the security of a bureaucratized process. Those best equipped to carefully assess the qualifications of prospective teachers are the principals who will be responsible for them and the colleagues who will teach with them. It is principals accountable for school performance who will have the strongest incentive to seek out and recruit effective teachers.

Three commonsense measures for revamping personnel policies have been proposed by the New Teacher Project, a nonprofit outfit that has worked to recruit talented teachers for troubled school systems. First, districts have accepted collective bargaining language that often permits resigning or retiring teachers to hold off on informing their principal until summer or even the beginning of the new school year. Second, districts have granted unions' "seniority transfer" privileges that give current teachers the first pick of any new opening before any new teacher can be hired. Third, weak financial management at the district and budgetary uncertainty at the state level leave district officials overly cautious about hiring for the new academic year. While these steps won't force district officials to become quality conscious, moving up the required notification date, restricting seniority transfer, and strengthening district financial management will improve the ability of the worst-off districts to begin hiring in the spring and early summer and recruit more promising candidates into the worst-served schools.[28]

What do the status quo reformers have to say about all of this? Reg Weaver, the president of the National Education Association, may have put it best. While one might expect Weaver to criticize arrangements that frustrate new teachers and sensible hiring practices, he took the opportunity to once again blame "the systemic and historic lack of funding that has most districts struggling to meet the needs of students. This includes money woes that result in last-minute hiring decisions."[29] As always, the status quo'ers are sure that the only answer is more money.

Training and Supporting New Teachers

Instead of attempting to stuff knowledge into aspiring teachers so that we can declare them "certified" or otherwise ready to go, a commonsense reformer recognizes that many of the key skills teachers need are developed through professional practice. New teachers should have time to observe and get feedback from colleagues, and receive training while practicing their work. One state that has been particularly lauded for its efforts is Connecticut, which has aligned its teacher standards with the material students are expected to know and developed a Beginning Educators Support and Training system that provides mentors throughout a teacher's first year. Commonsense reformers applaud sensible efforts such as these.

One promising approach is to encourage schools and school systems to train new hires. Such a model would be a rough approximation of the medical model, where residents learn the softer, more practical skills of medical practice by working under the supervision of veteran doctors. New hires would ideally receive some formal instruction in key areas prior to the beginning of the school year, teach about half the standard teaching load, receive mentoring, and be provided with a network of peers. As with hospital residents, these teachers would likely be paid at a low level, as much of their compensation would come in the form of free training.

A commonsense reformer doesn't for a minute doubt the value of high-quality teacher preparation or induction. Because the way in which teachers are readied for and introduced to the schools is so important, trying to ensure readiness with a crude, one-size-fits-all paper barrier is counterproductive. In a world with flexible hiring, districts and schools would be able to make arrangements to ensure that their new teachers are prepared, inducted, and supervised in a manner appropriate to the challenges at hand.

When Equal isn't Fair

Rafe Esquith, 49, is a bearded, 20-year veteran who teaches fifth-grade at Hobart Boulevard Elementary, a school in the Los Angeles Public School system. He teaches his class of 32 from 6:30 A.M. until 5 P.M. and skips his nine-week vacation in order to meet with students. Esquith can offer the extended school day and school year only because families choose to enroll in his class, reminding us of how choice helps create room for innovation. Esquith teaches his charges algebra, gives a daily grammar test, has students reading adult novels by authors like Steinbeck and Dickens, and has the class perform Shakespeare regularly. In 2002, his students read at the eighty-eighth percentile while the school's fifth-graders overall scored at the forty-second percentile.[30] The suggestion that Mr. Esquith ought to earn the same salary as any other 20-year veteran is a travesty. He works longer, harder, and more effectively than his colleagues. Simple fairness demands that he be paid more, far more, than the typical fifth-grade L.A. teacher.

Equal pay and equal treatment are fair only if individuals are equal in their effort and their contribution. If they are not all working equally hard or confronting similar challenges, then treating them equally is manifestly *unfair*— and that's what we do today. The status quo response is offered by union officials who argue that "teachers almost never treat salary as a competitive concept" and that they are not bothered "when an ineffectual teacher earns the same salary as . . . high-quality teachers."[31] If you accept these claims, then it's a safe bet that commonsense reform isn't for you. Our existing compensation system encourages career-squatting by veteran teachers tired of their labors, discourages talented young college graduates from entering the profession, frustrates those educators who pour their weekends and summers into their work, and attracts candidates who are often less motivated than those who got away.

Teacher union officials claim that it is nearly impossible to gauge teacher quality and that, even if the occasional principal can, principals in general cannot be trusted to treat teachers fairly. As an editorial in the National Education Association's *NEA Today* proclaimed, "Basing teacher pay on student performance is no answer—it's a thinly disguised assault on us. Every day, we educators do the best we can, often under horrific conditions, with the best of intentions. No single determining factor—least of all student achievement—should dictate who among us will be paid more than others."[32] Howard Nelson, a senior researcher at the American Federation of Teachers, the nation's second-largest teachers' union, has declared that allowing principals to evaluate teachers "is one of the most irritating, unfair, inaccurate things that could happen."[33]

A very different line, however, was taken by the man who founded the AFT, Al Shanker himself. "I'm worried about how to prevent the pay-for-performance issue from becoming dysfunctional, dog-eat-dog," Shanker once said. "But I'm sure that we can develop such a system and that it would be pretty good. Its flaws would be very small compared to what we have now or compared to what you would have without such a system."[34] Classroom teachers generally agree. A 2003 Public Agenda survey found that 78 percent of teachers agreed "in [my] building, it is easy to spot who the truly great teachers are," and 72 percent believed that "most teachers in [my] building could pretty much agree on who the truly great teachers are."[35] Even in the world of higher education, where there is less hard evidence on performance than in K-12 education, faculty raises are based in large part on assessments of how much faculty members are contributing as scholars, teachers, and community members.

Skilled and accountable school leaders will have self-interested reasons to identify and protect good teachers. Meanwhile, the research suggests that principals who do not have to abide by certification requirements are especially likely to hire and reward teachers who attended high-quality colleges, who possess strong math or science training, or who put in more instructional hours.[36] For all its imperfections, accountability gives principals a better gauge of employee performance than is available in professions like architecture, law, accounting, or engineering where evaluations are rendered on an annual basis.

It would be an enormous mistake, however, to rely simply upon assessments of student performance to gauge teacher quality. A commonsense reformer knows there's a lot more to schooling than standardized test results and that these are imperfect and incomplete measures of learning. It would be unwise to define teaching excellence this narrowly, yet that's a mistake that some would-be commonsense reformers risk in rushing to embrace performance-based compensation.

A teacher can contribute to student learning in a slew of ways that may not show up on a given assessment. A teacher may mentor other teachers or help to improve the effectiveness of colleagues in other ways. She may counsel troubled students, help maintain school discipline, remediate students on material that will not be tested, and so on. It is unfortunately true that this obesrvation has often been used by status quo reformers to excuse ineffectiveness.

However, there's nothing to be gained—and much to be lost—by going overboard in response. Rather than trying to judge teachers with mechanical precision, we ought to develop sensible instruments for evaluation and permit managers to make reasoned decisions. This is an area where public sector and private sector firms have made enormous progress in the last 15 years and where a wealth of models and experience are readily available. There's common ground here between commonsense reformers and status quo reformers who agree that we must hold teachers responsible for the progress of their students but who recognize that teaching is a complex profession in which performance should not be reduced to a simple number.

Beyond teacher effectiveness, however it is measured, there are several other considerations that districts should acknowledge and compensate: the relative challenges an educator faces, the desirability of the work environment, and the relative scarcity of the teacher's skills. Educators who take on low-achieving or unpopular schools may find it exceptionally difficult to produce performance gains or to attract students. To make challenging venues appealing to good educators, compensation and evaluations should reflect such circumstances. Moreover, compensation ought to reflect that it's often harder and simply less fun to teach low achievers in a gritty, crowded school than to instruct more advanced students in a well-lit, spacious, comfortable school. For instance, researchers have estimated that Texas school districts could retain teachers with three to five years teaching experience in low-achieving, high-minority schools at the same rate as in suburban schools if pay were boosted by about 26 percent.[37] Differential pay need not rely on guesswork but can be based on this kind of deliberate analysis. The truth is that restructuring teacher pay could help solve many of the seemingly intractable staffing problems that schools face.

A commonsense reformer knows it is also necessary for districts to end the fiction that they should pay English, social studies, and physical education teachers the same amount that they pay science or math teachers. As a former social studies teacher, it pains me to say this, but there are many more competent candidates for English and social studies jobs than for math or science positions. School administrators report that it was "very difficult" to fill elementary teaching positions less than 6 percent of the time but "very difficult" to fill math or physical science positions more than 30 percent of the time.[38] This is an international truism, with principals in Organization for Economic Cooperation and Development countries reporting that more than 30 percent have trouble finding qualified science, math, or foreign language teachers, but that fewer than 10 percent have trouble finding enough social studies or physical education teachers.[39]

Status quo reformers worry, in the words of one union official, "You're going to send the message that some teachers are more valuable than others. Feelings will be hurt.... We've worked [hard] to create a sense of community in schools—this would [destroy it]." The problem is that the public doesn't fund education salaries to bolster teachers' self-esteem but to provide for our children. If a district can hire good social studies teachers for less than it now spends and use the savings to hire the caliber of math teachers its students need, it is irresponsible not to do so.

The status quo reformers find the subject of compensation immensely distasteful and argue that parents don't want teachers who are "money oriented." A commonsense school reformer believes that parents care mostly whether teachers are going to educate their children. Sensibly enough, the public seems fine with lawyers or doctors who profit from their good works. It's not clear just why we would imagine material rewards to be at odds with good education, but it's an expensive conceit we can no longer afford.

Evaluating and Compensating Teachers

The conceit that compensation should be unlinked to a professional's performance is a strange one to those unfamiliar with the world of schooling. Today, just 5.5 percent of traditional public school districts report using pay incentives such as cash bonuses, salary increases, or additional salary steps to reward excellent teaching.[40] Just five states offer retention bonuses to keep teachers in high-need schools.[41] However understandable uniform treatment may have once been, when school leaders were unaccountable and reliable measures of teacher performance were absent, they now pose significant problems. As one teacher observed in endorsing extra pay for teaching challenging students: "A person like me, I don't want it. Let her have that extra $10,000. I'll take the easy class. But you'd have plenty of people like her that want the extra money and are willing to take a hard class."[42] The majority of teachers also back differential pay. The 2003 Public Agenda Survey of teachers found that 70 percent supported giving extra pay to teachers in "tough neighborhoods with low performing schools," that 67 percent supported it for "teachers who consistently work harder...than other teachers," and that 62 percent supported it for teachers "who consistently receive outstanding evaluations from their principals."[43]

School districts frequently provide piecemeal stipends for coaching or teaching English as a second language, yet they don't reward those teachers who mentor colleagues, critique lesson plans, or otherwise work to make the school successful. Few things are more frustrating for outstanding teachers than to be treated exactly like their less committed peers. Today, the profession repels too many energetic practitioners by expecting teachers to willingly sacrifice professional growth, advancement, and reward.

Compensation

Commonsense reformers reject the notion that teachers' compensation should be based on their experience and credentials rather than their performance. Districts determine salaries using a negotiated "grid" in which pay is strictly a function of the years a teacher has taught in the district and the number of degrees or credits he has accumulated. A school district will pay all teachers who have a B.A. and 5 years local teaching experience one amount and all who have an M.Ed. and 12 years local experience another amount—regardless of the quality of their work.[44]

A commonsense reformer believes that teachers who do well, those in unpleasant circumstances, those taking on special challenges, and those with critical skills ought to be pulling in very different base salaries. Paying for performance does more than deliver rewards to the most deserving workers. When done sensibly, it sends a vital message about the organization's priorities and values. Russell Miller, a principal with Mercer Human Resource Consulting, has bluntly observed that for organizations that fail to reward excellence, "The biggest risk is mediocrity. Your stars are going to look elsewhere, and your average and below-average employees will say 'I'm going to stick around.'"[45] Managers require the leeway to pay employees in accord with the difficulty of their job, the scarcity of their skills, and their performance.

This is not to say that managers should be given license to pay any employee whatever they choose. Just as traditional companies structure compensation to keep the pay of those doing similar work within a general range, a sensible system would utilize broad "pay bands" of the kind long utilized in the private sector and favored in civil service reform. These proposals are hardly radical. In the last couple years, the federal Department of Homeland Security and the three-quarter-million civilians working for the Defense Department have been shifted to a pay system that uses five career groups and four pay levels—rather than the bureaucratic 15-grade general schedule long used by most of the federal government. Dozens of studies of test projects involving more than 30,000 Defense Department employees have found that the system improved performance and morale while retaining essential safeguards.

In the case of the Defense Department, the safeguards have included the creation of an independent Merit Systems Protection Board through which employees can seek a review of decisions.[46] Systematic performance data and sophisticated information technology can prove invaluable in equipping managers to make good choices and in flagging problematic management decisions. For instance, enterprise compensation management software produced by companies like Kadiri Inc., Workscape Inc., and Advanced Information Management Inc. uses "disparate impact analysis" to determine whether any minority groups are being treated unfairly or whether the compensation for any individuals is out of line. These kinds of checks and balances would help protect educators from managerial malfeasance.

Such a system in a district might specify that teachers with 7 to 10 years of experience would earn between $40,000 and $80,000, depending on the difficulty of their assignment, the demand for their skills, and their performance. If districts were paying $80,000 to 33-year-old math teachers who were doing an effective job in troubled schools, and recapturing the cost by paying $40,000 to history or English teachers in comfortable schools, we would find it miraculously easier to find and keep the teachers we need.

Districts like Charlotte, Denver, Cincinnati, Dallas, and states like Kentucky, North Carolina, and Arizona are gingerly experimenting with "school-based performance awards" and more flexible pay systems that reward individual teachers for excellence on a number of measures.[47] These efforts to modify teacher compensation have typically been timid and tepid, tacking small bonuses onto the existing salary system. For instance, states and districts devise plans to provide a bonus of $1,000 or $2,000 to teachers who are already making $35,000 or $50,000 a year. Bonuses that are one-time awards of 3 percent or 4 percent of annual salary are unlikely to have much impact.[48] The president of the Wilson Group consultants, a firm specializing in performance-based reward systems, has derided merit increases of 4 percent as "a joke.... The after-tax difference [in pay] is a Starbucks coffee."[49] Robert Heneman, a professor of business management and human resources at Ohio State University has observed, "[The] research shows that you need [a] seven percent or eight percent [compensation increase] just to catch anybody's attention."[50]

Proposals to reform teacher pay routinely suffer from several flaws, all readily remedied through commonsense adjustments. First, the dollar amounts usually add up to a small percentage of teacher pay and are not linked to broader professional incentives. Second, these rewards are often structured in ways that limit the ability of individuals to influence their chance of winning. Many of the rewards are granted on a schoolwide basis, which, though a nice sentiment, means that even a massive effort on the part of an individual teacher has only a tiny impact on whether she will win the bonus. Such systems encourage everyone to work more or less as they always have, while hoping the others will shoulder the burden. Group bonuses are a healthy way to build cohesion when mounted atop systems that already recognize and reward individual effort, but are not by themselves effective at motivating individuals. Third, rewards are frequently given for acquiring certificates, like the one issued by the National Board for Professional Teaching Standards, rather than one's classroom performance. Finally, especially when rewards are sizable, as in the case of California's $25,000 bonuses, they are one-shot deals that feel like a lucky lottery ticket and which teachers expect to pocket about as frequently.

It is far better to provide more moderate incentives that committed employees can realistically expect to claim year after year.

Pensions

Public school "defined benefit" retirement plans were designed for industrial-era jobs in which employees did not move or change careers and reflect a mindset that assumes personnel should be strapped into a district for 20 or more years. These plans provide a formula-driven retirement benefit that disproportionately rewards educators who stay in place for 15 or 20 years at the expense of those who depart sooner. Most states mandate that educators stay in the retirement plan for 6 to 10 years before they become "vested" and can collect even a portion of their benefits. Matthew Lathrop, of the American Legislative Exchange Council, has noted, "The guaranteed benefit is only good for those who spend a substantial part of their career with one employer. That's an enormous drawback in today's economy, when even public employees are less likely to stick with a single employer."[51] Or, as one veteran educator phrased it to me, "This retirement system is a death trap. I'm ready to retire but I can't afford to bail out until I fully qualify . . . so I'm stuck here—and the [students] are stuck with me—for another three years."

This strategy made a certain sense when teaching was a profession for married women without other career choices, but it's a handicap in today's world where workers routinely switch jobs every few years. Dramatic rewards are provided for those who hang on for 25 years at the expense of those who don't stick around that long. For instance, as of 1998, 35 percent of major teacher retirement systems required that teachers remain for at least 10 years before collecting any benefits at all. In other states, teachers are typically required to remain in place for 5 or 6 years before becoming eligible for any benefits.[52]

With its emphasis on time served, the defined benefit model is hostile to entrepreneurs, discourages risk-taking, and is a better fit for a factory than a knowledge-based profession. Existing pension policies reduce worker flexibility and leave teachers hesitant to consider positions in new districts, charter schools, or new start-ups. The result fosters excessive caution and stifles creative thinking. A commonsense approach would provide benefits in a more flexible fashion and one less conditioned on long service. The most important step to take is shifting schools from traditional pensions to "defined contribution" arrangements, like 401(k) or 403(b) plans. Such a step would reduce the number of veteran teachers who feel compelled to put in their time in order to collect their full pension, ease exit from and reentry into the profession, give teachers more geographical flexibility, and make teaching more attractive both for talented 20-somethings and for midcareer job-changers. Reducing the obligation to fund pensions would permit districts to pay employees higher salaries in the here and now. Alternatively, districts could provide a generous contribution on behalf of each employee, perhaps 5 percent or 10 percent of salary, to an account that is readily portable if and when the worker takes a new job.

Such a shift in retirement benefits would simply reflect broader changes in American life. In 1980, just 20 percent of employers offered the more flexible defined-contribution plans; by 1998, more than 40 percent did. Meanwhile, the percentage offering defined-benefit plans declined during that same period from 39 percent to 22 percent. In other words, most employers are responding to a new and more mobile world by making it easier for workers to enter or exit their workforces without having to put retirement benefits at risk.[53] School systems, on the other hand, retain pension plans that can make it hard for exhausted teachers to walk away, that make teaching unnecessarily costly for candidates unwilling to make a 20-year commitment, and that may nudge career-changers with financial obligations to rethink their interest in teaching. None of this is necessary.

Non-Monetary Rewards

Another way to recognize excellence is to provide offices and the other trappings of professional accomplishment. The notion that all teachers ought to be treated identically shapes the educational workplace just as much as it does compensation and the career track. In most schools, teachers share a common workroom or lounge. Simple private offices are almost nonexistent. This excessive workplace democracy undermines the professionalism of outstanding practitioners, makes life especially difficult for those who shoulder additional responsibility, and sends the message that excellence isn't honored. While it is not feasible to provide offices for all faculty this should not prevent us from giving them to lead teachers who need room for counseling, planning, or mentoring colleagues.

It's not just about money, of course; it's about working conditions and professional opportunity. Recognizing that people teach for different reasons, it makes sense to reward teachers in different ways. Teachers can be rewarded not only with increased compensation, but with professional training, new resources, new responsibilities and opportunities, fringe benefits, or workplace perks. In almost any line of work, we take it for granted that employees who do good work ought to be treated accordingly—and there are a lot of sensible ways to go about this.

Professional Opportunities

New teachers, especially talented and ambitious young teachers, grow frustrated when they watch their college friends in other professions take on new roles and responsibilities while they enjoy no similar opportunities in teaching. To address this, over the years a variety of approaches have been proposed, most of them only to fade away. Reformers have proposed paying veterans a bonus for mentoring junior teachers. They have proposed "career ladders" in which teachers climb the rungs on the basis of accomplishments. Such proposals make sense but have generally been nothing more than symbolic sprigs, soon wilted by the broader culture of incompetence. Union leaders resist them because they threaten to create division among teachers and to change teaching in unpredictable ways, while reformers happily move on to the more agreeable subject of professional development and across-the-board pay raises.

A commonsense reformer is less concerned with any specific approach than with creating opportunities for teachers to advance in their profession, grow as professionals, tackle new challenges, and be rewarded for their successes. One school district might create positions for veteran teachers who spend half a day teaching and the other half working with colleagues to develop lessons. Another district might create a position for some teachers to take on classes with the most troubled students and then counsel those students during an extra period or teach half-time and serve as a coach and mentor to other teachers during the rest of the day.

A lack of emphasis on performance has encouraged teachers to view professional training as ticket punching to help meet state licensing requirements. States generally require teachers to obtain about six semester hours of credit every five years. Since the state's focus is upon ensuring that courses are completed, not the effectiveness of the teacher or the quality of the training, teachers typically seek the least demanding and most convenient courses available. The result is a cottage industry of mediocre courses and seminars. So mediocre in fact that 50 percent of teachers report that their recent professional development made "little difference" in their teaching.[54]

School districts spend more than $3 billion a year on professional development. This is not an entitlement for teachers, it's an investment of public money. There is no reason that it need be offered equally to all educators. Companies are unashamed when they provide training to promising employees and not to others. Rather than provide low-grade professional development to all comers, districts should target programs and support in ways that advance the larger needs of students and that help to attract, retain, and develop excellent practitioners. This may entail providing support to all personnel, but it may not. The determining factor should not be what will satisfy the teachers but what will serve the students.

Squeezing Out the Lemons

Currently, it is virtually impossible to fire poor teachers, especially after they serve 2 to 3 probationary years and become "tenured." In 2002, the Los Angeles board of education encountered fierce resistance when it tried to remove about 400 of the 35,000 teachers in the chronically low-achieving district. In the end, the board was able to remove only three, and two of the three removals were overturned on appeal. New York City's troubled school system, with over 72,000 teachers, sought to dismiss only three over a 2-year period. In two large Georgia counties, not a single tenured teacher was fired over a period of more than 5 years.[55] More than 80 percent of superintendents and principals report that the local union fights to "protect teachers who really should be out of the classroom."[56]

Nationally, public school districts report dismissing about one teacher a year for low performance. This amounts to a rate of well under 1 percent, compared to a rate of 4.9 percent in charter schools.[57] Public school teachers have been caught sticking a child's head in a toilet, reading the newspaper while children gambled in the back of the room, missing weeks or months of school at a stretch, and yet have kept their jobs.[58] Moreover, the paperwork required to prove teacher malfeasance is so onerous that principals find it easier to tolerate incompetence. In the words of one Washington state principal, "If I tried to remove them, it would be two years of paper, two months of my life, a lot of tension, and then it would still be a long shot." The protections that union contracts grant to teachers, particularly those who have lasted 2 or 3 years and earned tenure, are extraordinary.

The notion of "tenure" originated in higher education, where it was primarily intended to secure scholarly inquiry by protecting scholars who pursued unpopular lines of research. Tenure has always been less obviously applicable to K-12 schools in which teachers are hired to provide instruction rather than to create new knowledge. Aside from that larger issue, however, higher education itself has spent the last 30 years struggling to reduce the percentage of tenured faculty. The percentage of full-time professors with tenure or on the "tenure track" fell by more than 30 percent from 1975 to 1995, while the percentage working on short-term contracts increased by 50 percent during that period. From 1970 to 1998, part-time faculty grew from 22 percent to 42 percent of all instructors nationwide. Colleges and universities have taken these steps due to concerns about staffing inflexibility, lost efficiencies, and employee motivation.[59]

Unable to remove inept or lethargic faculty, principals and superintendents learn to simply work around them. One Los Angeles teacher explained, "A couple of years ago I had a terrible partner, but I had a very good principal who wrote everything down so they were able to ship her off to a different school. But that was terrible, because she went in and ruined the life of another school."[60] The simplest way for administrators to remove bad teachers is to encourage them to transfer to another school. In return, principals provide these teachers with positive evaluations. The result has been nicknamed the "dance of the lemons." In one troubled district after another, poor teachers receive good evaluations from principals eager to pass them along. Teachers themselves recognize how hard it is to purge their ineffective peers, with 36 percent reporting that "between tenure and the documentation requirements, it's too hard for administrators to remove any but the very worst teachers" and just 14 percent reporting that inability to remove bad teachers is not a problem.[61]

One assistant superintendent from another district explained: "It's still not in the district's mind-set that we can get rid of people. We don't do it. We haven't equipped principals to do this or let them know what to look for. We use 'dismissal for cause' to encourage problem teachers to leave, but...we're talking maybe fifteen a year, out of four thousand plus, and we're not even firing them—we're just trying to counsel them to depart on their own.... Removing the incompetent is just not part of our culture." The director of human resources in the same district reported the district had only just created a form enabling it to fire novice teachers during their initial probationary years, noting, "When we started working on HR, a denial-of-tenure form didn't even exist."

These routines are embedded in collective bargaining agreements and accepted by many administrators as a normal part of doing business. One high-ranking Texas district official explained what it takes for her district to fire a teacher in that nonunion state: "Firing incompetent teachers for poor performance or for engaging in misconduct is as time consuming and demanding as trying to convict someone of a crime. In cases of misconduct with students, the victims are almost always required to testify because teachers want to exercise their right to face their accusers. If the victim is unwilling or unable to testify because they are no longer available or mentally challenged, we can pretty much count on losing the case. . . . As for perform-ance, that is almost impossible!! You miss the deadline for the appraisal and [the appraisal] is null and void. The assessment instrument is so full of time-line requirements, that any misstep can result in a dispute, hours of time meeting to process the dispute and often resulting in rendering the assess-ment null and void. Then of course you have to put them on a Growth Plan and they have to give input. [If] you don't give them an opportunity for input, you're sunk. While the teacher is awaiting the hearing, he/she is still on the payroll, then add to that the cost of the substitute, attorney's fees, court reporter costs, hearing officer costs, transcripts, copying files and doc-uments, and most importantly, staff time. . . . Are we saying it can't be done? Of course not. What we are saying is that it requires almost 100 percent of a principal's time to *hope* to win a case to fire one bad teacher. Who is willing to do that with all the other demands of the job?"

Even teachers agree that tenure protects teachers who should not be in the schools. Seventy-eight percent of teachers report that there are at least a few teachers in their school who "fail to do a good job and are simply going through the motions" while 58 percent say that tenure doesn't necessarily mean that teachers have worked hard or proven their ability.[62] One New Jersey union representative has confessed, "I've gone in and defended teachers who shouldn't even be pumping gas."[63] A Los Angeles union repre-sentative said: "If I'm representing them, it's impossible to get them out. It's impossible. Unless they commit a lewd act."[64]

A commonsense reformer is perplexed that status quo reform groups like the National Commission on Teaching and America's Future can issue exten-sive reports on improving teacher quality without ever addressing the need to remove ineffective practitioners.[65] Private sector managers regard purging low performers as a routine part of the job. In fact, widely admired firms such as General Electric have made it a point to eliminate the least productive 10 percent of its workforce every year. As former GE CEO Jack Welch has explained: "Making these judgments is not easy, and they are not always precise. Yes, you'll miss a few stars and a few late bloomers—but your chances of building an all-star team are improved dramatically. This is how great organizations are built. Year after year, differentiation raises the bar higher and higher and increases the overall caliber of the organization."[66]

Accountability provides new safeguards for flexible firing. Measuring a teacher's value added helps flag ineffective teachers and protects good teachers from unfair treatment. Districts can use these measures as a way to monitor school management and detect individual principals who may behave irresponsibly. In an era when 78 percent of superintendents evaluate principals on their ability to judge and improve teacher quality, the case that teachers need to be insulated from cavalier management is an increasingly difficult one to make.[67] The fact that just 16 percent of teachers even concede that union protections can impede actions to improve schooling illustrates why it is perilous to rely on teachers for policy advice.[68] This is a case where the interests of children and practitioners simply diverge.

Educators protest, "Teachers want to know that their jobs won't go away." This is all well and good, but it is also irrelevant. Pilots, mechanics, and engineers who also have mortgages and kids would like an employment guarantee. However, they know that they deserve to keep their jobs only if they do well. Across America, employment is normally "at-will," with workers free to quit any time and employers equally free to fire workers. That sensible standard should be the model for schooling.

Rethinking the Job

The effort to bring more flexibility into teacher hiring, compensation, and professional growth suggests an obvious need to rethink the job itself. While I will have much more to say on this front in chapter 6, it is worth quickly highlighting a few points. The constancy of the teaching role from one school to the next and one classroom to the next that characterizes schools today makes it difficult to take full advantage of the various talents that educators possess and prevents us from cultivating future leaders or developing essential skills. One of the attractions that charter schools hold for many experienced teachers is that working in a charter school often permits them to take on new curricular or leadership responsibilities without having to abandon the classroom. Once we alter the hiring and compensation systems, it will no longer be a bureaucratic nightmare to invent positions in which a teacher combines teaching, administrative, and technical or mentoring responsibilities. This will allow us to put more teachers in leadership roles where they lead small groups or handle managerial tasks. It will also permit us to promote faculty and utilize their organizational or coaching abilities without pushing them out of the classroom.

The Status Quo Reform Remedies

Beyond demanding more money, the status quo reform crowd has three remarkably unproductive proposals. One is to erect new hurdles for people interested in the profession. The second is to have a committee of education types identify a national cadre of "master teachers" based on hundreds of pages of essays and other materials submitted by applicants. The third is to endorse a "new unionism" in which we trust union leaders to willingly sacrifice member benefits out of the goodness of their hearts.

Raising Licensure Barriers

Status quo reformers, led by Stanford professor Linda Darling-Hammond, have sought to raise certification standards and make it harder for potential teachers to enter the profession. They want to demand that all applicants receive education degrees or complete an "alternative" program run by a school of education. They advocate requiring any would-be teacher to take more education school classes and to spend a longer time performing a student internship. The problem with this approach is threefold. First, as we mentioned earlier, there is no evidence that this training makes teachers more effective. Second, they will discourage even more potential teachers— especially those with attractive options. Third, this approach tightens the grip of education school professors on teaching, squelches competing ideas, and protects training programs from healthy competition.

The National Board for Professional Teaching Standards

A second approach is embodied in the National Board for Professional Teaching Standards (NBPTS). Since its 1987 launch by a consortium of teacher unions, schools of education, and professional organizations, the NBPTS has sought to "professionalize" teaching by establishing a national standard for excellence. Proponents like Stanford professor Linda Darling-Hammond claim that, "National Board certification—just like board certification, architecture, and accounting—is granted only to highly accomplished teachers who have demonstrated their abilities on rigorous assessments."[69] In theory, this is an interesting idea.

In execution, it is a disaster. The NBPTS judges excellence not on the basis of student learning, but on a bundle of lesson plans, student work, videotapes, essays, and other materials that applicants submit. To finance the process, applicants pay a fee of $2,300, a charge that's at least partially covered by school outlays in 31 states. Based on the materials submitted, NBPTS "experts" then decide whether or not to certify the teacher. Thirty-two states pay cash bonuses to NBPTS certified teachers regardless of their actual performance in the classroom. In fact, while we have spent well over $200 million to certify and reward more than 24,000 National Board teachers, there is no large-scale research that has thus far examined how effective these teachers actually are at educating children.[70]

The NBPTS model presumes that collecting enough teacher essays and student work samples allows evaluators to judge teacher competence without actually examining student achievement. To that end, NBPTS has proclaimed "exemplary" standards for teachers in 27 fields, none of them based on whether students learn anything. A number of problems have resulted. For instance, there is the Massachusetts social studies teacher who was denied NBPTS certification because he failed to meet the "Collaboration in Professional Community" standards, even though the teacher had authored four books on teaching and had helped launch two successful public schools.[71] Scholars at the Urban Institute and the University of Washington have found that African American and male applicants are systematically rejected at higher rates than their peers.[72] Not surprisingly, researchers have assailed NBPTS for the capricious way in which the standards are used and argued that there is no evidence that NBPTS-certified teachers are more effective than other teachers.[73]

The NBPTS approach undermines commonsense efforts to link teacher compensation or recognition to their effectiveness as a classroom teacher, faculty colleague, and member of the school community. Instead, it has constructed an exhausting, expensive process that wastes time and money while suggesting that the measure of teacher quality is not whether students learn but whether teachers write sufficiently passionate essays about their "commitment" and "reflectiveness."

The "New Unionism"

Finally, some well-intentioned scholars have called for a "new unionism" in which unions partner with the superintendent and school board to promote school improvement. They point to a handful of districts where unions and management have reached tenuous agreements that feature a rhetorical commitment to student performance and mild steps to promote improved teaching in return for generous compensation concessions. Some districts have introduced observations in which teachers evaluate each other, allowed principals to reject senior transfers in favor of more junior teachers when filling staff vacancies, and expanded teacher responsibilities to include more contact with parents. Even heralded efforts in locales such as Toledo and Rochester have had little sustained success and typically faded away within a few years.

The larger problem with the "new unionism" is that union leaders rightfully view their role as promoting the security and well-being of members. Consequently, they will refuse changes that could result in pressure or pain. The role of union officials is to serve teachers, not students. This doesn't make union leaders venal, it's just a fact of life. Any union leader who forgets that simple fact is not likely to remain in a leadership position for long, as a candidate more attuned to the shared requirements of the membership will come along. While the new unionism is a nice idea, it rests on an unrealistic faith in the generosity and selflessness of union officials and the willingness of teachers to voluntarily sacrifice protections they have long taken for granted. The result is that even some ardent proponents of the new unionism have begun to grow skeptical of its prospects.

Many hardheaded public officials and business leaders have been snowed by the status quo proposals, taken in by honey-laden words like "professionalism" and "standards." These values are important and valuable elements of school improvement, but real reform needs to rest on firmer foundations.

School Choice Alone Won't Solve These Problems

Some would-be commonsense reformers promise that school choice alone will be enough to remedy the workforce problems. Because the teacher unions are responsible for so many of the constraints on teaching, choice proponents hope that introducing choice will either force unions to change their ways or permit a new set of more flexible schools to displace the old.

In fact, many choice-based reforms are accompanied by measures that extend the regulation of teaching to choice schools. Of the 40 states that have adopted charter school laws, more than half impose rules that limit who a school may hire or the terms of employment. In January 2003, the Illinois state legislature doubled the number of charter schools that would be permitted in Chicago. Receiving far less notice was the legislature's decision to couple this concession with a requirement that the new schools hire traditionally licensed teachers. In other words, an expansion of charter schooling or school vouchers can have no effect on how the workforce is managed or can even extend status quo regulations to areas where they previously didn't apply.

Most charter schools have adopted personnel systems that look remarkably like those in the traditional district schools. Most hire certified teachers, pay teachers primarily on the basis of seniority, and fire few teachers.[74] Why? Because most are run by conventional educators who can't conceive of running a school in any other fashion. In many locales state regulations limit the freedom of charter schools to hire or compensate teachers, while the ability of charter schools to attract staff has been impeded by pension rules that leave teachers and principals hesitant to change positions. Education school professionals have fully formed notions of what schools should look like. So long as they produce nearly all of the nation's teachers, merely opening new schools won't suffice to change the status quo.

Conclusion

Commonsense reformers should not get caught up bashing the teacher unions or casting union leaders as villains. Workers have every right to organize. Unions have played a critical role in securing rights and fair treatment over time. The problem is not with the unions, but with contracts in which states and districts have negotiated away essential management freedoms and with a system that neither encourages nor empowers school or school district officials to resist union demands.

Moving to a more flexible system of hiring, firing, and paying teachers is part and parcel of moving to an emphasis on accountability and competition. Our traditional approach to teacher licensure is based on funneling teachers through rule-bound education school programs that may or may not ensure or enhance classroom effectiveness. Standards-based reform seeks to move school governance from that same industrial-era assembly-line model and toward a less regulated system that focuses more on educational performance than on ensuring that teachers have completed one of the nation's 1,300 teacher preparation programs. Such a model implies two approaches to enhancing teacher quality, both of them inconsistent with existing certification systems.

First, leaders need the flexibility to monitor and reward personnel in sensible ways. Second, it is necessary that leaders identify and then either assist or remove ineffective teachers. Both sets of tasks become easier as states develop more systematic and reliable evaluation systems.

It is in the most troubled systems that commonsense workforce reforms will have dramatic effects. In these schools, administrators have tremendous difficulty finding qualified teachers. It is in these districts, with their large numbers of long-term substitutes, burned-out veterans, and unqualified teachers, that new applicants will be welcome, that offering generous compensation for effective teachers or those with critical skills will have the largest impact, and that explicit pressure and individual-level incentives will make a huge difference.

Reforming the teaching force in this way will foster a more flexible, welcoming, rewarding, exciting, and performance-focused profession. A culture of competence will summon and energize the kinds of adults we want in classrooms: impassioned, hard-working, and effective teachers and communicators who know the content they are teaching. Of course, the status quo reformers are right in noting that fulfilling the promise of these reforms requires attending to the support, training, and working conditions of teachers. Making this a reality requires that we provide teachers with the school and district leadership they deserve. Good teachers will be frustrated and alienated by unfocused leadership, incompetent performance assessments, or a lack of support. Competitive and tough-minded accountability can encourage performance-conscious and creative leadership, but the next two chapters will discuss how we can make that potential into a reality.

CHAPTER FIVE

Leadership

The genius of a good leader is to leave behind him a situation which common sense, without the grace of genius, can deal with successfully.

—Walter Lippmann

Tough-minded accountability and competition will drive improvement only if school and district leaders turn away from the path of least resistance and reject the temptation to make their peace with the status quo. This may entail leaders shutting down popular programs and shifting those resources to more vital concerns, firing teachers whose students do not show acceptable academic improvement, or reassigning outstanding teachers to low-achieving classrooms or schools. In each case, the visible hand of tough-minded accountability or the invisible hand of competition is prodding superintendents and principals to do things they would prefer not to do.

Accountability makes inaction unpalatable by holding superintendents and principals personally responsible for student learning. Pressing leaders to brush past obstacles and giving them more control over their employees won't do much good, however, unless leaders possess the requisite skills and tools. In chapter 4, we addressed those changes that would give leaders the tools to recruit promising educators, cultivate and reward excellence, and remove ineffective personnel. I will now turn to how commonsense reform can help to recruit, support, and reward the leaders we need.

Somehow, insulated from the broader world by licensure requirements, schools of education and experts in educational administration have propagated a belief that managing schools is different from managing anything else. Even though business leaders and professors of management recognize that there is a lot of common ground in managing a hospital, a bank, a computer firm, a city government, or an airline, we have indulged educational leaders in this conceit. As a result, school leadership has managed to remain largely unaffected by the management revolution that has swept through the American public and private sectors in the past decades.

Today, we routinely accept in educational leadership the kind of incompetence that prompts shareholder revolt or even criminal prosecution in the private sector. When investors buy into private sector firms that make mundane products like hot dogs or soap, the first thing they seek out is a skilled, competent management team. Commonsense reformers are always puzzled that we seem ready to settle for less when it is our children themselves who are at stake. Managerial malfeasance like losing track of millions of dollars, not knowing how many employees are on the payrolls, or failing to file required state documents is a common occurrence in many large school systems. While we appropriately pursue the executives of an Enron, Tyco, or WorldCom for misusing investor funds or falsely reporting on the financial health of their firms, we show a puzzling tolerance when superintendents or school district officials conduct themselves in a similarly troubling fashion.

In 2002, the Oakland school system was forced into default after Dennis Chaconas, the acclaimed new superintendent, had hired hundreds of new teachers and handed out a 24 percent teacher pay raise even when warned by a state Fiscal Crisis and Management Assistance Team report that "the district's future financial solvency is in serious question." The Oakland school board had hired Chaconas in February 2000 based upon his dynamic personality and exciting reform strategy, though the reform effort turned out to rest largely on ramping up spending in the hope that this would improve school performance. While Chaconas was predictably hailed for his "innovations," his mismanagement produced an $82 million two-year deficit and eventually forced the district to seek a state bailout of more than $100 million. Even after this debacle, the Oakland school board remained supportive of Chaconas and his "reform" agenda. As the leader of one of Oakland's most influential African American churches explained, "Chaconas has inherited a bad situation. Since he's been superintendent, he's done good work. He can't pull rabbits out of hats. He can't turn water into wine. He can't raise the dead. He's just a man." Chaconas's defense for the debacle was to concede that he had ignored issues of financial oversight and "concentrated on academics [because]...I thought that was the most important issue." Eventually, in order to get the bailout from the state, the school board was forced to fire Chaconas in June 2003—though only after paying him $389,000 in severance.[1]

In March 2003, the Washington, D.C., public school system, with a budgeted workforce of about 10,600, discovered that it actually had 640 more employees than its budget permitted, at a cost of more than $30 million a year. Officials reported that, "Employees were hired without anyone checking to see whether their jobs were covered in the budget." For 71 employees, it wasn't even clear what job they supposedly held. City council member Adrian Fenty said: "I am staggered by some of the numbers here." After a 2001 request for an employee count, it took the system's chief financial officer and human resources officials 18 months to produce a list of employees and budgeted positions. This would be cause for broad and instantaneous firings in any well-run private sector firm, but was shrugged off by the superintendent as "an accumulation of past ills...that have to be cleaned up." Hundreds of the employees weren't even educators. The district had 192 employees in transportation whose positions were not supposed to exist.[2]

In November 2003, the Baltimore City public schools frantically laid off 710 personnel when the leadership realized that the district faced bankruptcy due to a multi-year $52 million deficit if it didn't chop $24 million in spending by the end of the school year. Even as she announced the layoffs, Chief Executive Officer Bonnie Copeland reported that she was still uncertain how much the system owed in unpaid bills and pleaded with staff to turn in invoices that might amount to $13 million or more. The cuts were concentrated in the central office, which the district had failed to trim in a more disciplined fashion even as its enrollment shrunk steadily during the 1990s. By 2001–2002, Baltimore City had 581 central staff for 94,000 students, while larger Maryland systems, including Baltimore County and Prince George's County, needed less than 300 central staff for more than 100,000 students. Reducing the size of central administration to a comparable level would have saved Baltimore City roughly $15 million a year.[3]

This sort of management is unacceptable. Leaders are responsible for determining where resources are being used well, where they're being wasted, and to move them accordingly. "In tight economic times, if you're going to be efficient and effective, there's no way you should be running the same number of schools," the chief executive officer of the Detroit schools, has observed.[4] Closing just nine schools allowed the Birmingham, Alabama, school district to immediately save $5 million in 2002–2003.[5] Of course, shutting down even one school almost always provokes fierce opposition from the affected community. As a result, district officials generally make such cuts only as a last resort. In truth, no employer wants to close facilities or upset employees. The problem is more intense in democratically controlled services like public education or the post office in which the affected communities will fight any closure, regardless of the larger social benefits.

Why have we been able to overcome this reluctance in so many other fields yet remained stymied in schooling? The problem is one of will and of skill. In chapters 2 and 3, I discussed how a commonsense reformer seeks to strengthen the will. Now I will turn to the question of skill. Education leaders are former teachers focused on managing procedures and appeasing the teachers and the community. They are not good at making tough financial choices. They are not skilled at managing finances. They do not have the information technology, the skilled staff, or the incentives to control costs. We have created a school leadership culture that honors neither the tenets of financial prudence nor student performance. We have a leadership culture in which leaders, believe it or not, think they should not be held accountable for student learning. A 2003 Public Agenda survey of school principals found that 45 percent thought it a "bad idea" to "hold principals accountable for student standardized test scores at the building level," and just 41 percent thought it a "good idea."[6]

In the private sector, CEOs are expected to provide strategic direction, solid management, and responsible fiscal oversight. As one school reform analyst has trenchantly noted, "Business leaders would scoff at the idea that the financial side of a business should be isolated from the production side. In the world of education, however, the ability to provide 'instructional leadership' is considered separate from and more important than mere financial management."[7]

In the popular imagination, a great school leader is a larger-than-life figure who inspires through her own powerful convictions or uplifts through relentless optimism or dazzles through creative genius or motivates through a passionate commitment to disciplined performance. We have these models tucked in the back of our minds, summoned from our own experiences and popular culture.

We look at the successes of these outsized figures and say, "Geez, it is possible. Why isn't everybody doing as well?" Then we look at these leaders, try to distill the qualities or skills that helped them finesse the system, and set out to replicate those skills. Fawning newspaper and magazine stories convey the implicit message, "Here, all good leaders should be like *this*." We fail to recognize that these success stories may not offer especially good direction for reform. How can that be?

Today's effective education leaders are successful in spite of their jobs. They're successful because they have such strong personalities, so much energy, or such creativity that they are able to work around the procedures and arrangements in place. In a sense, these leaders are artists—finding ways to coax improvement without incentives, accountability, support, or an ability to overturn outmoded regulations. They do this by charming, cajoling, and brow-beating subordinates and community members into cooperating, often at great personal or professional cost.

By focusing at any one moment on the handful of leaders who are passionately self-motivated and unconcerned with rewards, the status quo reformers have managed to conclude that incentives, institutions, and management tools don't matter. Since these leaders are self-propelled phenoms, at least until they burn out from exhaustion, status quo reformers presume that tough-minded accountability and competition are unhelpful distractions. Unfortunately, given that our schools employ more than 85,000 public school principals and about 15,000 superintendents, seeking to fill all of these positions with preternaturally gifted or messianic candidates is not a particularly promising long-term strategy.

District Governance

The nation's schools are governed by some 15,000 independent school districts, each of which covers a distinct geographic area and most of which enroll fewer than 2,500 students. About 95 percent of districts are governed by elected school boards, with the remainder typically governed by appointed boards named by the mayor. Most boards include five or seven members who stand for election every four years. Boards are relatively amateur affairs, with most board members earning no salary, having few resources, and devoting less than five or eight hours a week to school affairs. Because elections tend to draw low turnout, with most voters having little detailed knowledge on candidates or their positions, it is easy for school district employees and other organized groups to exert significant influence on election results.[8]

These arrangements make it difficult for board members to firmly support commonsense measures that are going to require educators and school personnel to give up longstanding privileges and protections. Commonsense leadership requires that boards provide oversight but do not hamper district leaders in responding to the dictates of accountability. Boards in large districts, in particular, overstep their role and engage in micromanagement, allow strong leadership to be vetoed by active political constituencies, provide unfocused direction, endorse rigid union contracts that tie the district's hands, and fail to forcefully confront central staff bureaucracy or resistance to change.[9]

While commonsense reform is more about providing a blueprint for running schools than dictating management structures, school boards are too often unstable, unserious, and insufficiently focused on management. It will be hard to promote the commonsense agenda without addressing board governance. There are a number of alternate strategies that have been suggested for accomplishing this. Various reformers have suggested adopting mayorally appointed boards, taking steps to make board elections more transparent and competitive, and providing board members with more resources. Each notion has merit and deserves consideration. Another approach that has significant commonsense appeal is the suggestion that districts themselves should be remade into competitive entities, ending the geographic monopoly attributed to each. Instead, districts should be empowered to operate schools beyond their traditional confines and there should be an approval process that permits new nonprofit and for-profit entities to similarly begin authorizing and managing schools.[10] Such possibilities remain necessarily speculative at this juncture. The key commonsense point is the need for governance arrangements that promote board accountability and provide management with coherent direction.

What Education Leaders Do

There are three kinds of education leaders the commonsense reformer should keep in mind: principals, superintendents, and the superintendent's staff. The nation's school districts vary dramatically in size, from those rural districts with a few dozen students and one school to New York City with its one million students and one thousand schools.

Principals manage schools. They supervise teachers, coordinate curricula and assessment, handle discipline, ensure school safety, communicate with parents, represent the school to the community, supervise the facility, and otherwise assume responsibility for their charges. In elementary schools, which tend to be only a few hundred students, principals generally play the gentle role of den mother. They usually oversee no more than about 30 teachers, have limited disciplinary responsibilities, and operate with only a secretary and a receptionist. In high schools, principals often manage staffs of 60 or more teachers, confront serious disciplinary issues, and run front-office staffs that can include a handful of assistant principals and assorted other staff. In 47 states, principals are required to be former teachers, and even in the few exceptions almost every principal is a former teacher trained in a school of education. Nationally, 99 percent of principals are former teachers.[11] Like teachers, principals are paid primarily on the basis of their formal credentials and how long they have been with the school system.

Superintendents are appointed by school boards to be the executives in charge of a group of schools and the services that support them. Depending on the district, superintendents may be responsible for managing a handful of schools or hundreds of them. From their perch in the district's central office, superintendents are responsible for the district finances, managing the principals, school staffing, curricula and assessment, professional development, transportation, school safety, public relations, athletics, food services, maintenance, construction, and all the other services that it takes to support a system of schools. Especially in a district of 15 schools or more, superintendents spend so little time in the schools or directly tackling issues related to teaching and learning that they often benefit more from management experience than education training. Nonetheless, 43 states require superintendents to be former educators with an advanced degree from a school of education. Despite high-profile exceptions in recent years, only a handful of the nation's 15,000 superintendents don't fit that traditional bill. Superintendent pay is much more variable than principal pay. While school boards have a pretty free hand at paying superintendents in the manner they see fit, only a tiny percentage of superintendent contracts link compensation to district performance.

The executive district staff consists of those central office managers who work as part of the superintendent's team. Such officials serve as deputies to the superintendent for the accounting department, human resources, transportation, professional development, information technology, assessment, security, and other similar tasks. Many of these tasks, such as accounting or human resources, entail no particular expertise in education at all. Their responsibilities largely mirror those of their peers in any software company or textile manufacturer. Nonetheless, most districts staff many of these positions with former teachers and principals. In many cases this is to comply with state regulations and contractual agreements; in others it is a painless way to move mediocre educators out of the schools.

The Allure of "Instructional" Leadership

In the 1980s, school reformers embraced an idea they termed "instructional leadership," acknowledging that principals and superintendents in effective schools focused on the core questions of teaching and learning. At the time, this was an important reminder that leaders could not afford to spend their days obsessing about bus schedules and textbooks. Unfortunately, over time the mantra of "instructional leadership" has become an albatross that has romanticized the abilities of former teachers, caused sensible management practices to take a backseat to overhyped pedagogical and curricular innovations, and obscured the different leadership capabilities called for in different circumstances.

Ensuring that instructional personnel are monitored, evaluated, mentored, and supported is obviously a critical component of the job for principals and superintendents. Instructional leadership, however, must extend to providing leadership in terms of culture, human resources, management, external development, and strategy.[12] It may be less essential that leaders be prepared to personally coach teachers than that they be able to establish accountability systems, build a culture of excellence, deal firmly with unproductive personnel, manage information, improve business practices, recruit good supporting personnel, cultivate a strong leadership team, and negotiate political and parental pressures. In successful schools where students are doing well, faculty members are engaged and self-policing, and competent management practices are established, leaders can be effective by focusing narrowly on coaching and supporting faculty. In other schools, it may be necessary to overhaul the organization before it makes sense to seek a traditional "instructional leader." Clearly, every school needs someone to take responsibility for helping teachers to improve curriculum and instruction. However, because most schools have a number of faculty members who can potentially play such a role, it is not mandatory that each and every principal personally play this role.

In any event, researchers have found that principals and superintendents spend only a limited portion of their time on the curricular and pedagogical aspects of the job. Few principals spend even a quarter of their time on questions regarding instruction and those in low-performing schools spend almost none.[13] Rather, the tasks principals deem most demanding have less to do with classroom instruction than with more conventional managerial challenges like firing unfit employees, addressing employee grievances, and handling an extended workday.[14]

Other things equal, a commonsense reformer would naturally prefer that educational leaders have instructional expertise. However, it is rarely the case that all things are equal. In only considering former teachers, we rule out leadership candidates who possess critical organizational or culture building skills that may be in short supply among former teachers. The problem with the notion of instructional leadership is not its healthy focus on teaching and learning but its presumption that this means *only* former teachers are suited to be education leaders. This creates two major problems. First, teachers, by definition, have worked in the schools. This means they have learned the culture and routines of public schools from the inside. At times, this can be tremendously helpful for a leader. At other times—as when it is necessary to impose painful change or overhaul a troubled organization—such attachments can create blind spots or cause leaders to drag their feet on necessary actions. This is especially true when principals and district officials are drawn from the ranks of people who have formerly taught in that very system. Second, classroom instruction develops many skills, but not necessarily those suited to managing personnel, a leadership team, or million dollar budgets.

Today, schools provide few opportunities for teachers to develop leadership skills and limited room for entrepreneurship. Teachers have little or no opportunity to gain experience managing teams, evaluating adults, changing organizational routines, or leading with a light touch. The result is that very few principals are authoritative without being authoritarian. Far more common are principals who retreat to their office and permit teachers to police themselves or principals who imagine that leadership requires that they be dictatorial and abrasive. For instance, superintendents rate just 11 percent of their principals as excellent at holding teachers accountable for instruction, just 16 percent as excellent at making sound recommendations on teacher tenure, and just 7 percent as excellent at moving ineffective teachers out of their building.[15] *This* is why tough-minded accountability systems have so often resulted in small-minded micromanagement of teaching practice rather than sparking the kinds of ingenuity and collaboration that we have so often seen in other professions.

Contrast the cases of mismanagement discussed earlier in the chapter with what transpired in St. Louis in 2003 when the school district hired Alvarez & Marsal, a New York–based private corporate turnaround firm, to get the district's finances and operations in order. The district faced a shortfall of at least $55 million in its $400 million budget. Darnetta Clinkscale, the school board president, explained, "Our goal is to get the system going in the right direction . . . so we can attract a world-class superintendent." Within the first three months, the new team had saved $15 million by closing 16 underenrolled schools, laying off 1,400 employees, and outsourcing many district operations in the 40,000 student school district. Stunned, the president of the local American Federation of Teachers chapter reported, "It just seems like everything has been done behind closed doors, and then, bam! This is what it's going to be."[16] Leaders unschooled in the compromises of public education may be more willing and better able to make hard but vital decisions about using and allocating resources.

The Reality of "Defensive" Leadership

The reality is that schools and school systems are led by former teachers who typically have little experience managing adults, are unfamiliar with how organizations other than public K-12 schools operate, possess slapdash training in management, and are discouraged from thinking creatively about education management. Coupled with aggressive lawyering and extensive state regulation, this state of affairs has produced a cult of "defensive leadership." Efforts to ensure that all children are adequately served have produced an onslaught of judicial directives in recent decades governing special education provision, how students may be punished, what classes schools must offer, and any number of other matters. Principals who have never worked outside of K-12 education, have a limited managerial toolbox, and enjoy few rewards for excellence but severe travails for even small missteps, too often respond by embracing a narrow proceduralism that stifles energy and talent. As another principal admitted, "If I think there might be anything [relating to harassment] . . . I go right to the compliance officer immediately. I just kick right into the procedure . . . I don't want my judgment in any way to come in."[17]

Consider one Washington, D.C. elementary school wracked by disorder, teacher absenteeism, and miserable student achievement. This is exactly the kind of school where a ruthless commitment to excellence coupled with support for dynamic teaching is most needed. So, what did the principal do? In a pretty typical example, she adopted a policy that prohibited teachers from having any kind of bodily contact with students. Explained one teacher, "We were told that even positive reinforcement through touch is considered corporal punishment because you could withhold that, and that is cruel." Teachers were not permitted to punish violent students or even to tell a student to stand in the corner or copy words from the dictionary. Observed another teacher, "The only thing you could do is ask the child, 'Why are you angry, what made you feel like doing that?' "[18] How this would improve the environment and enhance the education of students is unclear. Principals can get in grave trouble for any incident and receive little reward for running an outstanding school. One result is that only the self-starters tend to run great schools.

As one Massachusetts principal related, "You've got to be nuts to take this job. I go to these leadership seminars where they talk about proactive management, building your team, [and] managing by walking around . . . but it sounds like they're in another world. I work with who I'm given, beg central for information I need, negotiate with personnel to get positions filled. . . . Look, unless you say, 'Screw it, I'm going to push for achievement and if I piss off central or ruin my career, so be it,' unless you do that, you just wind up spending all your time trying to stay out of the penalty box." As a 2003 Public Agenda study noted with careful understatement, "For many principals and superintendents, avoiding lawsuits and fulfilling regulatory and due process requirements is a time-consuming and often frustrating part of the job."[19]

Effective leadership requires promoting a culture of competence, even when that means challenging angry parents, employees, or community members. Unfortunately, the compliance culture, the elevation of former teachers, and the cult of instructional leadership have combined to produce a culture in which leaders learn to be inoffensively ineffective and practice "defensive leadership." Rather than seeking talent or attacking problems, defensive leaders primarily work to avoid embarrassment and ugly conflicts. This is not because they are unconcerned with the plight of their students but because we have constructed a world in which the personal and professional rewards for results-driven improvement are minimal, the obstacles to tough minded action are imposing, the costs of upsetting employees or the community are large, and too many principals or superintendents are unprepared to lead. The challenge for the commonsense reformer is to consider how we get the leaders we need, equip them to perform, and motivate them to excel.

Who Should Lead?

Today, we have institutionalized a very narrow, particular idea of who can serve as an education leader. Generally, in order to be licensed, administrators are required to have taught for three years, completed graduate coursework at an education school in classes like school administration and curriculum, and done an internship. The administrators themselves explain the problems with this approach. Just 8 percent of superintendents and 21 percent of principals report that certification ensures that a principal has what it takes to be a good administrator.[20] Asked about what provided the most valuable preparation for their current position, just 2 percent of superintendents and 4 percent of principals mentioned their required education coursework.[21]

We funnel all kinds of leaders, facing very different challenges, through this same pipeline. The results have been predictable: a shortage of effective leaders and a lack of innovative thinking on management or leadership. A recent national survey of superintendents found that fewer than 40 percent were happy with their principals' ability to make tough decisions, delegate responsibility to staff, involve teachers in developing policies and priorities, or spend money efficiently. When filling a principal position, 60 percent of superintendents agreed they have had to "take what you can get."[22]

At the level of the superintendency, matters are no better. In 2002, Paul Houston, the executive director of the American Association of School Administrators (AASA), said: "The pool of good [superintendent] candidates is shallow. Five years ago, the pool was fairly shallow, and I thought it was as bad as it could get. I was not nearly pessimistic enough. It's gotten worse."[23] In various districts, we now have human resources systems that manage 20,000 or more employees overseen by former middle school teachers and billion-dollar budgets monitored by former algebra teachers unschooled in accounting.

Today, one in three principals is a former gym teacher.[24] While this makes a certain sense—since the current job of most principals emphasizes the skills of discipline and crowd control—if these are the primary qualifications, it is likely that lots of nonteachers might also be equally well equipped. If these are not the primary qualifications, the troubling implication is that gym coaches fill the principal ranks because they regard administration as a safe, comfortable job and because they were not too invested in their classroom teaching.

The problem with leadership licensure is similar to a problem we discussed in the last chapter regarding teachers. Given the imprecise nature of management, asking licensure to bar the door against unsuitable leaders disregards much of what we know about leadership. After all, the general business credential (the MBA) is *not a license*, but a degree that employers value as they see fit. Even in day care and higher education, where we typically require formal credentials for entry into the profession, we do not require additional ones to pursue leadership positions.

Thirty years ago, when leaders were unable to monitor or control their staff, licensure made a certain sense. If all leaders could do was sit in the occasional classroom, review lesson plans, and try to charm and cajole teachers into doing better, then hiring former gym teachers who had completed education school programs ensured that leaders would be comfortable managing large groups and familiar with the rhythm of the school.

The reliance on former teachers rests on the presumption that only former teachers can monitor classroom personnel or support instructional improvement. Today, both assumptions are dubious. The first may have been plausible when we lacked outcome data on teacher performance and the capacity of administrators to judge teacher effectiveness was consequently limited to observing the occasional class and monitoring parental complaints. Today, however, we have a wealth of information on achievement and entrepreneurial managers gather data on various facets of teacher performance. The always minimal value of sitting in the back of a teacher's classroom a few times a year has diminished further, while the value of understanding and applying data is at a premium. Meanwhile, superintendents and principals have almost universally come up through the public schools, frequently starting as teachers and advancing through the ranks of the same systems where they now play a supervisory role. Raised in that culture, principals and district officials tend to recoil at the notion that they should routinely and aggressively monitor or push their employees.

The claim that only former teachers can mentor is equally problematic. In those schools or systems where no one else is available to work with teachers on curricular or instructional issues, administrators must play this role. Such situations are quite rare, however. More typically, principals and superintendents head teams that include a variety of individuals with different strengths. An administrator who utilizes her team wisely can provide more useful assistance than an overstretched solitary leader drawing upon only her personal knowledge.

Finally, any teacher accumulates mastery over only a small slice of educational content and pedagogy. Much of the expertise of a high school history teacher does not translate to math or science, and only a limited amount even transfers to elementary school history. A middle school teacher's expertise does not necessarily provide much specific guidance for working with first- or second-grade teachers. A high school math teacher (much less a gym teacher) who becomes a middle school principal will have some expertise to share with the 20 percent of the faculty who teach math, but little beyond a practiced eye and sensible generalizations for other faculty members. Many non-teachers may be prepared to provide as much. Even in school systems where teachers share common objectives, differences across subjects, grades, and performance levels can leave good teachers hesitant to offer their colleagues much specific instructional advice. Any effective principal or superintendent needs to draw upon the skills and talents of the entire faculty, whatever their personal experience.

Commonsense reform seeks to broaden the talent pipeline while recognizing the sensitive and unusual demands on education leaders. The proper standard is not dissimilar to that posed in the previous chapter. Candidates should hold a B.A. or B.S. degree from an accredited college or university and pass a rigorous criminal background check; demonstrate relevant experience sufficient to exhibit essential knowledge, temperament, and skills for the position; and demonstrate mastery of essential technical knowledge, to the extent that we can pinpoint such knowledge (in areas like education law or special education) and where a state figures that an individual administrator must have personal command of the subject matter. Do these criteria imply that anyone who wishes is entitled to serve as a school administrator? Absolutely not. As we discussed in chapter 4, being permitted to seek work does not equate to the right to hold a position. Training, experience, preparation—these qualities are encouraged and rewarded in a sensibly designed system.

There are many institutions besides schools that help to raise and educate children. These include tutoring programs, counseling programs, youth clubs, preschools, and so on. There are a wealth of non–K-12 personnel running literacy and youth programs, especially in urban environments, who have demonstrated a passionate commitment to children and who are experienced at managing the education, mentoring, and counseling services that schools provide. Why would we not search for school leaders among such candidates? In other lines of work, we don't presume that architects need to have started as bricklayers, senators as civil servants, airline executives as pilots or baggage handlers, or hospital administrators as doctors. We understand that different roles may require different talents and training; that competence in one role may not translate to another; and that narrow selection criteria stifle creative thinking, shrink the talent pool, and require us to push effective employees into jobs which may not play to their strengths.

Though proponents of licensure argue that education leadership positions are so challenging that nobody wants them, in fact enormous numbers of accomplished individuals are eager to pursue such positions. In 2003, New Leaders for New Schools had 1,012 candidates apply for 70 fellowship slots. In its principal cohort, the Broad Foundation's Urban Superintendents Academy had over 650 inquiries and more than 160 applications for 20 slots, and the KIPP (Knowledge is Power Program) principal academy selected 11 fellows from more than 250 applicants. In Washington, D.C., a district in dire straits and plagued by a chronic shortage of competent principals, the New Leaders for New Schools program was inundated with 291 applications for just 11 positions.[25]

In a few states, legislators are starting to take the commonsense route and open up school leadership to a wider range of promising candidates. In 1999, Michigan abolished state licensure of school administrators. In 2002, California radically streamlined administrative licensure. Today, three states permit nontraditional candidates to apply to become principals, and seven permit them to become superintendents. Unfortunately, even districts in these states make little use of this flexibility and disregard candidates without teaching experience. It is time for the rest of the states to follow these few leaders into the twenty-first century and for districts to seize the opportunity to pursue the talent they need.

How to Prepare Leaders

Preparation for education leaders should begin by recognizing that different kinds of leaders need very different skills. A district technology coordinator or accounting chief needs particular skills that have little or nothing to do with classroom issues. A superintendent in a large district is charged with supervising a staff of managers, while a school principal may run a management team or, in a very small school, may serve as a jack-of-all-trades. As a result, there is no one-size-fits-all formula for preparing educational administrators.

Today, education administration is an insular subspecialization of management, taught by professors who are often unfamiliar with the larger body of research on management and instead offer their own "educationally unique" formulations of leadership. Prominent thinkers, such as Thomas Sergiovanni in *Leadership for the Schoolhouse*, argue that corporate models of leadership cannot work in education and that "we [must] accept the reality that leadership for the schoolhouse should be different, and . . . we [need to] begin to invent our own practice."[26] The status quo crowd is convinced that schools are different from any other organization, given the fact that educators are already working flat-out to do all they can, and that leaders need to reject corporate-style management that presumes workers need to be pushed, rewarded, or monitored. This is nonsense. There is no one style of corporate leadership, nor is there a unique brand of education leadership. This thinking has helped create an isolated and intellectually suspect ghetto.[27]

Existing training programs do not teach important skills. Administration preparation programs are incoherent, ask little of students, and provide weak substantive training.[28] Despite claims that leaders need training in pedagogy or curriculum, it is not clear that trainees receive even this preparation. A national survey of 1,400 middle school principals found that more than a third had taken no coursework on middle school education practices, that 52 percent reported that their university coursework was of moderate or little value, and that 55 percent said the same of their university field experiences.[29]

Unlike business schools or graduate programs in public administration, even elite programs in education generally impose little quality control. Instead, certification requirements drive off the strongest candidates, many of whom would rather pursue an MBA than a degree that has no value outside of education. James Guthrie, chairman of education leadership at Vanderbilt University, and Ted Sanders, chief executive of the Education Commission of the States, lamented in 2001, "University preparation of education administrators has fallen into a downward spiral dominated by low-prestige institutions, diploma mills, outmoded instruction and low expectations. Many . . . programs have virtually no entrance requirements, save the applicant's ability to pay tuition."[30] Compare the standards used by business schools to those of the education schools housing the nation's top-ranked education administration programs. In 2002, when the *U.S. News and World Report* rankings placed Penn State University's business school forty-third, the school accepted 24.5 percent of applicants, and admitted students had a mean GMAT score of 624. Meanwhile, the Penn State school of education, with the nation's eighth-ranked education administration program, accepted 49.1 percent of its *doctoral* applicants, and admitted students had a mean verbal GRE score of 475. Ohio State University's twenty-fourth-ranked business school accepted 28.9 percent of applicants. Admitted students had a mean GMAT score of 645. On the other hand, the OSU education school, home to the nation's third-ranked administration program, accepted 54.9 percent of doctoral applicants (and 74.3 percent of M.Ed. applicants), and admitted students had a mean verbal GRE score of 476.

Education management training ought not be distinct from every other kind of management preparation. Managers of technology or accounting should not necessarily be plucked from inside the school system or the ranks of educators. Such candidates should be free to obtain the most appropriate training, and then school districts should recruit from that pool.

Principals and superintendents should be permitted to come to their roles through various routes, providing a diversity of experience and the most expansive possible talent pool. This does mean that some administrators will need training before assuming their job and others will need professional support once on the job. Candidates should not be required to pass through any particular program. The question ought to be their suitability for the job and their performance on it. Rather than providing desultory training to a captive audience of gym coaches, training programs will have to offer programs useful to voluntary candidates. Some candidates may enroll in MBA programs, others in traditional education leadership programs, and others in hybrids. Nonprofit programs like New Leaders for New Schools and the Broad Center for Superintendents are developing new ways to train both traditional and nontraditional candidates. This diversity will permit school districts and administrators to opt for the most useful approaches and will compel less effective programs to improve or shut their doors.

Performance Evaluation

Executives are notoriously bad at managing for the long term, a discipline that can be readily swamped by the demands of the here-and-now. Executives should not be judged only on their short-term efforts, but also on how they are preparing their people for challenges that may be five or ten years down the road. Especially because overhauling information technology or personnel practices may not have an immediate effect on student performance, it's vital that executives and managers be evaluated with a full appreciation of their actual role. Absent clear pressure to focus on these issues, it is far too easy for officials to slide into the habit of shortchanging the future in order to simply dump all available resources into employee pay and short-term classroom needs.

This does *not* mean that we cannot rigorously evaluate leaders, only that we should not rely entirely upon measures of student performance. Creating appropriate evaluations for managers is something that well-run companies and nonprofits routinely address with "balanced scorecards" that factor in multiple measures of organizational performance. What might a balanced scorecard look like in education leadership?

Managers ought to be evaluated using four key components: the performance of their charges, their market performance, the nature of the challenge they have taken on, and their ability to mentor and develop personnel.[31]

Principals and superintendents ought to be rewarded based upon the rate at which their school or district boosts student achievement and its success at attracting students. Districts ought to establish guidelines that measure improvement on each measure along two distinct four-point continua. Each continuum should be graded into excellent, good, average, and below-average gains. For instance, boosting enrollment by two percentage points might be regarded as good, and gains in excess of four percentage points as excellent. Districts should set guidelines that reflect local conditions.

Two concerns arise. One is the fact that principals in different schools face vastly different challenges, and the second is the possibility that such an approach might encourage principals to adopt unscrupulous tactics in order to boost test scores or enrollment. How is such a risk to be minimized? First, the combination of tough-minded accountability and competition helps limit the incentives to engage in such behavior. Schools normally drive up test scores by shedding students who are improving very slowly, while the easiest way to increase enrollment is by pursuing every child in sight. However, because tough-minded accountability focuses on the rate at which students are improving, it's not clear that principals are going to come out any better by enrolling high achievers rather than low achievers, especially if disadvantaged students bring more funding with them. Meanwhile, pressures to attract enrollment argue against efforts to shed students.

This safeguard alone, however, is not enough. Some troubled schools are hemorrhaging students, have mediocre test scores, and already have difficulty attracting effective principals or teachers. Other schools enjoy strong reputations among parents and have accomplished faculties that are a pleasure to lead. It would be ludicrous to adopt an evaluation strategy that made tough environments even less attractive while funneling incentives to principals in comfortable schools. Consequently, district leaders should adjust expectations for principals accordingly. The simplest way to do this is by designating "hardship" schools and establishing special criteria for principals in those schools. The other important way to address this problem, which we will discuss momentarily, is through compensation.

The biggest challenges to fairly and fully evaluating leaders emerge in the area of organizational maintenance and employee development. Useful data on managerial performance should be collected from subordinates, appropriate parents and community members, and supervisors. Thoughtful scorecards can draw on employee satisfaction and turnover, evaluations from parents and external partners, relative efficiencies, and the performance of support services for which the manager is responsible. This kind of evaluation can ensure that managers are recognized for their overall performance while minimizing temptations to manipulate the system. When evaluating principals, superintendents can survey faculty views regarding the school leadership and school climate and parents regarding their satisfaction; monitor faculty turnover or school efforts to reach out to parents; observe school discipline and cleanliness; gauge how responsibly they use resources, and so on. Similarly, superintendents and central office staff should be appropriately evaluated by staff and community members with whom they interact. While today's schools routinely lack useful assessments like these, that is a product of the inattentiveness to performance characteristic of the culture of incompetence and not because it is impossible to evaluate educational management. In fact, the same lack of managerial accountability that we find in schools has at some point bedeviled every public organization and private firm. In every sector, holding managers accountable required thinking creatively about how to measure and gauge managerial performance.[32]

Compensation

Commonsense reform requires education leaders to continually seek ways to improve teaching and learning. Some education leaders will rise to this challenge out of personal commitment but the commonsense reformer is not content to rely on good intentions. We have already talked in the previous chapters about incentives and how to structure compensation. As with teachers, the problem is less with the amount paid to educational managers than with the fact that we pay far too little to effective administrators in tough roles and too much to ineffective or unnecessary officials. Nationally, in 2002–2003, the average annual salary was $126,000 for a superintendent and $99,000 for an assistant superintendent. In districts with 25,000 or more students, average superintendent pay was $170,000. Average principal salaries were $75,000 at the elementary level, $81,000 at the middle school level, and $86,000 at the high school level. Assistant principals averaged about $65,000 to $70,000.[33]

There are three principles to keep in mind when thinking about addressing administrative compensation. The first is that leaders should care intensely about how well their people perform. The second is that we want to be sure to motivate leaders in ways that serve the best interests of all their children. The third is that we want leaders to care not only about the short term, but also about the long-term health of their school or school system.

Principals and Superintendents

Performance should drive compensation. Salaries ought to reflect success at improving student learning and at serving the needs of local families. Of course, all leaders don't face equal challenges. It is much easier to maintain high levels of student achievement in Westchester, New York, than in Harlem. It is easier to compete successfully in an area with no charter or private schools than in communities like Philadelphia or Milwaukee, where there are dozens of charter schools or voucher schools.

Performance incentives ought therefore to be linked to improvement rather than to absolute level of performance, except in those special cases where a school or district is sustaining an exemplary record. Principals whose schools excelled on both dimensions might earn a 25 percent or 35 percent bonus, while those whose schools achieved average gains might be entitled to a smaller amount.

Commonsense reform dictates adjusting base pay for principals in accord with the difficulty of their position, a policy that makes tougher assignments more attractive. As the superintendent of Palm Beach County, Florida, has observed, "If you don't have your highest-performing principals in your highest-need schools, then you're just exacerbating the problem." Palm Beach County permits principals to earn up to 20 percent above their base pay depending on the size of school enrollment, the percentage of poor students, and the number of extracurricular activities offered. While that 20 percent maximum adjustment is probably too low, it reflects the commonsense thinking that can make demanding leadership positions more attractive and rewarding.[34]

Finally, it is important to ensure that principals be recognized not only for short-term performance but for developing faculty, building external relationships, and forging a cohesive school community. This dictates lending substantial weight to the feedback obtained from staff and parents and other appropriate measures collected in the evaluative process.

District Staff

Because central district staff are not directly responsible for teachers and students, their compensation cannot be readily linked to student performance. Instead, they should be evaluated on how well they perform their particular role, whether that entails managing information technology, human resources, or professional development. Staff should receive variable raises based upon the quality of their work. Reviews should be based upon both supervisor evaluations and measures of performance that are determined by the director in consultation with their supervisor. An information technology director might be evaluated on criteria such as response times to schools, frequency of system outages, rate at which district personnel are trained, the implementation of new software, and so on. We might evaluate a reading trainer on measures such as student gains in the schools she worked with, teacher evaluations, and number of teachers trained.

Termination

Just as in the case of teachers, it is essential that it be easier to terminate ineffective administrators. Most observers find this notion less objectionable and some districts have made real strides in putting an end to the idea that a principalship or central office appointment carries a lifetime guarantee. In Houston, the district succeeded in putting all principals on two-year performance contracts. If principals failed to perform adequately, they could be fired at the end of the contract without cause. In San Diego, superintendent Alan Bersin removed 90 percent of the district's 180 principals in his first five years as superintendent.

The point is not that removing administrators will somehow make problems disappear. Simply firing the coach is not an effective way to turn around a troubled team. However, the ability to hold leaders accountable for performance, to have them always aware of expectations, and to remove those individuals who do not live up to their roles is essential to constructing a culture of competence. Firing a principal cannot mean simply hiding them in some comfortable job in the district office. Too many large districts have failed principals, inept assistant principals, and burned out teachers stacked like cordwood in downtown departments like payroll, human resources, and curricular development. Commonsense reform does not settle for making it easier to hide poor administrators in these warrens but insists on ridding schools of them altogether.

Rethinking the Job

Last chapter, I noted that reconfiguring faculty jobs could give teachers new responsibilities and provide them with new opportunities. For instance, in the fashion of many private schools and charter schools, a school might do away with the positions of one or two assistant principals who are assigned to handle parental contacts, discipline problems, and scheduling on a full-time basis. Instead, the school might apportion the roles among three teachers, each of whom adopts a reduced teaching load. Such a course offers a number of benefits. One key benefit of allowing teachers to take on more coaching or engage in more team-based work without leaving the classroom is that it allows faculty to develop leadership skills and deepens the district's talent pool. This approach can ease the principal's job by providing the staff with a diverse set of skills that she can rely on. Having staff who are experienced at coaching, working with parents, scheduling, analyzing performance, or whatnot narrows the scope of tasks for which a principal is responsible and allows districts to concentrate on hiring principals with particular strengths. Expanding the teacher role also creates more room for teachers to grow as professionals without having to change schools or leave the classroom, making it easier for principals other than those in the most attractive suburban schools to develop and retain "player-coaches" in their classrooms.

Support Services

In the case of principals and superintendents, one can at least plausibly claim that experience in education is helpful. However, most districts also use teaching experience to screen staff for many positions that are unrelated to the classroom. Districts routinely look first to their teachers when recruiting managers for positions in school security, human resources, transportation, and any number of other functions for which teachers have no particular training or suitability. There is the district where a former junior high math teacher is in charge of accounting for a $500-million-a-year business. There is Los Angeles where, until just a few years ago, a $6 billion facilities operation was managed by a former gym teacher earning $80,000 a year.

John Fullerton, vice president of the Urban Education Partnership in Los Angeles, has observed, "Many critical business managers in large school systems rose into these positions 'through the ranks' and may have started out in an unrelated position, such as a teacher or principal. While such an organic process of 'growing your own' can result in strong employees who know the specific issues and details of the district, these employees have not been exposed to approaches outside the closed world of education and... may inherit inefficient and tremendously outdated processes with no clear ideas on how to improve them."[35]

In fact, because teachers have spent their career in the classroom, they are especially *unlikely* to have the requisite skills and knowledge appropriate to vital support positions. By trying to fill central administration with former teachers, districts ensure that they do not consider many highly qualified candidates. By favoring licensed administrators, they reject veteran professionals who don't want to spend their entire career working for a school district.

Putting the Doers in Charge

One reason the culture of incompetence has proved so intractable is that those responsible for student learning often find significant parts of the school system are beyond their grasp. Critical functions like human resources, information services, facilities, and technology are run as independent fiefdoms by longtime district employees. As one assistant superintendent confided, "When we've tried to aggressively recruit nontraditional teachers, we've run up against stiff resistance in the [human resources] department.... First they endorse the most cautious possible interpretation of state regulations, then they tell us why their software won't do what we need or why [the changes] are impossible given their timelines, and then they drag their feet and call anything that upsets their routines 'irregular' or 'problematic.' They get away with this because it's just too exhausting to fire them or make them cooperate."

It's vital that the superintendent have clear and unquestioned authority over support functions and personnel. While a smoothly running human resources or transportation operation won't make poor schools good, balky support services can waste energy and get in the way. It must be clear that the metric for performance in support services is not procedural compliance but how well departments help the district to staff, manage, and operate effective schools.

Managing Support Services

For positions removed from instruction—like those in transportation, accounting, human resources, evaluation, payroll, buildings, and so on—barriers restricting the hiring of noneducators should be dismantled. In fact, for many districts, a more attractive alternative to running each of these departments may be to hire outside firms to take on specialized tasks such as payroll services, accounting, bus transportation, food preparation, or building maintenance.

Even more troubling is that rules on hiring, firing, and compensation designed to address status quo concerns about holding teachers accountable for student learning often apply to administrators in jobs utterly divorced from teaching and learning. There is no cause for personnel in transportation or accounting departments to be treated any differently from their counterparts in any other transportation or accounting firm. Their performance can be readily evaluated using established benchmarks. The Houston Independent School District, for instance, has developed an impressive annual assessment that measures the performance of its various support services on multiple dimensions. The pressure to attract and retain the best people has led to the introduction of performance-based pay in many jobs, such as university fund-raising and health-care management, where it was once seen as insufficiently idealistic.

Experience has shown that breaking down barriers and rewarding excellence has improved worker quality, morale, and the quality of service. Again, nothing here is especially complex. It is only a matter of applying common-sense principles to an area from which they have too long been absent.

Giving Leaders the Tools

Effective leaders need tools. Leaders need to be able to recruit the right personnel, evaluate performance, promote deserving individuals, reward excellence, and remedy or purge ineffective teachers or staff. Without the power to do these things, even the right leaders with the right skills and incentives won't amount to much.

A critical tool for any leader is the ability to assemble their own team and to rid their organization of ineffective personnel. Yet, as we discussed in chapter 4, administrators cannot easily dismiss even clearly incompetent personnel. In fact, 30 percent of principals surveyed reported that it is "virtually impossible" to "fire a tenured teacher who was terrible in the classroom" and 97 percent said it is either "difficult" or "virtually impossible." Among superintendents, 96 percent said it would be "difficult" or "virtually impossible" to fire such a teacher.[36] As one superintendent confided to me, "In theory, I suppose I could get rid of some of these clowns, but the process would be so long and sticky and would raise so many hackles that it just wouldn't get me anywhere. Anyway, I'd never get the people I'd need. The pay scale guidelines wouldn't let me recruit them competitively, the [collective bargaining] agreement would make hiring them a nightmare, and the whole thing would get me painted by a couple of board members and by the paper as a 'union buster.' Is our finance department a mess? You bet. I'd love to overhaul it. But it would be a self-defeating battle, so I just have to accept that and try to nip and tuck them into better shape and focus on the areas where I can make a difference." Superintendents accommodate themselves to these barriers by focusing on the smaller, status quo changes that they can make, while leaving the system's fundamental problems untouched.

I have already discussed many of the requisite tools in earlier chapters. They include the ability to monitor the performance of teachers and other employees, to provide good information to employees, to hire based on merit, to assign personnel where they are most needed, to reward excellence, and to fire poor performers. Two of the tools, the ability to collect good information and to utilize technology, will be discussed at length in chapter 6. Unless we pursue this broader agenda of commonsense change, leadership reform alone won't amount to much.

Status Quo Remedies

Status quo reformers have posed two reforms of their own in response to the leadership challenge: one tries to increase the education establishment's control over who is permitted into leadership positions and the other seeks to dictate more narrowly the content of leadership training. Neither tackles the challenge of evaluating or rewarding performance or deepening the talent pool. Instead, the status quo remedies try to improve education leadership by further constricting the pool of eligible candidates while giving the schools of education and professional associations a tighter grip over who is allowed into the profession.

Standards for School Administrators

The education leadership community has endorsed a push for standards that is modeled on the troubling National Board for Professional Teaching Standards that we discussed in the previous chapter. In the case of school leadership, the Interstate School Leaders Licensure Consortium (ISLLC), a group that includes the organizations representing school administrators, schools of education, and their various allies, has developed "Standards for School Leaders."[37] Today, the ISLLC standards have been incorporated into policy by more than 35 states, and the Educational Testing Service has developed a School Leaders Licensure Assessment that is modeled on the standards. The problem is that ISLLC standards are not based on performance but on ensuring that potential leaders embrace the values of the professional education community. The six standards assert that school administrators should "promote student success" by doing things like "facilitating...a vision of learning" and "collaborating...with community members." In other words, ISSLC is trying to ban from leadership anyone who believes schools should focus on teaching academic skills, that performance-based accountability is important, or that teachers should be judged based on results.

The ISLLC School Leaders Licensure Assessment, which more than a half-dozen states—including Kentucky, Maryland, and North Carolina—now use to assess principal candidates, is supposedly grounded in research on what makes for effective school leaders. However, the exam does not ask any questions about what superintendents or principals actually need to know about the law, budgeting, management practice, or education research. Instead, the questions focus on making sure that leaders have absorbed ISLLC-approved values. As the ISLLC's chairman, Ohio State University professor Joseph Murphy has said, "[The exam] is a statement of values about where the profession should be"[38]—or at least, where the status quo reformers think it should be.

One question asks candidates to write an essay based on following case: A high school senior failing a class asks the principal if he can drop the class although it is "contrary to school policy." The principal permits the student to drop the class. Test takers are asked to assess whether the principal's action served the student's "best interest." While most sensible people might think this at best a complicated question, or incline to answer that a policy should be adhered to as any breach sets a bad example and does not teach the student responsibility for his actions (or lack of them), the ISLLC folks think it is clear that leniency is the obvious course. Endorsing the principal's action earns a perfect score; telling the student to tough it out gets a candidate marked down. In fact, in the sample materials, this answer receives a zero: "The principal's action is wrong.... Much more is learned in high school than academics. Students must learn that there are consequences for their actions.... If this student is allowed to graduate, the lesson he will learn is that he does not have to accept the consequences of his actions."[39] Apparently, the key to school improvement is ensuring that no principal be permitted to think that high school students should be responsible for their decisions. This is the push for "standards" in leadership. It is not merely another harmless status quo reform, it is a decided step backward.

Regulating Leadership Training

A second troubling push by the status quo reformers is an effort by the education schools and experts in "education leadership" to tighten their grip over who is allowed to train principals or superintendents. The National Policy Board for Education Administration, another group that consists of the same status quo interests that formed ISLLC, has started writing standards for leadership training so that the National Council for the Accreditation of Teacher Education can start approving leadership programs.[40] Unfortunately, but not surprisingly, the standards focus on paperwork, the degrees held by professors, the program's commitment to "diversity," and so on. In short, they are based on proceduralism and ideology.[41] The answer is not to further restrict who can train education leaders but to encourage a variety of preparation programs to compete to provide the highest-quality training in the most useful fashion and at the best price.

Romanticizing Nontraditional Leaders

A third approach, one that has ensnared many would-be commonsense reformers, has been to romanticize the nontraditional executive. Too many reformers echo the philanthropist who declared: "If we could just get the right kind of [nontraditional leaders] into these big districts, it would change everything. The good ones have got the savvy and the know-how to make organizations work. Forget all this complicated stuff about teacher licensure or competition, leadership is the answer." Captivated by the generals, attorneys, politicians, and businesspeople, who have assumed superintendencies in San Diego, Seattle, New York, Los Angeles, Chicago, and elsewhere, some have imagined that just the right outsider will somehow wipe away all the real constraints that confront executives. Hiring a single well-regarded leader doesn't address the underlying problems and too often winds up delaying the consideration of far-reaching change.

There is nothing wrong, per se, with pursuing high-profile nontraditional superintendents. However, as Harvard business professor Rakesh Khurana cautions in *Searching for a Corporate Savior*, pinning an organization's hopes to a high-profile superstar can backfire by distracting attention from fundamental problems.[42] Most current nontraditional superintendents were hired not on the basis of a reasoned assessment of their strengths and skills but because they were thought to be forceful and accomplished individuals. The fascination with "leadership" that can be readily transferred from one field to the next has sometimes been shockingly simplistic.

The logic behind these decisions often amounts to little more than stereotyping, with military officers sought because they are thought to run taut organizations and attorneys because they're familiar with law and politics. Nontraditional recruiting can repeat the worst excesses of "celebrity CEO" hiring by the private sector. When businesses are doing poorly, directors often seek to bring in a white knight by focusing on candidates with outsized reputations. This produces a thin, hard-to-recruit pool of uncertain suitability. Important skills may not be attached to sexy resumes, and pursuing glamorous names narrows the nontraditional pipeline to a trickle. Recruitment of nontraditional leaders should be pursued in a measured fashion, with a focus on transforming management and not on cherry-picking a few famous names.

Conclusion

Commonsense reform requires taking steps to build a pipeline of quality leadership candidates and then reshaping the tools and role of management so that leaders have a real chance to be effective. We need leaders who can leverage accountability and technology, devise performance-based evaluation systems, reengineer outdated management structures, recruit and cultivate nontraditional staff, drive decisions with data, and build professional cultures. Far too many current leaders are ill suited for these challenges. However, simply finding such candidates won't suffice. We don't need a couple of dozen superintendents gamely swimming against the tide, but tens of thousands of competent superintendents, principals, and administrators working in tandem. They will best be able to do so when they are part of a system that grants them the tools and flexibility they need and that holds them, and their employees, accountable.

Because few executives enjoy being the bad guy, the costs of inaction must be high enough that they find it more painful not to act than to let matters drift along. The mistake is to think that finding tough-minded leaders for our schools is simply a question of recruiting the right individuals. When we do find such leaders and plop them into today's districts, too often they accommodate themselves to the realities of their job by standing firm less and less often. The commonsense solution is not to hope that we will stumble across or miraculously train bushels of superheroes, but to change the school house culture so that both nontraditional and traditional leaders will answer complaints by explaining: "This is what we must do. If I go, your next hire is going to come in and have to do the same thing. So you might as well accept it."

Leadership reform is the linchpin that makes commonsense reform work. Increased accountability, borne of performance assessment and competition, requires leaders who will use the tools of accountability to stimulate and not to stifle teacher ingenuity and professional judgment. Competition will create room for entrepreneurship and reinvention in running schools and school systems, opening a door for leaders equal to the challenge. The capacity to evaluate performance on the basis of student achievement, faculty feedback, and parental satisfaction makes it possible to judge the effectiveness of principals, superintendents, and other officials in ways that are far more useful and sophisticated than licenses or checklists.

In the years immediately following World War II, business administration was a minor profession, and business schools were institutions of modest reputation viewed as intellectually suspect stepcousins to economics departments. As the centrality of management grew in the postwar economy, businesses were forced to discipline their hiring and business schools became increasingly selective and focused on teaching critical economic, accounting, and quantitative skills. Today, America's executive workforce is admired across the globe, and business schools are among our universities' most prestigious units. This all transpired without formal licensing; neither business schools nor America are any the worse off because Bill Gates or Michael Dell never obtained an MBA. The world of education leadership is ripe for a similar revolution.

CHAPTER SIX

Reinvention

Science is a first-rate piece of furniture for a man's upper chamber, if he has common sense on the ground floor.

—Oliver Wendell Holmes

Commonsense reform will not work as intended if school districts do not change in fundamental ways. If leaders lack the tools to increase efficiency, streamline their workforce, and find ways to allocate resources effectively, then neither tough-minded accountability nor competition are likely to produce significant change. Commonsense leaders do this not by making people work harder or longer hours but by helping professionals to take full advantage of their skills, eliminating unnecessary or redundant tasks, and concentrating resources and effort where they are needed most.

During the 1970s, New York City was overwhelmed by sanitation problems. The Fund for the City of New York rated 6,000 city streets and reported that 43 percent qualified as "filthy." Up to that point, the city had always taken a compliance-based approach to street cleaning. Officials made sure that a truck was assigned to each route, that each truck had a full complement of workers, and that trucks kept to their schedules. Using a new system called Scorecard that focused on street cleanliness instead of cleaning schedules, the city assigned crews to the dirtiest streets and rewarded those crews that produced the biggest improvements. A decade later, the percentage of streets qualifying as "filthy" had declined to 4 percent.[1]

Baseball's Oakland Athletics have less money to spend than almost any other team in the sport. Yet, in the years since general manager Billy Beane took over the team in 1997, they have consistently gone to the playoffs by whipping teams that spend two or three times as much. In 2002, the A's spent $40 million to make the playoffs alongside the New York Yankees, who spent $126 million. In recent years, the A's have paid about $500,000 in salary for each victory, while teams like the Baltimore Orioles have spent over $3 million per win. How did the A's do this? Beane assembled a nontraditional management team, one light on baseball insiders and heavy on data wonks, that took pains to rethink the process of assembling a baseball club. They made it a point to count and measure everything that mattered, used data to systematically reconsider the importance of everything players did, and used cost-effectiveness to guide hiring decisions. The transformation only became feasible with the advances in computing and information technology, but the technology was only a tool. The same tool languished unused by Beane's peers.[2]

The annals of public and private management are replete with such successes, with several incisively documented, for instance, by management guru Jim Collins in his heralded book *Good to Great*.[3] These triumphs are produced not by people working longer hours or by executives issuing new regulations. Instead, they emerge when leaders set a clear direction, establish a culture of competence, use information to inform decisions, reimagine staffing and organizational management, squeeze out waste and inefficiency, and more fully utilize employee skills.

Reinvention requires giving entrepreneurs the opportunity to create wholly new ways to organize schools and deliver instruction and the incentive to carry these beyond their school or their classroom. Creating such a world begins with stripping away the barriers that inhibit fresh thinking about how schools are staffed, organized, and managed. Radical improvement will only emerge if entrepreneurs are allowed and encouraged to use new technological advances as tools to manage information, resources, staff, and services in new and more effective ways.

Commonsense reform only became feasible as new technology enabled educators to collect and utilize performance information in a fashion that renders compliance-based regulation unnecessary. We can now empower educators to easily monitor the performance of each student, of each class, and each school; to readily diagnose student weaknesses; to determine what parents want and where they are enrolling their students; and to evaluate the quality of services ranging from transportation to professional development.

Reinvention is not about fancy technologies. Technology only supplies tools. Reinvention is about helping managers and teachers use those tools in ways that create breakthroughs in performance and productivity. As a 2003 Institute for the Study of Knowledge Management in Education wryly noted, "Technology implementation does not necessarily improve decision-making ... [or] outcomes."[4] Despite the seductive ease of dumping computers and technology into schools, such a course won't do much to improve student learning or school effectiveness. In every line of work, from library management to policing to higher education, technology matters most when used to rethink how people go about their work. In schooling, technology can grant educators immediate access to critical information on performance and spending, enable schools to ignore geographic boundaries in providing instruction and obtaining services, and permit staff to be used in more effective and more efficient ways.

Reinvention in schooling is not a pipe dream. Radical rethinking is not the province of a few companies or even a few industries. Between March 2001 and August 2003, for instance, the nation's largest 100 companies improved productivity so rapidly that nine workers were able to do in 2003 what took ten workers in 2001. These results highlighted a decade-long stretch of rapid growth in dozens of industries, including service sector fields like health care, insurance, and law.[5] Economists have long recognized that potential productivity growth is more limited in service sectors, like education, than in fields like manufacturing or retail. Nonetheless, even the service sector has witnessed productivity gains of about 1 percent a year during the past three decades. Appropriate cautions regarding limits on service sector efficiency have been wielded by status quo reformers eager to claim that efficiencies cannot be found in schooling.

Given the chronic plea of the status quo reformers for more resources, you would think they'd be eager to support reinvention that will yield heightened efficiencies. Finding ways to get the same work done with less money and fewer personnel would allow schools and school systems to free up educators to focus on needy students, address new challenges, and pay employees more generously. Finding ways to do more with less frees up resources and makes schools more effective at any given level of funding. Moreover, the evidence suggests that there is a significant amount of waste in public schools. In 1999–2000, total overtime in the Los Angeles Unified School District was 228 percent over budget, with auditors finding that much of the time was never approved or even documented. In 2001, auditors found at least $21 million in fraud and waste in the L.A. central administration. In Chicago, the former superintendent discovered $250,000 in equipment, including 24,000 pieces of furniture, sitting apparently forgotten in a district warehouse.[6]

Despite the frequency of such occurrences, or the kinds of problems in Washington, D.C., Baltimore, or Oakland mentioned in chapter 5, status quo reformers routinely attack efforts to find new efficiencies as a conspiracy to promote a corporate agenda. Proposals to use technology to downsize the workforce, alter instructional delivery, or improve managerial efficiency are inevitably attacked by status quo reformers as part of an effort to "[t]rans-form public education ... [in order] to expand the profits of investors, edu-cate students as consumers, and train young people for the low-paying jobs of the new global marketplace."[7] This tendency to imagine that the respon-sible use of public money is part of some shadowy global conspiracy evinces a fundamental lack of seriousness about serving either our children or the nation.

The State and Federal Role

Historically, American schools were governed locally. During the nineteenth century and well into the middle of the twentieth century, the federal government played almost no role in K-12 schooling. While states passed general laws requiring all students to attend school, mandating the length of the school year, and setting some conditions for personnel, most decisions regarding curricula, policy, and school affairs were the province of local school boards.

During the latter part of the twentieth century, state governments grew steadily more active in school affairs as they sought to reduce funding inequities and to improve school quality. In the past two decades, states have become much more active in dictating policy with the most significant efforts in the area of accountability. These efforts were briefly discussed in chapter 2. While adopting increasingly muscular accountability systems, states have generally not made complementary efforts to prune procedural regulations. In fact, many states are continuing to tighten these regulations—governing teacher certification, class size, curricula, and so on—thereby effectively choking off promising opportunities for reinvention even while demanding continuous improvement and new efficiencies.

In the past four decades, the federal role in education has increased steadily. The federal government became an ongoing presence in K-12 edu-cation for the first time through the Elementary and Secondary Education Act (ESEA) of 1965, which provided federal tax dollars to help support disadvantaged students. Over time, the federal government has played a growing role in supporting low-income students, mandating services for chil-dren with special needs, and providing support for programs like early childhood education. The federal role radically expanded in 2002 when

President Bush signed the No Child Left Behind Act (NCLB), with its extensive accountability requirements. Federal efforts to enhance accountability have not been matched by similar moves to promote flexibility.

At both the state and federal levels, reticence on the part of would-be commonsense reformers and status quo efforts to retain established protections and procedures have produced a situation in which educators are responsible for results yet remain mired in a culture of incompetence which they have little ability to change. In a new century marked by the decentralizing and democratizing forces of technology, mobility, and communication, school systems continue to embody all the flexibility of a nineteenth-century shoe factory.

State and federal officials are too far removed from any given school or classroom to make fine-tuned decisions. Instead, they render broad policies that are, as a matter of course, less than ideal for any given school or classroom. Each time state or federal officials try to dictate educational process through another regulation and limit permissible practices regarding staffing, school management, or instruction, they essentially criminalize any approach that requires relaxing even a part of that guideline.

State and local officials should provide the means to hold school districts accountable, supply the appropriate resources, and then allow the educators to educate. Within districts themselves, superintendents ought to establish accountability systems, set the ground rules for compensation, monitor principal performance, and then work to give principals control of their money and personnel.

Management

Commonsense reform requires that school managers be accountable for performance. This accountability is possible only when managers control their own budget and resources, know how much is being spent on various programs and people and how well students are doing, and are able to flexibly deploy people and material. In short, there is a need for easily accessible, finely grained information on costs, performance, programs, and people.

Decentralization

Because no two schools have the same student populations, no two schools have identical needs in terms of staffing or scheduling. Rather than have central officials issue regulations or broad commands, decentralization permits school leaders to analyze the needs of their students, determine the teaching and staff resources needed to meet those needs, and make sensible judgments about instruction and school operations.

Edmonton, Canada, is the mecca of decentralization, a locale where American school reformers repeatedly trek in order to see how it is done. In the 30 years it has been committed to decentralization, the Edmonton public school system, which was once regarded as a disaster, has become a model and has come close to putting the local private schools out of business. Today, 88 percent of Edmonton seventh graders and 92 percent of twelfth graders score at or above grade level on the Alberta Provincial test. In Edmonton, schools are free to hire part-time instructors instead of regular staff, to launch special programs, or invest in extensive laboratory facilities or tutoring services. Because schools are funded on the basis of their enrollment, with difficult-to-educate students bringing substantially more money than more advantaged children, schools have the resources to provide the services their students need.[8]

One readily grasped illustration of decentralization is provided by the practice of "lean production," which revolutionized automobile manufacturing by shifting as many tasks and responsibilities as possible to line employees and promoting quality control "that quickly trace[s] every problem, once discovered, to its ultimate cause." Lean production relied on teams of responsible employees using readily available information to quickly respond to problems and monitor performance. By 1989, Japanese factories produced higher quality cars than the old-style mass production plants in North America and did so in less than two-thirds the time. A comparison of General Motors and Toyota plants, for instance, showed that the GM plant took 31 hours to produce a vehicle and had 135 assembly defects per 100 cars whereas the Toyota plant produced one car every 16 hours and averaged only 45 defects per 100 cars.[9] The key to the success of lean production is not some newfangled technology or business school scheme, but the ability of decentralization to put employee knowledge and skills to good use, to hold employees accountable, and to boost morale by giving employees more control over their work.

There is no magic involved in decentralization. Decentralization enables teachers to do a better job at the mundane things they do every day. A teacher may need to devote extra time to a particular student, explain a concept in a different way, or acquire supplemental materials for a student. Different learning and teaching strategies are effective with different students. Teachers with good information on student performance and control over additional resources can more readily make use of their professional know-how. Teachers and principals with more leeway to alter lesson plans, substitute texts, group students, discipline students, and reconfigure classes will find it easier to make sensible decisions.

Now, while flexibility and decentralization are desirable, it is important to avoid romanticizing decentralization for its own sake. It's neither necessary nor desirable for each and every school to reinvent the wheel by experimenting its way toward an approach to reading or math instruction. Districts seeking to accommodate mobile student populations, cultivate sustainable systemwide expertise, or facilitate faculty movement among schools have good cause to adopt standardized approaches. Starbucks executives would think it irresponsible to have each new franchise operator hunt for his own beans or devise his own method of brewing coffee because there are some areas where shared expertise and intensive training have a proven track record. Similarly, there are a number of demonstrably effective approaches to reading or math instruction that districts might choose to adopt. There is nothing wrong with accountable district leadership insisting that all schools use a particular approach to reading instruction so long as the possibility of competition ensures that this coordination doesn't become stifling.

School Budgeting

Business professor Bill Ouchi relates the story of asking a principal the size of her school's annual budget. She told him it was $50 million. He thought the figure sounded a little big high, so she checked and realized it was more like $17 million. She explained, though, that it didn't really matter—because she controlled only $32,000 of that money. The rest was spent by the central school district and beyond her control.[10]

This is a familiar experience to anyone who has spent much time around schools. Traditionally, school districts have run schools by assigning staff and managing services out of central office. Money is allocated at the district level for salaries, benefits, books, and services, and these are then parceled out to the schools. That a principal might prefer two inexpensive assistants to a full-time secretary or an extra reading teacher to a set of new computers doesn't matter. For instance, in 2003 New York City decided to have parent coordinators in the schools and proceeded to spend $43 million to hire one for every school. It made no difference if a school already had an active parent network, an assistant principal who handled the role, or two teachers well-suited to teaching half-time and serving half-time as a coordinator. Principals had no leeway to determine whether the money could be better spent. Staff, services, and supplies have traditionally been issued by school districts in accord with strict formulas, creating no incentive for principals to be either creative or disciplined.

A school district might issue a school one teacher for every 23 students or an assistant principal for every 250. Schools have neither the ability nor the incentive to use personnel more effectively. Because there are no rewards for fiscal discipline or prudent financial management, systems encourage sensible principals to fight for as much stuff as possible. Utility bills and substitute teacher costs are paid out of one big pot. Irresponsible schools don't come out any worse than penny-pinchers. In fact, the penny-pinchers wind up having their savings used to pay for the lights left on at less responsible schools. As one official reported in Edmonton, "When we paid our utilities centrally, we had a guru from Europe who was exhorting our people to save energy. And we didn't save. We got rid of the guru and we gave the utilities money back to the schools. The first year we saved $2 million."[11]

An important part of such reforms, as I mentioned in chapter 3, is making sure that the money a school receives for a student actually reflects the cost of educating that student. For instance, Seattle has worked out a sliding scale in which the amount a school receives for a given student can range from $2,600 to more than $24,000 depending on the student's educational needs. While there are a number of reasonable ways to design such systems and to weight the needs of various students, the central logic is straightforward.

Decentralizing budgets means shifting more control over resources to the school level. Of course, principals are free to continue existing staff arrangements if they think those to be optimal. Otherwise, a principal might bring in an extra teacher instead of an assistant principal, might reduce two teaching slots in order to purchase supplies or contract for a tutoring program, or make any number of similar adjustments. Meanwhile, all schools have a new incentive to keep a careful eye on electricity, maintenance, substitute teaching, field trips, and supplies, because every dollar saved will come right back home.

New Kinds of School Systems

Commonsense reformers need to be open to systems of schools that don't fit into our traditional models of what school systems look like. New "education management organizations" (EMOs) are operating charter schools and bidding to manage traditional public schools. As of 2002, the Education Policy

Studies Laboratory at Arizona State University reported that 36 education management organizations were operating 368 public schools. These EMOs provide an opportunity to expand on the success of individual schools and to reap the potential cost savings produced by big systems without serving as a monopoly provider for every student in a geographic community.

Aspire Public Schools in California, the KIPP Academies, Edison Schools, and the National Heritage Academies are all examples of organizations that operate a geographically dispersed network of schools. Thus far, each has shown academic promise and provided popular alternatives in a variety of communities, typically by targeting children ill-served in the local schools. Especially significant is that these organizations are pioneering cost-effective approaches that commonsense competition would force other schools to mimic or match, out of simple self-interest. Operating in multiple locations without the facilities infrastructure of a traditional school district, it can be a challenge for nontraditional school operators to locate school buildings, arrange transportation, provide food, or recruit personnel. There is a critical role for providers that can help school districts, charter schools, nontraditional systems of schools, or private schools arrange for these various needs.

Using Data to Inform Decisions

Tough-minded accountability requires ready access to information up and down the education hierarchy. States need prompt access to complete information in order to evaluate schools. Superintendents and principals need information in order to assess their subordinates and identify weaknesses. Teachers accountable for student performance must have ready access to updated information on student achievement, so that they know where students stand and can adjust their efforts accordingly. As we observed in chapter 3, information is just as important in the case of competition. Competition in the absence of information will emphasize concerns other than school performance.

Typically, conversations about education technology focus on classroom technology. This is a mistake. The real power of technological change is its ability to help us reimagine the way that school systems are governed and the way that schools are staffed and managed.

Information management has the capacity to help schools become dramatically more effective. Data systems that track information on individual students permit teachers to easily and quickly check performance on specific tasks, can permit school-site personnel unprecedented control of budgets and hiring, and can increase flexibility regarding resource allocation.

In the words of Sy Fliegel, the famed New York City administrator, "Leaders are only as good as the information they get." Historically, districts have done a poor job of collecting information needed for management while concentrating on gathering the information they were required to report to the state and federal government. This meant counting the number of students enrolled in the district, the number of students in each school, and overall district expenditures. Obtaining data on anything more detailed, like what classes or programs students were enrolled in or how money was being allocated, was a crapshoot. Even on the simplest measures of performance or spending, there has long been little agreement on what should be tracked or how to measure it. The result has been a hodgepodge of tracking systems, often within a given district, that made it difficult for educators, parents, or public officials to monitor either effectiveness or efficiency.

Measuring What Matters

A compelling illustration of how accountability coupled with technology can improve public services comes from the remarkable success that New York City and other cities have enjoyed using new tools to combat crime in the 1990s. These efforts drew heavily upon new approaches to data analysis that helped the police assign patrols and focus their energies in more effective ways. The department's system was called Compstat, short for "computer statistics" or "comparative statistics," a system that compiles data from street cop reports, crime complaints, arrest and summons activities, crime patterns, and police activities. Over time, the system was broadened to include 734 categories of concern, measuring even the incidence of loud parties and of police overtime.[12]

In the first five years after the 1993 introduction of Compstat, the number of homicides in New York City fell from 1,946 to 629—a rate of decrease three times that of the nation as a whole. In Philadelphia, Compstat was implemented in 1998. In the first year, the police cut both the murder rate and the auto theft rate by more than 15 percent. Similar results were experienced in other cities that successfully implemented a Compstat system, including Los Angeles, New Orleans, Albuquerque, Sacramento, and Omaha.[13]

Nothing about Compstat is surprising. It makes it easier to hold officers accountable, to pinpoint areas of concern, and provides the information that can help all police focus on using their skills. All members of the police force can readily access these data. In New York City, precincts were required to update crime statistics on a weekly or daily basis, rather than on the monthly or quarterly basis that had traditionally been the norm. New mapping software allowed department officials to plot clusters of crimes on the map of a neighborhood, correlating them with drug sale sites, addresses of people previously released from prison, areas of gang activity, schools, shopping centers, public housing, and other relevant locations, and to share information departmentwide within seconds. Timely information gives chiefs a way to hold district commanders accountable for responses to crime and forces police at all levels to communicate and coordinate their efforts to fight crime.

The system worked equally well in other venues. When New York City police extended the system to traffic control in 1998, after six months vehicle accidents had dropped 38 percent and pedestrian fatalities had declined 36 percent. These improvements were credited to the system's ability to highlight the need for small changes like fixing a stop sign, changing light timing, and placing orange nylon mesh at intersections to prevent pedestrians from stepping too far into the street.[14]

In education, student assessment and familial school choices can provide a wealth of information on what's working, what families find satisfactory, and how students in various schools and classrooms are faring. It's hard for many private-sector veterans to believe, but only the exceptional district is able to readily pull up such information. Districts have had little or no idea how much they spend on a school or how much is being spent on particular students. When one asks principals or teachers for this information, those that have it available almost inevitably turn to large binders rather than more nimble electronic interfaces.

We manage most schools in the same way stores managed inventory in the 1960s. If a principal wants to know how many days a teacher has missed, how much is being spent on janitorial services, how long it's been since the school replaced its science texts, or when an order of new manila folders are arriving, there is maybe one district in 50 where she can find this information in the computer. I remember sitting with a principal in a well-regarded district and asking if he could pull some data on teacher absenteeism or staff training costs. He spluttered, almost knocking over an award in catching himself, and asked: "Are you kidding me? ... Do you know what I do if I want substitute teacher data? I have [my secretary] go through the files and tally it up. She keeps a running total on graph paper for me. ... If I want to check on a supply order, I call the deputy [superintendent] for services because we're old friends, and I know he'll actually have someone pull it for me. For texts, I just ask the department chairs. They remember that kind of stuff."

District Data Challenges

Surprisingly, in this day and age, the typical district spends 40 or more minutes a year *per student* collecting, processing, and reporting the data required by the U.S. Department of Education under No Child Left Behind. That equals 6,000 hours in a district of 10,000 students. The tremendous delays in processing data and the staff time consumed are the consequence of districts having personnel fill out written forms and retyping data from one software package to another. Simply equipping districts to report data electronically and acquire data from existing databases is a daunting challenge.[15]

School districts regard it as a triumph when they simply get their information technology systems integrated and are able to manage payroll and budgeting in a reliable fashion. The notion that districts should routinely make available fine-tuned data on performance and management at the school level is regarded as a pipe dream. If there's anywhere we'd expect districts to have gotten serious about using data strategically, it's in Cleveland and Milwaukee, where the nation's two major voucher programs have operated for an extended period, or in Dayton, Ohio, which has lost nearly 20 percent of its students to charter schooling. Yet, even these districts have done little or nothing to survey departing parents, analyze which students are leaving, or systematically examine what different families are seeking from their schools. When asked why they don't collect it, principals and district officials tend to look puzzled and to respond as did one deputy superintendent, who told me, "We're busy trying to run a school system. We're trying to serve the children that are here. ... Where would we be if we spent our time collecting trivia? Nobody with any sense is going to waste time and money trying to pile up that [trivia]."

Tracking which schools and programs are attracting or losing students can inform district and school decisions regarding school performance and services. Why don't educators collect it? As one Michigan deputy superintendent explained, "We're an urban district, so we have a lot of natural mobility. Close to a quarter of our students may change schools in a given year. So that makes it hard right there. Collecting information on their addresses and contacting the parents for satisfaction, you may not fully understand how difficult that would be. ... It's true we have home addresses for all students, but sending out surveys and analyzing them would be very demanding. And, as far as students enrolled in charter schooling ... the names of students are available and I guess we could [match them with our enrollment], but that would be pretty painstaking. I doubt we could get them all [and] ... if families have gone to charter schools, I wonder how eager they would be to provide us information on why they left."

It is true that collecting information takes time and that districts cannot survey every family or track every number precisely. However, neither objection is really a problem, especially when the alterative is blind guesswork. A moderate investment by the school district in understanding the needs of local families is likely to result in higher levels of local support and satisfaction. The idea is not to build a pristine data set, but to collect enough information to be useful. It's really a simple question of deciding to invest in the information technology rather than something else, collecting data systematically, and making the data available to district personnel in a timely fashion.

Modern technology offers a wealth of straightforward, time-tested ways to make the necessary information widely and instantly available. Some districts like Houston and New York City have taken pains to retool their technology systems. Others like Cincinnati and Seattle have taken aggressive steps to determine how and where money is spent, permitting sensible budgeting. To be useful, this information has to be at people's fingertips. This isn't all that difficult. Huge and complicated organizations and businesses, from Wal-Mart to the Internal Revenue Service, track productivity figures, costs, and evaluative measures. The information management industry is built on designing the systems to collect this information, slice and dice it, and immediately provide the necessary information to decision makers.

Some promising efforts are being pioneered at the national level. One promising development is the joint effort that the National Center for Educational Accountability (NCEA), the New York–based firm Standard and Poor's, the Los Angeles–based Broad Foundation, and the U.S. Department of Education launched in 2003 to systematically collect data on performance, student population, and school finances at each school in every state. Assembling these data will make it possible to evaluate the level of student performance and the gains posted at each school in comparison with similar schools in the state. NCEA has already done this for seven states, making it a simple proposition for any parent to gauge how well a Tennessee elementary school that's 80 percent minority and 70 percent low-income compares with other Tennessee elementary schools educating a similar student population. Such advances in data analysis will help address concerns that schools are being asked to perform the impossible and identify schools that are performing exceptionally poorly or well given the challenges they face.

Making Information Available

Fortunately, states and school systems are beginning to make real progress on the collection and dissemination of information. Spending money on technology platforms or simply providing information isn't enough. Huge investments in information management have run afoul when they've ignored cultural and behavioral realities. Nonetheless, using data to inform decisions must begin, sensibly enough, with good information being available. Obtaining good information on performance requires three things. First, each student's performance on a battery of assessments should be tracked over time, and that includes other relevant information on student progress and performance such as attendance, special needs, and so on. Second, districts and schools should track personnel, their salary information, their work history in the district, and how that links to information on costs and student performance. Third, officials must be able to track enrollment and costs, not merely in terms of the number of students in the system, but to the most precise and incremental level. How many students are being taught using reading program X? How much does it cost? How much money is being spent on computers at this middle school versus that middle school? Believe it or not, a frightening number of education managers can't readily find out this kind of information.

The ready availability of performance data can help strong leadership and creative teaching to coexist. The data allow principals to monitor teachers without having to micromanage them and permit effective teachers to demonstrate that their approach works. At the same time, the information permits the principal to intervene in the case of ineffective teachers. One administrator in Aldine, Texas, told me how the district posted dramatic gains in student achievement during the late 1990s, gaining national attention: "In theory, we're fine with giving teachers a lot of autonomy and trusting their judgment, but ... whatever we were doing wasn't working. If teachers really wanted to do something, we'd tell them, 'You show us the data ...' We didn't get into any arguments with them, we just said, 'Let's look at the data.'"

Using Information in the Schools

Thus far, I may have given the impression that collecting quality data is primarily an issue of accountability. While that is one important function, sensible data and information management are necessary not only to hold teachers and administrators accountable, but also to help teachers and schools improve instruction and devise new programs. Comprehensive and accessible student achievement data allow teachers to identify student needs and then target resources and instruction accordingly. Timely and thorough achievement data permit teachers to use their pedagogical and curricular expertise to the best effect.

How does such a system actually work? It starts with administrators and teachers working together to analyze data and come up with solutions. One Maryland principal explained how such collaboration can work, saying, "When we looked at the data we found out ... that reading for literary experience was our weakest area. So we had to then become informed as to what we needed to do strategically in the classroom to improve in this area, which meant looking at things like current research and books that were provided to us in the area of reading."[16] An administrator from a district hailed for its data-driven improvements confided her district's technique to me: "Each year, we look at how our schools are doing, grade by grade. Then we take our curricular staff and target those schools, especially those grades, where performance isn't where it needs to be. The staff goes into that school and works under the principal's direction. They'll sit down with faculty, discuss performance data and what it shows about strengths and weaknesses, show them how to use data, model strategies and lesson plans, or whatever they need." Just as the New York City Police Department learned how to use data to pinpoint problem areas and design tailored solutions to create a safer city, so can teachers and administrators together use data to ensure high levels of student achievement.

Timely data collection and data-driven decision making empower educators by involving teachers, administrators, and other team members in identifying areas that need improvement and tackling them in an informed manner. For example, when the superintendent of the Reynoldsburg, Ohio, schools was informed by a parent that her eleventh-grade child was reading at a fourth-grade level, he immediately went to find out how many of his students in grades 7–12 were reading at that level. Thanks to the web-based data management and decision support system in place in the Reynoldsburg school system, the superintendent determined in less than 15 minutes that the 6,300-student district had 84 students in such a plight. He designed a reading program targeted to meet the needs of those students, and a year later the district reported that those students had demonstrated reading improvement that averaged a year and half's worth of growth.[17]

Rethinking the Organization

The rhetoric of the status quo reformers has so permeated our understanding of schooling that the terms "efficiency" or "cost-effectiveness" sound frighteningly radical. The very words can set the teeth of parents and educators on edge. Yet efficiency is about finding ways to accomplish goals with fewer resources, a process that frees up time and money and makes new achievements possible. The problem with frowning upon cost-effectiveness and efficiency is that school reform winds up being about efforts to load more stuff on top of the existing structures—never about uncovering waste, discarding the ineffective, or freeing up resources to do new things. As Stanford University economist Eric Hanushek remarked a decade ago, in an observation that remains depressingly true today: "Unfortunately, schools today have few incentives to use technology effectively. Not only are teachers not rewarded for using technology well ... [but] schools districts seldom make cost saving a high priority. The most frequent use of computers and other technological programs is to enrich the curriculum, providing presentations that are interesting and entertaining but that may not be central to the instructional program."[18]

Piling on more is not a recipe for radical improvement. Effective organizations don't drive improvement by doing the same thing with the same number of people or by pouring *more* people or technology into a static organization. Sustained improvement results when technology is used to shift routine tasks and mundane obligations from people to machines, freeing skilled practitioners to focus on the areas where their skills are critical and where creative endeavors add value.

These changes reduce the need for employees, making management simpler and less onerous. Shrinking the workforce frees up resources and makes it possible to pay employees more. Automation eliminates some rote or unpleasant tasks, which frees up personnel for more rewarding work. Perhaps more important, by automating routine functions, technology helps employees focus on the more creative responsibilities that add substantial value—enhancing their contribution, making the organization more productive, and thereby increasing both the benefit to the customer and the resources available to reward employees. Reducing time spent on rote tasks allows people to concentrate their efforts and focus on what they do best, makes it easier to judge performance, and reduces the number of talented workers we need to secure.

The travails and resurgence of the American steel industry illustrate how quality organizations rewrite the rulebook as technology permits. Faced with cheap imports, rising energy costs, and outmoded labor practices, 30 companies have filed for bankruptcy in the past few years. These traditional companies relied upon "integrated steelmaking," a production model that required vast amounts of energy, labor, and capital to smelt iron ore in enormous blast furnaces. Meanwhile, the surviving companies have harnessed new technologies to reinvent the production process in ways that require less of all these resources.[19]

The leading new company is Nucor, an upstart founded in 1969 that now produces more steel per year than perennial leader U.S. Steel. Nucor has abandoned the traditional integration technique, instead developing "mini-mills" that use energy-efficient electric arc furnaces to recycle scrap metal into fresh steel and that requires fewer workers to produce each ton of metal.[20] The mini-mill process has revolutionized the steel industry by lowering costs while boosting productivity.[21] The success of Nucor was not produced by wedging new technologies into an existing organization but by using break-throughs as a tool for rethinking management and operations. Nucor offers large incentives for productivity and efficiency gains, with employees earning 65 percent of their pay in performance incentives.[22] Another upstart, International Steel Group, has slashed management, devised flexible work rules, and offered incentives to employees for gains in efficiency. International now produces more steel than did LTV, the now-extinct firm that it displaced, with less than half the workforce.[23] Today, American steelworkers are the best-paid steelworkers in the world, yet American steel firms remain competitive because reengineering has allowed them to produce higher quality steel than their international competitors with just a fraction of the man-hours.

Doing More without Getting More

Status quo reformers will deny that the case of steel has any possible relevance for schooling. I know this because they have taken pains to tell me so, time and again. So let's consider an example a little closer to home. In 2003, Long Beach Unified School District, with a highly diverse student population of 97,000, won the national 2002–2003 Broad Prize for Urban Education despite having cut nearly $40 million from its $840 million budget during the school year. The district posted steady student improvement despite having imposed hiring freezes, limits on staff travel, and holds on all discretionary programs. As district information officer Richard Van Der Lann noted, "We tapped the brake pedal when we saw leaner times coming. We're doing more with less."[24]

During 2002–2003, the Florida Virtual School enrolled more than 6,800 students in its 75 course offerings. Florida Virtual provides web-based classes, instruction, and assessments to students in a variety of academic subjects and electives. Like virtual schools operating in 15 other states, Florida Virtual allows faculty to provide courses to a scattered student population. Programs like Florida Virtual may make it possible to provide quality academic instruction to some students and for some courses much more cheaply, freeing up resources for other needs.

Alternatively, we might consider several examples highlighted by the Learning First Alliance, which in 2003 documented success of five high-achieving, high-poverty districts that had posted significant achievement gains over three or more years. The five districts—Aldine, Texas; Chula Vista, California; Kent County, Maryland; Minneapolis; and Providence—all made gains without a significant infusion of new resources. In fact, these districts were funded just like other local districts that were going nowhere. What explained their miraculous success? The answer won't surprise a commonsense reformer. The districts retooled their leadership, used data to drive decisions, focused relentlessly on student learning, devised a systemic approach to instruction, and reallocated resources accordingly. As the Learning First Alliance reported, "[The districts] looked carefully at how to stretch and prioritize their dollars … [and] worked hard to ensure that funds were available for principal training, teacher leader training, and other priorities."[25]

Perhaps the most significant impact of education technology is its ability to eliminate barriers posed by geography. Technology makes it easier for schools in different locales to communicate or share staff and makes it possible for central administrators to deliver support or instruction to a campus that's hundreds of miles away. Nowhere has this become more of a reality than in small schools, which can readily combine to share teachers and, by broadcasting classes though fiber optic connections, offer their students a choice of languages, advanced courses, and tutoring that would have once been prohibitive.[26]

Is Teaching Like Performing a Mozart Quartet?

Despite the testimony of the Long Beaches, Florida Virtuals, and Aldines, status quo reformers insist that it is impossible to educate children more efficiently, that each and every component of schooling is entirely dependent on having more educators in the schools to do the work and that there is no way technology can be substituted for anything that teachers do. This line of argument cites the true arts: where the act of creation itself is the end product, it can be difficult or impossible to use technology to improve performance. As Patrick Moynihan, the legendary U.S. Senator and Harvard professor, was fond of saying, producing a Mozart quartet two centuries ago required four persons, four stringed instruments, and, say, 35 minutes. Producing the same Mozart quartet today still requires the same people, instruments, and time. Despite breathtaking technological advances, productivity has not changed.

In the case of schooling, this analogy is incomplete and ultimately misleading. In the arts, what has changed over two centuries is that, through radio and records, and then through television and other electronic media, the number of people able to *hear and appreciate* a given performance has increased dramatically, at ever decreasing cost. Changes, improvements, and increased efficiency in technology has made what was once the preserve of the elite available to the general public.

Technology is most effective when it allows people to do the *same thing* as before in a *cheaper and more efficient* fashion, including reaching more people through the same effort. "Productivity is not about people working more, it's about people working more efficiently. That's where technology comes in," in the words of the chief economist at the consulting firm Retail Forward, Inc.[27] In 2003, the U.S. Postal Service trimmed its workforce by 16,000 after offering early retirement to mail clerks, sorters, and other workers no longer needed due to automation. The 2003 cuts followed staff cuts of 23,000 during 2001 and 2002.[28] Mail delivery didn't get slower or more erratic because of the layoffs. Rather, technology was substituted for people on tasks that were routine or that machines could otherwise handle more efficiently.

Rethinking Staffing

Historically, educators in the schools have been expected to perform a mass of responsibilities. The nation's schools are almost entirely staffed by teachers, teacher aides, principals and assistant principals. More than ninety-five percent of these folks are teachers or teacher aides. Each teacher is expected to run discussions, lecture, help students use computers, grade essays, mentor their colleagues, supervise homeroom, patrol the cafeteria, and design lesson plans. We've got a slew of complex and demanding tasks and dozens of adults with different strengths and weaknesses. Yet, districts and schools have each teacher duplicating the work of dozens of other teachers in the school and hundreds or even thousands in the district.

Teachers today do pretty much the same job that teachers did in 1950. Think about that. In medicine, progress has been matched by specialization—with different doctors taking on more precisely defined roles and new, less expensive paraprofessionals like registered nurses and physical therapists taking on tasks that don't require a doctor's training. In law, attorneys have taken on more narrowly defined roles and have hired increasing numbers of paralegals to take on responsibilities that don't require an attorney's training. Meanwhile, both fields have used new technology to replace mundane tasks like typing and record-keeping that used to consume a wealth of time. The result is a profession in which skilled and expensive professionals are able to spend an increasing percentage of time on the tasks that most effectively deploy their training. The same is true in almost every line of work.

In schooling, however, nearly every teacher is still a lecturer and group leader, grader and hallway monitor, curriculum developer and test designer. Every year our high schools have tens of thousands of teachers giving variations of the same lectures on the Civil War, right triangles, the digestive system, and what have you. Every teacher is asked to be a master of both content knowledge and developmental psychology and group dynamics and Socratic inquiry, and is then loaded with a heap of mundane tasks. The natural result is that these presentations tend to be of highly uneven quality, delivered by teachers who have not been selected for their skills as lecturers or storytellers, and require thousands of hours of teacher time spent preparing variations on the same material.

Imagine a law firm or an engineering firm or a consulting firm of 50 or 90 adults where every single employee focused on one particular set of substantive challenges but otherwise did variations of the same job. Imagine a hospital with no nurses or physicians' assistants or physical therapists, where doctors performed every task. We would need a slew of additional doctors, each would have less time to devote to any particular specialty, and costs would skyrocket.

In justifying the need for more spending on teacher salaries, status quo reformers routinely bemoan the difficulty of finding enough good teachers to staff the nation's schools. In 1999, public schools employed 2.9 million classroom teachers and 620,000 instructional aides.[29] Those figures are enormous. Just the smaller 2.9 million figure alone, excluding instructional aides, represents about one out of every 45 people employed in the United States. It is more than twice the 1.4 million active duty personnel who serve in the U.S. Army, Navy, Marine Corps, and Air Force. It is nearly three times the 1.1 million active attorneys in the nation.[30] Simply finding and training 2.9 million competent individuals is a consuming challenge, one that we have made more difficult than is necessary.

We need that many teachers only because we've spent the last two decades frenetically trying to shrink class size come hell or high water. The truth is that we could probably instruct, mentor, and support students at least as well as we do today with a much smaller teaching force. Using international data from the Third International Mathematics and Science study, researchers have found that countries with small class sizes are able to afford large teaching forces because they hire relatively less effective teachers. Further, the researchers found that "capable teachers are able to promote student learning equally well regardless of class size" while less capable teachers "do not seem to be up to the job of teaching large classes." Reducing the size of the teaching force by deploying teachers more thoughtfully would permit managers to attract higher quality teachers and to be more selective about who they hire, to provide more intensive training and support, and to manage more personally.[31]

It's not that class size is unimportant, it's just that the benefits of class size tend to be outweighed by the need to find ever more teachers, the dilution of teacher quality, the required sacrifices in other areas, and tend to vary significantly with the students, the teacher, and the subject taught.[32] Imagine trying to improve medical care by insisting that every medical practice have a doctor for every twenty-two patients, whatever the needs of the patients or the other resources or personnel available. Practices would have to seek out more doctors, slash pay in order to afford them, and reduce spending on technology or support staff. Doctors with healthier patients would certainly appreciate the lighter workload, but we'd probably all wind up with better health care if doctors handling chicken pox and sprained knees saw more patients and neurosurgeons saw fewer.

As I mentioned in chapter 4, thinking creatively about the teacher's role can create new opportunities for teachers to tap their talents and develop professionally. In Iowa, by 2003, the Iowa Communications Network linked 750 school videoconference sites across the state and allowed participating schools to offer subjects such as Spanish or physics without each school having to hire its own teacher.[33] "Virtual schools" offer web-based instruction to thousands of students even in remote locations. At the university level, where nearly two million students took at least one course online in fall 2003, a 2003 national survey of nearly 1,000 college administrators conducted by the Sloan Consortium found that 57 percent of the administrators reported that Internet-based courses were already at least equivalent to traditional courses in educational quality. One-third of the administrators thought that the web-based courses would be superior to in-class instruction within three years.[34] Rather than using these resources as a last resort, commonsense reform dictates that school systems think creatively about how they might use these to help improve instruction, target resources, and reduce costs across the board.

Increasing Cost Effectiveness

Consider the Texas district that received an infusion of funding to improve student learning and achievement. Research into the effects of that money revealed that it hadn't made any difference in student learning at 13 of the district's 15 schools. How could that be? Unsurprisingly, researchers determined that the problem was what the schools did with the money. The schools dumped most of it into reducing class sizes without ever deciding how to leverage that for significant improvement. In the end, reported the former superintendent, the schools "didn't change the way they were doing things. . . . All they did was take that support, lower pupil–teacher ratios, still use the same curriculum, still use the same instructional methods. You'd go over there and they'd actually have . . . ten students in a class, but guess what they would be doing? You'd have two rows of five students, and the teacher would still be sitting up there in the front of the room, and still using ditto sheets like they were before. You can do that with thirty students as easy as you can ten."[35]

Such "reforms" serve neither teachers nor students. They waste valuable resources, stoke public frustration, soak up money that could otherwise fund higher pay, and do nothing to improve instruction. Unfortunately, such expenditures are the norm. Absent any incentives to either limit or even reduce expenditures, leaders of school systems do not seek cost-cutting measures. But many are available, through consolidation and outsourcing.

Trimming Overhead

School districts are not lean organizations. Bloated school systems like Los Angeles and New York City have central office staffs that include at least one central administrator for every 60 students in the schools. The same rate holds even in "reformed" systems like Houston and Seattle. These ratios don't even include the principals, assistant principals, secretaries, and other administrators based in the schools. Meanwhile, the Catholic school systems in Chicago, New York City, and Los Angeles enroll tens of thousands of students in hundreds of schools and yet make do with one central administrator for every *5,000* students.[36]

Nationally, about 16 percent of district funds are spent in the central office. Now, such calculations are tricky, because public education's uncertain accounting standards mean that a lot of spending on services like special education or professional development can be apportioned in various ways. Nonetheless, these figures raise real questions. In the corporate world, central administration is much leaner. Let's take the case of supermarkets, since they are a business that requires a lot of centralized logistical coordination. In the grocery business, central management costs typically equal just 5 percent of spending.

Efficiencies are not impossible in schooling. Disciplined leaders have succeeded at cutting central office spending by a third to a half. For instance, under superintendent Steve Adamowski, central office spending in Cincinnati was cut from 11 percent to just under 5 percent, and the office staff—which had consisted of 600 people in the early 1990s—was cut to about 220.

Flexibility and Outsourcing

Choice-based reform can break the stranglehold that conventional school districts and state bureaucracies have over who can deliver education services and how they are delivered. Today, we think of every school district as a self-contained unit responsible for providing food, transport, shelter, books, leisure activities, sports stadiums, health care, and a menu of other services to all its employees and students. Efforts to revisit these arrangements by shifting some services to other agencies or by contracting with vendors to provide some of these services generally erupt into holy war, with critics bewailing the "privatization" of schooling and the end of civilization as we know it.

Educators must distinguish between their core responsibilities and other obligations. Core functions are those relating to teaching, learning, assessment, and supporting faculty. Then there are the marginal tasks—like maintenance, food services, and transportation—that districts have to be responsible for but that should probably be contracted out to specialized vendors. Such functions include tasks like printing and payroll, which distract management from their central tasks and where a lack of competition and public sector work rules have kept even the largest districts from turning their size and scale into cost savings.

Contracting permits principals and superintendents to shrink their responsibilities by turning them over to specialists. For example, many companies contract with independent vendors to manage their payrolls. This allows a firm to specialize in what it does best, accumulating expertise while spreading the costs of its specialists and systems over a large number of clients. On the other hand, nearly all school systems manage their own payroll operations, requiring that they buy the computer systems and hire payroll managers. Districts struggle with a chore at which others have much more experience. Meanwhile, district payroll employees work under a civil-service pay scale and in an organization where their role is clearly peripheral. As a result, it is hard for districts to recruit the kind of talented personnel that a private sector payroll company can attract. Not only do school districts wind up performing these functions less effectively than a specialized vendor, but they are often forced to draw upon a talent pool that is weaker than that available to private vendors. Consequently, many districts have former teachers rather than trained professionals running the human resources or accounting departments for $500 million operations.

In Oregon, the School Boards Association reports that one-third of the state's 198 school districts contract out for bus service, 32 do so for food services, and 17 for custodial services. Are there potential problems with contracting? Of course. There are unscrupulous vendors and districts do need to negotiate sensibly. However, there are also unscrupulous district employees. The key is for districts to have a small professional staff that writes contracts with specific performance benchmarks, that monitors the performance of vendors, and that ensures that vendors fulfill their obligations in terms of both the amount and the quality of service provided.

Each niche market would create opportunities to tap the expertise of firms that already provide the service on a routine basis. Outsourcing will permit schools and school districts to focus upon educational issues, hand peripheral services off to specialists who do them full time, and dramatically shrink the number of people that educational leaders must manage. Schools can become leaner, nimbler organizations.

However, few school or district leaders really want to choose a food services firm, a transportation firm, and a security firm each year. So, there are two accommodations commonsense reformers should encourage. The first is the emergence of "bundling" firms to arrange packages of services for schools and districts and allow schools or districts to obtain food services, accounting, maintenance, and other services with a single call. By supervising provision for many clients, bundlers will be in a position to evaluate vendors on an ongoing basis, simplifying the job of monitoring and rating performance. The second is to help schools or small districts form purchasing consortia, each led by a manager or management team responsible for picking through various providers and forwarding recommendations to individual members.

The Status Quo Critique: Demanding "More"

The signature belief of the status quo reformers is that, as one esteemed education school professor forcefully told me, "The word efficiency has no place in education. Schools are not factories. ... They are gardens, and gardens demand nurturing." Status quo reformers ridicule the very idea of cost-effectiveness as a consideration in school management. Imagine the signal that sends to those competent, hardworking educators who know that inefficiency soaks up money we could use to pay them more, provide new resources, expand professional development, or invest in facilities.

If You Want Change, It'll Cost You

Status quo reformers repeatedly insist, "If you want schools to change, it's going to cost you. You've got to be willing to pay for it." Commonsense reformers just don't buy it. Why should change cost more? Most private sector firms remake themselves only when forced to find ways to survive on less, meaning they are expected to pursue radical change while spending *less*.

Organizations transform themselves by refocusing on the essentials, tackling contract language and staffing routines once viewed as untouchable, and finding ways to use new technological and management tools to rethink their work. Companies on the verge of bankruptcy cut salaries, shrink investment, find ways to make do with less, or find a way to scale back services. Workers are laid off or take salary cuts. Managers find ways to use technology more effectively. Service sector firms like law firms, newspapers, accounting firms, and insurance companies have slashed a majority of the support positions that 40 years ago were required to maintain files, handle correspondence, keep schedules, prepare documents, and handle the other assorted tasks that have today been automated. As new tools became available, market pressures to contain costs pressed firms to use technology to downsize and to streamline operations.

When faced with such pressures, educators, on the other hand, have rarely taken such steps. Take the case of John Wilhelmi, a principal in Portland, Oregon. After the No Child Left Behind Act enabled students in his low-performing Marshall High School to attend other local schools, his school lost a lot of students, including more than a third of the incoming freshman class. How did Wilhelmi respond? He wrote an open letter to President George Bush complaining about his rating. Did he seek savings or try to reallocate resources more productively? No. He cycled through a bushel of status quo reforms while explaining, "We can only do good things to the extent that we have the staff to do them. If we lose staff, then we lose the capacity to do good things."[37] That is not how effective organizations respond to competition. Effective organizations free up resources by cutting labor costs and using technology to streamline operations. Only in education do we presume that there is no fat to cut and no employees to spare or believe it impossible to deliver new services without new resources. Only in education do we imagine that inefficiency is a natural state of being.

More Technology ... and More Employees

The status quo reformers seek to keep padding the ranks of teachers, while pushing for more spending on technology in schools and classrooms. Nowhere is this more evident than when we look at a comparison between technology spending and teacher hiring over the last 30 years. The federal, state, and local governments spent a negligible amount on technology in 1970. By 1995, they were spending $3.3 billion, or $75 per student, and by 1999 they were spending $5.5 billion, or $119, per student.[38] In 1994, just 3 percent of U.S. classrooms had Internet access; by 2001, 87 percent did. From 1998 to 2002 alone, schools went from having an Internet-connected computer for every 19.7 students to having one for every 5.6 students.[39] We've spent more than $20 billion in the past five years just linking schools and classrooms to the Internet through the federal E-rate program. With this kind of investment in technology, a commonsense reformer would expect school systems to find ways to use personnel more effectively.

Instead, during a period of no noticeable improvement in student performance, schools dramatically *increased* their workforces. Between 1970 and 2000, a massive increase in the teacher workforce drove the student–teacher ratio from 22 students per teacher to 15 per teacher.[40] Expensive new technology is dumped into schools without much discipline or forethought, with computers too often winding up as high-priced typewriters that sit mostly unused in the back of classrooms.[41]

In 2000, Maine governor Angus King proposed giving laptops to all of the state's seventh graders. The $50 million proposal included no notion as to how the investment could be used to improve school efficiency, how it might be used to wring out future savings, or why this represented a disciplined use of funds. Rather, King had decided he wanted to "do something different from what everybody else is doing" and reveled in the national and international attention that resulted.[42] A commonsense reformer is all for issuing laptops to students if the technology is being used to rethink the delivery of schooling. Unfortunately, the status quo instinct is to ladle computers into classrooms, pay little attention to pursuing complementary change, and then sit back and hope that magic will happen.

No accountant or radiologist or defense attorney expects to get paid more for seeing fewer patients, much less for doing so while working with expensive new technologies. When doctors see fewer patients or accountants serve fewer clients, they get paid less. In schooling, the problem is that the increased revenues needed just to cover the cost of new hires makes it nearly impossible to provide generous rewards for excellence.

Technology for Technology's Sake

Status quo reformers in schools of education and in consulting have earned acclaim and money by pitching glitzy new approaches to classroom computing. Offerings include personal digital assistants (PDAs) to help student take notes or do math, web-based social studies course materials, interactive curricular supplements, expensive plans to issue a laptop to every student, and so on. It's the same old cry for more of anything and everything. When the results suggest that all of this spending hasn't done much to advance student learning, status quo reformers are confused and express disappointment that teachers haven't utilized the expensive new toys in ways they should. Is the solution to rethink school management or the use of technology? Nope. It's ... of course, a need for more money and more training.[43]

In districts, education technology is too often an isolated preserve, one where tech coordinators purchase and install computers that are rarely used. Managing technology contracts is not easy—the vendors know all about the products and the costs, while the customers don't. To even the playing field, organizations need tech-savvy, sophisticated, experienced representation. Unfortunately, the situation related by one district technology chief is all too typical. He confided, "[My predecessor] was a former school technology coordinator who liked working with classroom computers and software, didn't think about the system's information technology needs, couldn't explain why we should invest in data management, ... wouldn't push people to retire all these old data systems we're still running, and didn't seem to really [care] about aligning tech with the rest of the program." Districts seeking information technology platforms often wind up with white elephants or uncoordinated systems that make it hard to integrate information or determine the cost-effectiveness of programs.

Status quo reformers imagine that, in the face of all evidence, sprinkling a bunch of computers through schools will somehow prompt teachers to integrate the new capabilities into their lessons and boost student learning. Most of what students currently do on classroom computers is write, e-mail, search the web, design web sites, write low-level programs, and use tutoring packages. None of this requires the latest hardware or software. Given the power and capacity of modern technology, most schools probably need to replace a computer only every five or six years, at most, in order to reasonably meet the needs of their students.

It's common sense to note that the purpose of education technology should be supporting the district's education mission. If teachers can't or won't use the tools, or if money is spent on programs that don't help the students learn, even exciting innovations are a waste of resources.

Protecting Adults First

Status quo reformers oppose contracting because they identify with the adults rather than the children. In California, former Governor Gray Davis signed legislation in 2002 that prohibited school districts from entering into any contract that would displace district employees. In effect, by only permitting contracts that did not save any money on personnel, Davis signed a law that made it illegal for school systems to become more efficient.

When private contractors are able to make do with fewer janitors or by paying food service workers less, observers should be delighted. This frees up money to spend on teachers, books, and other essentials. Instead, status quo reformers complain about the hardship suffered by workers. For example, in 2003, Collinsville, Illinois, signed a contract with food service company, Sodexho, that was expected to save the district about $225,000 a year. What was the primary source of the savings? Collinsville had previously paid cafeteria workers $16 an hour—the new salaries were expected to reflect the job market and be closer to $7.50 an hour.[44] While status quo reformers use the personal stories of these cafeteria workers to tug at our heartstrings, a commonsense reformer always need to remember that these overly generous salaries and padded payrolls are being funded by dollars steered out of the classrooms.

California offers up another instructive example. In June 1998, California voted on Proposition 223, the "95-5 Initiative," which sought to cap the percentage of school budgets spent on central administration at 5 percent. The idea was to cut bureaucracy and shift money to the schools. The measure was defeated at the ballot box after a coordinated lobbying effort by the school administrators, the California PTA, and small school organizations in a show of status quo muscle.

Conclusion

I've walked into the office of a school district official in charge of managing enrollment and watched in disbelief as he fished through the piles of computer paper stacked on his desk, table, chairs, windowsill, and floor to check which schools were losing students to charter schools. I've sat with school board members who had asked for an update on district spending only to be told it would be weeks before they could get the information. I've ridden along with teachers who could get performance information on their students only if they drove to the central office and hunted down test reports, and others who couldn't get feedback from November assessments until April.

These are not distant memories of schools from an earlier age, these are the realities of most schools and most school districts in the twenty-first century. We blithely operate schools in a fashion that was dated in the 1970s and that would be deemed irresponsible in a toothpaste factory. Rather than demand that schools be among our most thoughtfully managed institutions or that education dollars be spent with particular care, we pour money into school systems that operate in terribly inefficient ways and ignore the promise of new technological advances.

No school leader, no matter her gifts, is going to lead effectively in these conditions. Leaders need tools and the opportunity to use them. Commonsense reform will not work unless we reengineer school systems, and that requires reimagining management and leveraging the power of technology. Doing so will require that we begin by revisiting state statutes and employee contracts that use mandatory teacher–student ratios, standard staffing policies, and regulations on outsourcing and management.

In the corporate world, observers estimate that businesses routinely spend 5 percent or more of outlays on data collection, analysis, and management. In the financial services industry, for instance, the norm is 15 to 20 percent. In the case of K-12 schooling, however, Eduventures Inc., a Boston corporation that tracks the education industry, has estimated that total national expenditures on data analysis and management in 2003 were only $145 million amid outlays of more than $400 *billion*. Forget 5 percent. We are investing much less than *one-tenth of 1 percent* of education spending in data analysis and management. State and district officials have shoveled resources into continually expanding staffs rather than investing in data or information management and then are puzzled that anyone would critique them for failing to track spending, performance, or family satisfaction.

The ability to instantly share full information on student performance, school performance, and costs across vast distances permits a focus on results that was simply not feasible until the most recent decade. This technology is the engine that makes tough-minded accountability a reality and that makes commonsense leadership a real possibility.

Technology is not a miracle cure. It is a tool. Many efforts to harness technology fail, not because the technology is flawed but because technology is only as good as the organization that uses it. If technology is introduced without developing a comfort level among employees, without integrating it into organizational routines, without making it easy to use, or without using it to simplify the jobs and roles of employees, it will likely be brushed aside. As William Eggers, Global Director at Deloitte Research, has noted, "Success requires changing people's attitudes, belief systems and ways of doing business—helping move them from what they know to something new and strange."[45] This requires leadership that fosters a culture of competence and then tends sensibly to training, support, and implementation. As always, the commonsense reformer recognizes the centrality of these concerns and trusts that accountable managers equipped with leadership tools and guided by good information are the best bet to make the transition work.

In the end, the measure of reinvention is what happens to student learning. Reinvention offers educators new opportunities and then lets them practice their craft, in schools and classrooms and systems, as they see fit. Accountable educators are under no compulsion to adopt any change, only to perform adequately and efficiently. If they do, they will have the ability to reimagine their work as new possibilities and tools emerge. If they don't, someone else will find a way to do better. That is the nature of commonsense reform.

CHAPTER SEVEN

A Commonsense Challenge

What you have to understand is that most people in this country are men and women of common sense.

—Harry S. Truman

America's schools are in a state of crisis, though it is not the one that some critics would suggest. American schools are not awful, are not gutting our economy, and are not terribly unsafe. On balance, given the population they serve, they are probably doing as well as they did two generations ago. In that time, though, the importance of education and our investment in schooling have increased exponentially. In 1954, a high school dropout could reasonably expect to build a rewarding life. In 2004, such hopes are increasingly illusory. Given that schools are the lifeblood of a democratic nation, their importance becomes staggering when they serve also as the gateway to worldly success. In such an age, educational excellence becomes a democratic obligation and mediocrity an abomination. The crisis is that so few of our schools are excellent, so many are mediocre, and yet the adults responsible are content to tinker and theorize. The crisis is that performance we deemed adequate fifty years ago is neither tolerable nor defensible today, yet the status quo reformers steer us away from commonsense measures in favor of mawkish testimonials, pleas for patience, and a hefty helping of "expertise."

Meanwhile, tens of millions of children who hail from broken homes or broken neighborhoods rely on our schools to open the gate that would otherwise deny them the opportunities of twenty-first century America. Seeking to serve these children, we have doubled and then doubled again after-inflation spending on schools. In the nation's most troubled urban districts, we now spend more than $150,000 per child in the course of the typical student's K-12 education. Nonetheless, more than half of fourth graders in these districts cannot even read at a "basic" level on the National Assessment of Educational Progress.

It is true that schools have been asked to educate children who were previously excluded, more children from single-parent homes, and a larger population of students for whom English is a second language. It is equally true, however, that today's children are much more likely to benefit from being raised in smaller families and by more educated parents. The best that defenders of the status quo can muster is to claim that schools are better than overzealous critics suggest and that, thanks to continuous growth in spending, "American schools are not doing worse than in earlier times."[1]

Consider that. Of what other institution in American life would defenders claim that treading water was an accomplishment? From the Postal Service to urban policing, from industrial enterprises to fire departments, from welfare to the U.S. armed services, the last quarter-century has been a story of explosive progress, of learning to do more with less. If we're serious about improving our schools, we're told, the $10,000 per year we spend on each student is only a down payment. If we want school improvement, we're told we're now going to have to pony up "real" money.

This rhetoric has not changed in decades. Since 1994, elementary and secondary education spending has grown from less than $300 billion to over $400 billion a year. Today, amid painful budget deficits, states are asking public schools and other public services to absorb necessary cuts. Educators have reacted to these modest requests in a damning fashion, refusing to slim down school systems while frantically threatening to cut school days, lay off young teachers, or shutter popular programs. In every decade, status quo reformers have used complaints of pinched budgets to excuse mediocrity. This plea has grown old. The truth is that schools spend a lot of money. They probably spend enough money to teach every child at least the essential skills they need.

Would more money help? Of course—so long as it is spent wisely. A commonsense reformer is similarly happy to acknowledge the merit in many status quo reform proposals. Many recommendations for enhanced professional development, new leadership strategies, and improved instruction make good sense. However, no matter how much we might wish it were otherwise, neither more money nor even well-designed instructional reforms will magically bring a culture of competence into being. That must be done first and done deliberately. Then reformers can turn to other concerns.

The commonsense reformer believes that the challenges of the moment offer an opportunity to bring our schools into the new century. Belt tightening in the states and a looming era of federal deficits provide a chance to rethink whether we really want to keep educating our youth in institutions modeled upon the procedural, inflexible lines of a 1920s shoe factory. Tight budgets can bring clarity and create an opening to make radical changes that appear unnecessary in more sedate times.

The commonsense reformer understands that schools cannot be one-stop remedies for social inequality or the imperfections of the American way of life. When status quo reform groups such as the Children's Defense Fund see education as a popular, back-door way to fund their crusade for "social justice," they overpromise what schools can do and overburden educators. Good schools alone will not remove crime from disadvantaged neighborhoods, rebuild tattered families, or create jobs. What schools can do is educate our children and prepare them for citizenship. If this requires schools to establish clear priorities and prune back peripheral services, so be it.

None of the institutions of a free society—not schools or firehouses or city halls or churches—work as well when asked to shoulder all of a community's burdens. Institutions that are effective at meeting limited human needs often buckle when asked to become all-purpose social agencies. The truth, however, is that a lot of status quo reformers aren't all that interested in the small potatoes of making sure that children are literate and numerate, possess essential knowledge and civic skills, and are equipped to pursue further education or a desirable job. Status quo reformers have grander ambitions. Armed with their righteous agenda of social reconstruction and a naive faith in the ability of schools to reinvent society, these minor league revolutionaries have unwittingly marginalized the gatekeeping skills while earnestly suggesting that overwhelmed schools used to address challenges ranging from immigration to economic malaise to sexual conduct to single-parent households.

In the 1991 status quo tome *Savage Inequalities*, Jonathan Kozol profiled the miserable conditions of several urban school systems. At the close of this immensely influential book, after profiling the staggering dysfunction of these systems, Kozol offered advice to those who would address the abominations he depicted. What did he counsel? Strong measures? Tough-minded policy change? Nope. All he could think to offer was an indictment of American racism, a demand for more spending, and a plaintive appeal, "Surely, there is enough for everyone within this country. It is a tragedy that these things are not more widely shared."[2] Twelve years later, in 2003, American Education Research Association president Marilyn Cochran-Smith flatly rejected the premise of commonsense reform, arguing that, "The ethic of caring about students ... come[s] from the heart ... from deep beliefs about the importance and value of the life chances of all children, the morality of teaching, and the future of our democratic nation. Commitments like these cannot be forced, and they cannot be bought. But they can be informed, nurtured, and channeled into productive work in schools and communities."[3] I'm sorry, but answers like these are not good enough. Aspirations of social justice and a love for children are noble things. However, when homilies and dreamy visions of sugarplums serve to excuse inaction and incompetence, the high-minded can become blasphemous.

Sonia Nieto, professor of language, literacy, and culture at the University of Massachusetts School of Education, speaks for many status quo reformers when she declares, "Even under difficult conditions—one might well say *especially* under these conditions—public schools are the best hope for realizing the utopian vision of a democratic society."[4] The damning result has been an unwillingness to get serious about school improvement until all the preconditions they deem necessary are in place. By refusing to pursue school improvement until American society is reconstructed while reimagining schools as Swiss army knives that will solve every social malady, status quo reformers excuse mediocrity while justifying a steady influx of new dollars. Meanwhile, our children, particularly the most vulnerable among them, foot the bill in lost opportunities and fractured dreams.

In light of the militantly irresponsible language of the utopian status quo reformers, it is easy for commonsense reformers to be seduced by self-styled "structural reformers" who strike a much more sensible tone while gingerly side-stepping commonsense proposals. Commonsense reformers must resist the temptation to embrace painless "structural reforms" like tweaking leadership arrangements, adopting inconsequential accountability plans, changing the size of schools, or expanding public school choice when these are posed as an alternative to measures that will actually increase accountability and flexibility. Commonsense reform requires unleashing and then harnessing elemental impulses and entrepreneurial energy. Proposals that mimic some features of commonsense reform but fail to alter incentives, opportunities, or consequences are a distraction.

Some status quo reformers may imagine an irony in the commonsense case, given that my very first book, *Spinning Wheels*, is best known for its indictment of urban school reform efforts. Reform has indeed earned a bad name in education circles, deservedly so. Scholars like Stanford University education professors David Tyack and Larry Cuban and Brookings Institution scholar Diane Ravitch have noted the long and undistinguished history of school reform, critiquing most efforts as little more than ineffective tinkering.[5] However, we ought to avoid carelessly extending the gloomy assessments of traditional education reform efforts to the kinds of institutional redesign envisioned by commonsense reform. Traditional efforts have sought to change what educators do or how schools do it. Commonsense reform isn't about making educators do anything differently, it's about changing the world in which they work. Traditional reform has amounted to so little because, in a phrase favored by education policymakers, it is "like punching a pillow." The system absorbs reform efforts and oozes back into place. This happens because it can; comfortable inertia inevitably prevails, in schooling or anywhere else, except when disciplined by a culture of competence. Commonsense reform seeks to institute such a culture. While commonsense reformers will have particular preferences regarding what is taught and how teachers teach, commonsense reform itself is largely agnostic on these matters.

Let the Sun Shine In

While alternately pursuing educational elixirs and crusading for utopian visions of social justice, status quo reformers have quashed more sensible efforts to make sure schools do a few things well. The result is that even incremental improvement is rare cause for celebration.

Good organizations, in schooling and elsewhere, are characterized by clear goals, careful measurement of performance, rewards based on outcomes, the elimination of unproductive employees, operational flexibility, the ready availability of detailed and useful information, personnel systems that recruit and promote talent, and attention to training and professional growth. This describes few of today's public schools. How do we get from here to there?

The commonsense reformer is humble enough to know that she cannot prescribe exactly how to get there in a given community. She does not try to tell schools just what to teach, how to calibrate the balance between tough-minded and competitive accountability, how much schools ought to spend on research, how technology should be used to deliver instruction, or exactly how to structure teacher compensation or training. Rather, the commonsense reformer relies on certain principles that have been shown to increase effectiveness, enhance productivity, and align self-interest with the common good.

Bret Schundler, former mayor of Jersey City and a New Jersey gubernatorial candidate in 2001, has pointed out, "Newark's public schools now spend $16,000 per child, yet less than 20 percent of New Central High School's ninth graders graduate. Meanwhile ... [New Jersey Governor] Jim McGreevey says that $16,000 is not enough to educate a child in Newark."[6] When I talk about school spending, I am inevitably met by status quo reformers who will boldly declare, "If schools are spending $16,000 per pupil and failing to teach students to read, then we're clearly not spending enough."

Ultimately, the test of our seriousness about education is not whether we demand more but whether we are willing to funnel dollars into systems that violate the most basic precepts of common sense. After all, $16,000 a child is a lot of money. It is $400,000 for a class of 25 children. Heck, $10,000 a year per student is a lot of money. For instance, while the U.S. Census Bureau reports that Washington, D.C. is spending a total of more than $15,000 per pupil to produce abysmal results, 88 percent of private elementary schools and 60 percent of private secondary schools in the D.C. metro area charge less than $7,500 a year.[7]

A commonsense reformer wonders whether we aren't spending enough for well-run schools to get the job done. After all, status quo reformers have spent the past fifty years telling us that they don't have the resources they need, even as we doubled spending and then doubled it again. Despite these efforts, the relentless refrain of self-styled public school proponents like Californians for Justice is, "The crisis in our schools is a problem both of funding and of discrimination. We under fund schools generally, and we neglect some communities in particular."[8] Before taking these complaints at face value, a commonsense reformer merely asks whether any competitors can teach all children effectively with the money we are now spending. After all, evidence from private schools and charter schools suggests that they can perform at least as well as traditional public schools and for substantially less money. Results from districts like Aldine, Texas, and Chula Vista, California, suggest that the leaders of accountable public school districts can find ways to promote systemic improvement without more money.

If no one else can do any better than the public schools with the money that we currently spend, then a commonsense reformer will enthusiastically partner with the mo' money crowd to seek the necessary support. However, even as the status quo reformers insist that there is not enough money to get the job done, they bitterly resist proposals for cost efficiencies or to allow new competitors to prove their mettle. In Michigan, a 2003 proposal to merely increase the number of charter schools prompted a walkout by Detroit teachers that closed the schools down for a day and torpedoed the legislation. Public educators have harassed charter schools, fought to limit their funding, demonized proposed voucher programs, and attacked accountability measures that allow students to flee failing schools. Status quo reformers can't have it both ways. If our traditional public schools are being shortchanged, educators should welcome competitors with the confidence that none will fare any better. If they continue to squelch would-be competitors, they cannot be surprised when commonsense reformers raise questions about their efficiency or effectiveness.

Principles of Commonsense Reform

Commonsense reform rests on seven simple, straightforward principles.

- Schools must focus on doing a few crucial things and doing them well. The most important thing for schools to do is ensure that all children, at a minimum, master the gatekeeping skills of reading, writing, mathematics, and have a fundamental grasp of science and history.
- Educators should be held accountable for the work that they do and should have the freedom and flexibility to run schools and teach classes in accord with their professional judgment.
- School systems should relentlessly seek out talented and entrepreneurial teachers and leaders and should strive to nurture these individuals.
- All schools need not look exactly the same. We should allow schools to excel in different ways and permit families to find the school that matches their child's needs.
- Educators who excel at serving children, who contribute in meaningful ways to their schools, or who take on the toughest assignments should be recognized and rewarded.
- Ineffective educators need to be identified and either remediated or fired.
- School districts should promote flexibility and accountability by decentralizing, using modern technology, and rethinking how they are organized.

The fact that these principles are considered at all controversial in education circles suggests just how far out of kilter our schools really are. Status quo reformers like Michael Apple, education professor at the University of Wisconsin, insist that those who would have schools pursue flexibility or efficiency are relying on an "utterly romanticized portrayal of the business sector." They justify such claims by insisting, "Children are not plastic masses of raw material that can be 'processed' in the same way we make breakfast cereals."[9]

When they caricature the principles of commonsense reform as "business principles" or a "business approach," the status quo reformers do a tremendous disservice to students. These labels are a misnomer, and the fact that they are used at all is a travesty. They are a misnomer because there is nothing uniquely "businesslike" about asking that organizations be accountable, flexible, or efficient. These are not business principles—these are sensible guidelines for motivating adults and ensuring that they perform their chosen work. The travesty is that these qualities are labeled "businesslike" because they are the norm in the private sector, while we have permitted critical public organizations to totter along with little more than good intentions as a guide. Embracing accountability and flexibility in education is not an attempt to import business thinking; rather, it reflects the recognition that we should approach our children's education with at least the same degree of seriousness that we currently reserve for the production of breakfast cereal and designer jeans. The fact that we have not done so reflects an appalling lack of moral seriousness on our part.

Commonsense reform is not a miracle cure. It is only a beginning. It provides only the initial blueprints for a culture of competence. There are many important steps and sophisticated approaches to management that extend far beyond the basic structural elements of commonsense reform. Management and organizational behavior scholars like Clayton Christensen, author of *The Innovator's Dilemma* and co-author of *The Innovator's Solution*; Jim Collins, author of *Good to Great* and co-author of *Built to Last*; Daniel Goleman, author of *Emotional Intelligence*; and James Champy, author of *X-Engineering the Corporation*, have illustrated how great organizations forge a culture of competence through creative thinking, dynamic leadership, and careful attention to practices—not through some mechanical carrot and stick strategy.[10] They are, of course, entirely correct. The problem is that when today's education managers adopt the advice of a Christensen or a Collins and try to assemble the right people or create space for innovation, they quickly get mired in the regulations and routines that create the culture of incompetence. Visionary leadership requires a certain basic toolbox: that executives be able to assemble their own teams, reward excellence, remove the inept, measure performance, encourage entrepreneurial activity, access information, and reinvent operations when necessary. Otherwise it amounts to little more than high hopes. Commonsense reform provides not a final answer, but a chance to create the kinds of organizations where visionary leadership can flourish.

Making Schools Magnets for Talent

The most important factor determining school quality is the competence of teachers. The biggest problem with our schools today is that they repel talented candidates. While status quo reformers bemoan or deny this state of affairs, commonsense reformers tackle it. In the poignant phrase of Abigail Thernstrom and Stephen Thernstrom, authors of *No Excuses: Closing the Racial Gap in Learning*, "Teaching in a regular public school is a profession for saints, masochists, or low-aspiring civil servants. To do the job splendidly asks too much in the way of sacrifice; simply to meet minimum standards asks too little in terms of skills, knowledge, imagination, and dedication."[11]

This staffing strategy was never a particularly thoughtful one, and its flaws have become increasingly evident as schools have lost their ability to rely upon an abundance of talented women and black teachers. Today, the professional barriers that once forced those individuals into teaching have been dismantled. Even Sandra Feldman, the president of the American Federation of Teachers, the nation's second-largest teachers' union, concedes, "You have in the schools right now, among ... the teachers who are going to be retiring, very smart people ... [but] we're not getting in now the same kinds of people."[12]

Reaching out to the teachers and education leaders that we need will require three things. First, it requires that teaching be interesting, creative, and rewarding work. Teachers need a clear sense of purpose; they need to operate in safe and cohesive environments, and they need the opportunity and information to operate as professionals within a collegial community. On all of these issues, the commonsense and status quo reformers can find common cause. Teachers and education leaders need the freedom and flexibility to identify challenges, diagnose situations, and take action. Of course, granting this kind of freedom requires rolling back procedural rules and replacing them with a system of accountability premised on performance and competition.

Second, educators need to be fairly compensated. They need to be rewarded for their performance and for tackling outsized challenges. They need opportunities to grow professionally and advance in their careers. They need to know that lethargic or unmotivated colleagues will not become fixtures and that energy and entrepreneurship will be recognized. Districts can free up the necessary resources and develop new opportunities by slimming down and shedding ineffective staff, while developing staffing systems that take fuller advantage of faculty expertise.

Third, states and districts need to strip down licensure barriers and hiring procedures that discourage nontraditional candidates from applying for positions. This doesn't suggest that school districts should necessarily prefer such candidates, only that they should not arbitrarily rely upon regulation to restrict the applicant pool or stand in for good judgment.

Talented, energetic people seek out the opportunity to do good and important work. People want to teach and to work with children. Not only is there universal recognition of schooling's importance, but teaching is one of those jobs that inspires practitioners to muse, "I am happy and full of energy. I feel great, I am buzzing tremendously. ... It just never occurred to me that work could be something you actually enjoyed."[13] Schools need to welcome the best of these aspirants. The key to all of this is flexibility and allowing educators to operate as professionals.

The flip side of flexibility is accountability. A commonsense reformer knows that neither you nor I, nor any state or federal official, is as well equipped to make good teaching and learning decisions as is a responsible teacher. However, because it is our children in those schools and our taxes that finance them, you and I and our elected representatives have every right to set goals regarding what children need to know and to hold educators accountable for teaching that material. Commonsense reform does not seek to tell teachers how to teach, what materials to use, or to set rules about who should work in schools. Educators should be entrusted to make informed, data-driven decisions, and should be accountable for the results of their endeavors.

This openness provides ground for a rapprochement with status quo reformers. If status quo reformers drop their insistence on offering various prescriptions as alternatives to building an accountable, flexible system, they will find much room to try their various remedies. If status quo reformers wish to manage schools that do not link pay to performance, hire only teachers trained in education schools, hire administrators only from the ranks of teachers, and avoid contracting for services, they are free to do so. Commonsense reformers will not object, but will let the results tell the tale. There will be room for every approach that serves children and satisfies families, whether it be progressive, traditionalist, or something else.

This kind of "grand bargain" would create opportunities for teachers of all philosophical stripes. After all, many of the brilliant pedagogues hailed by the status quo reformers, innovators like Deborah Meier and Ted Sizer, have long bemoaned the procedural handcuffs that plague the public schools. Meier, the widely hailed founder of the Central Park East Schools, has acknowledged that one of the reasons she and her colleagues started Central Park East, "although we didn't often admit it—was our personal desire for greater autonomy as teachers. We spoke a lot about democracy, but we were also just plain sick and tired of having to waste so much time and energy negotiating with school officials over what seemed like commonsense requests, worrying about myriad rules and regulations, being forced to compromise on so many of our beliefs."[14] What status quo reformers forget is that this kind of procedural system is inevitable absent accountability. However, competition and tough-minded accountability make possible the flexibility and autonomy that nurtures the very schools—such as the Central Park East Schools or the Coalition of Essential Schools—that many status quo reformers hold up as models.

A Commonsense Reform Agenda

Commonsense reform begins with a powerful accountability system that clarifies goals, makes it easy for decision makers to monitor performance, and allows them to reward, remediate, or fire employees as appropriate. Accountability based upon student achievement in essential skills shows educators, parents, and policymakers how schools are faring at their core task. It provides assurance that decisions about employment or compensation are not being made on capricious grounds but by principals and other administrators who will be responsible for the results of their decisions. Once accountability is in place, it is easier for policymakers and voters to trust school leaders to make decisions guided by their knowledge of the students, the faculty, and the data on student learning.

The presence of tough-minded accountability makes competition both desirable and possible. Competition is desirable because focusing tough-minded accountability on core content will not, by itself, ensure that schools excel in other important ways. Competition allows different schools to adopt distinctive approaches that can meet the varied needs of local families. It's possible because the public will have assurances that all publicly funded schools are held to account for their performance on what matters most.

The federal No Child Left Behind Act (NCLB) has made the task of commonsense reform much easier. By requiring all states to test students in the gatekeeping subjects in grades three through eight and at least once in high school, NCLB ensures that the framework for tough-minded accountability is in place in every state. Although a commonsense reformer has real concerns about NCLB—especially its emphasis on the level at which schools are performing rather than on student growth, its mechanical emphasis on setting specific benchmarks, and its adoption of choice-based reforms that do little or nothing to promote competition—these can all be addressed in time. More importantly, NCLB has provided states with a foundation that can make commonsense reform a real possibility throughout the nation.

While NCLB has provided critical tools, however, the real changes that can enable and encourage excellence lie closer to home. Here, then, is the commonsense reform agenda.

Tough-Minded Accountability

Tough-minded accountability is the province of the states.

- States should construct straightforward standards specifying the knowledge and skills students must master in reading, writing, mathematics, and the essentials of science and history. Most states have taken these steps and are regularly assessing students in most grades, thanks in large part to the mandates of NCLB.

- Assessments must be aligned with the underlying standard, carefully designed, and rigorously tested. This may require tripling or quintupling spending on assessments. Such spending would still amount to less than 3 percent of per-pupil spending, a bargain price for high-caliber quality control.
- Assessments should focus on the gatekeeping skills. Measuring too many things dilutes the pressure on schools to ensure that all students are, at a minimum, mastering essential skills. The purpose of commonsense accountability is not to make all schools look alike or to dictate the entire curriculum but to ensure that no school is neglecting its most basic responsibilities.
- Performance must matter for students. Students ought not graduate until they have, at the very least, mastered the gatekeeping skills. This will ensure that no child is sent off without the basic preparation for adulthood.
- For educators, student learning must be the fundamental measure of performance. What matters is not the level of student achievement or the performance of any one group of students, but the rate at which students improve over time.
- States should provide readily accessible report cards that document the relative performance of each school and district and should encourage non-profit and for-profit groups that seek to disseminate this information.

Competition

Commonsense reformers do not endorse choice-based reforms because they believe charter schools or private schools are necessarily more effective than their traditional public counterparts or out of some mystical faith in parental rights. The reasoning is less grand. Allowing familial choices to steer education funding creates room for entrepreneurs and niche programs without compromising accountability.

- States should enact charter and school voucher legislation that will encourage the emergence of new schools. State departments of education should provide expertise, loan guarantees, and some start-up funding for authorized schools.
- Most or all of per-pupil spending has to follow students who change schools and the funding needs to reflect the real cost of educating the

student. It is essential that lost enrollment not vaguely impact schools but directly affect the compensation and job security of school personnel.

- States need to monitor authorization processes, academic performance, financial accounting, and school admissions practices.
- States should collect and make available information on measures of school quality that extend beyond student achievement on the gatekeeping skills. Although states need not plan to be the primary provider of this information, they should support efforts by self-interested educators to market themselves and efforts by nonprofit and for-profit parties to provide and disseminate information on school quality.
- Finally, an important caveat is that expanding autonomy and flexibility will require conscious action on the part of reformers. The modest school choice measures promoted by proponents will rarely suffice to foster meaningful competition. "Choice" alone will not necessarily increase school autonomy, personnel flexibility, decentralization, or operational freedom.

The Teaching Force

Taking advantage of accountability and competition requires a workforce prepared for that challenge.

- Licensure provisions that deter potentially qualified candidates from applying for teaching jobs ought to be stricken. This will also break the hammerlock enjoyed by teacher preparation programs, injecting new blood into the teaching force and subjecting these programs to healthy competition.
- Districts need to put quality-conscious personnel in charge of the hiring process and eliminate the excessive paperwork and lengthy delays that deter good candidates.
- Compensation strategies should recognize and reinforce commitment. Rather than paying teachers based on seniority or college credits, districts should base pay on the value of a teacher's skills, the difficulty of his assignment, his responsibilities, and the caliber of his work.
- Retirement plans should be shifted from "defined benefit" to "defined contribution" plans and changed so that educators vest much sooner. This will make the profession more attractive to a mobile population and to candidates who may not plan to teach twenty years, make it less costly for entrepreneurs to launch new programs or switch to charter schools, and reduce the number of veterans who feel trapped.

- Principals and superintendents should be empowered to terminate ineffective educators, subject to reasonable safeguards. The concept of tenure in K-12 schooling should be retired and educational employment should be made "at-will."
- The one-size-fits-all job description of the teacher should be made much more flexible. Teachers might play a variety of mentoring or administrative roles without leaving the classroom, for which they should be appropriately recognized and compensated.

Leadership

The opportunities and responsibilities of modern education management require a new breed of education leaders with the tools and experiences to address this changing world.

- The narrow notion of "instructional leadership" that requires principals to be former teachers should be retired. Educational administrators confront a number of managerial challenges and personal expertise in pedagogy or curriculum may not always be essential, especially if former teachers tend to lack other important skills.
- Licensure provisions that require leadership candidates to have taught or completed a certification program ought to be stricken. School and district leaders should be culled from as broad a talent pool as possible.
- Administrators ought to be compensated on the basis of performance, the challenge of their assignments, and the scope of their responsibilities. Terminating administrators for unacceptable performance should be a simple matter.
- Districts should cease drawing personnel in critical support positions like human resources, facilities, or information technology from the ranks of former teachers. Rather, districts should pursue trained specialists and pay them appropriately for their services.

Reinvention

None of the previous measures will serve to radically enhance school performance or efficiency unless educators have the tools to rethink and reinvent instruction and school management.

- States and districts should invest in information technology that provides information on student and teacher performance, expenditures, and personnel. Because much of this technology can be shared by many schools and districts, significant federal and state investment is appropriate. Ready access to detailed and integrated information allows managers to target support, permits teachers to address the needs of individual students, and allows school-site personnel to control budgets and hiring.

- Districts should decentralize resources to the school level to enable school personnel to take full advantage of their particular resources and familiarity with student needs. However, decentralization should not be pursued recklessly. In urban districts in particular, centralized decisions regarding instruction and professional development can make good sense.

- Districts should take advantage of technological advancements that have removed geographical barriers to the provision of schooling, support services, and professional development by exploring the possibility of contracting with specialized providers. Properly managed, such arrangements can help district leaders focus on core competencies while yielding less expensive and more effective service.

Above all, the commonsense reformer is a realist. The commonsense reformer knows that all good things do not go together, that adopting commonsense reform will entail real costs, and that some measures will require refinements or alterations with time.

The System and the Individual

The principles of accountability, flexibility, and competition may seem to unfairly burden the individual teacher or administrator. In truth, the opposite is the case. Accountable, flexible systems reward effort. In lieu of today's system, it is only those teachers in comfortable, high-achieving suburban schools where positions are in demand and where the work is pleasant who can be reasonably sure that many of their colleagues are enthusiastic and doing their fair share. One factor encouraging teachers to flee troubled schools is the desire to escape the burden of ineffective colleagues and go where they can trust that every member of the faculty will pull their own weight.

Commonsense reformers embrace tough-minded accountability and competition, in large part, because they foster an environment of cooperation and commitment. This is what the status quo reformers get wrong when they suggest that commonsense reform somehow undermines focused school cultures, faculty collaboration, professionalism, or a shared sense of mission. It's nearly impossible to build a professional culture in a school lacking in focus, devoid of leadership, dominated by ineffective teachers, or filled with teachers and leaders who feel helpless to promote effective change. When we create tools to purge the ineffective, reward hardworking employees, encourage teachers and administrators for taking on low-performing schools, and create more flexibility, we make it much easier and more appealing for committed educators to throw their hearts and souls into a school. A school culture defined by teacher apathy, isolation, or cynicism can erode the passion and undermine the effectiveness of even the most talented teachers. When others are pitching in, it's much easier to foster collegial relations and to keep schools civil, safe, and focused on student learning. When successful and hardworking teachers are visibly recognized for their efforts, it's easier for them to sustain their enthusiasm and to forge a culture where they are exemplars rather than eccentrics.

The Sequencing of Reform

One caution deserving special emphasis is that commonsense reform must not be pursued thoughtlessly or without discipline. Pursuing accountability or flexibility without regard to the other is likely to be ineffective. More to the point, though, there are better and worse ways to sequence the reforms. In districts with a dearth of strong principals, uneven teaching, and poor student performance, efforts to provide principals with more flexibility or to promote creative staffing are likely to be disastrous. In most districts, establishing clear performance goals, a coherent approach to instruction, and strong accountability mechanisms should precede efforts to decentralize and increase school-level flexibility. As district leaders establish clear expectations, cultivate the skills of the school-level leadership, and purge the weak principals, it becomes increasingly possible to safely shift authority to the schools.

Resistance to Commonsense Reform

Commonsense reform faces a number of challenges, some due to institutional barriers, others due to political opposition, and still others due to the ability of soothing status quo reforms to undercut the commitment to spiky commonsense reforms. Former President Jimmy Carter once characterized the nation's bureaucracy not as a source of fierce resistance but as a "giant

Washington marshmallow" that absorbed changes without really changing. It's hard to find a better characterization of the education establishment, with its ability to emulate the language of change while stripping it of all meaning.

The reality is that the political deck is stacked against commonsense reform. While this does not provide cause for despair, it does require commonsense reformers to survey the landscape with a clear eye. The organizations most active in education encompass the individuals who teach and run schools or work in schools of education. Teacher unions, education professors, school administrators—these influential groups all favor current arrangements that protect their positions, grant schools of education control over who is permitted to teach, limit accountability for student performance, and so on. This is not because the leaders of these groups are mean spirited but because their job is to protect the interests of their membership—whatever the larger results for schooling or America's children. They'd be irresponsible if they didn't take care of their members. We would look askance at a United Auto Workers (UAW) chief who put the interests of corporate investors ahead of those of her union members or a library director who did not try to protect his budget.

There is no need to bash the teacher unions or the various professional groups and associations. The problem is not with the unions or their allies but with arrangements in which public officials have negotiated away essential management tools while failing to create systemic pressures that counter union demands. In the private sector, as in the case of the UAW, competition at times forces the hand of union leaders. Because workers may lose their jobs if the business suffers, the union leadership has incentives to moderate demands that may harm the company—or even to take reductions or proactively seek to partner with the business if the market conditions warrant it. In fact, the UAW has today become an invaluable part of the resurgence of the U.S. automobile industry. This is not because the leaders of the UAW are especially enlightened or magnanimous, but because the imperative to protect workers has forced the unions to help the manufacturers remain healthy and profitable.

The problem with public-sector unions is that their employers do not face such competition, so they do not have the same enforced discipline. Civic leaders—some dependent on teacher unions for electoral support, others simply reluctant to criticize educators—have typically entered into tacit alliances with the educationists and unions, agreeing to push for more resources with insufficient attention to how they are spent. By forcing the public employee unions to pay more attention to performance, competition and accountability can help encourage them to adopt a more constructive stance.

Status quo reformers like to argue that there is scant evidence for the effectiveness of commonsense reform in education, conveniently omitting the fact that this is true largely because they have worked to block commonsense measures while spending hundreds of millions of dollars in public research support to profile status quo reforms in exquisite detail. Status quo reformers wave away examples from the Postal Service, higher education, industry, health care, policing, or the military as irrelevant because the circumstances are always "different from schooling."

Particularly troublesome for commonsense reformers is the ability of the status quo crowd to coopt the language of commonsense reform, and the willingness of journalists and policymakers to accept these ploys at face value. When commonsense reformers call for accountability and competition, the status quo reformers say, "Well, we're not necessarily *opposed* to those things per se, but they're a distraction. Let's focus on building community partnerships, paying educators better, and building expertise." Status quo reform proposals suggest a pleasant middle ground; they make hard-nosed reforms look uncouth, unpleasant, and unnecessary. Status quo reformers defang commonsense reform by rejecting painful measures as "uninformed" or "ideological" and offering "compromises" that increase spending while ensuring that little of substance changes. Because the status quo reformers are typically the "experts," their "moderate compromises" enjoy the imprimatur of professional consensus.

The professional education community is currently floating a number of status quo changes that have been gussied up to look like commonsense reform. We have discussed several of these along the way, but a few are worth flagging for particular attention. These measures have enjoyed particular success because proponents have sought to ape the promise of commonsense change without requiring any of the hard work.

One such proposal is the push for "procedural" or "opportunity to learn" standards. While status quo reformers reject performance-based accountability, they recognize the potency of the idea. So what they have done is repackaged rules and regulation in the guise of standards. The approach seeks to increase regulation over who can teach or lead schools, who can train educators, and how schools operate by promoting these as "standards." In each case, of course, the regulators will be either education bureaucrats, schools of education, or the professional education associations. The case of the National Board for Professional Teaching Standards, discussed in chapter 4, or the Interstate Leadership Licensure Consortium, discussed in chapter 5, are classic examples of this approach. Another wonderful illustration of the procedural standards approach was provided by the coordinator of Marylanders Against High Stakes Testing, a group of educators and parents seeking to dismantle the Maryland accountability system. Rather than measure whether students are learning, she explained that they seek to push school districts "toward school climate goals—class size, quiet places for one-on-one work with students, cheerful atmosphere, air conditioners [in the school], toilet paper, computers, books for all." Schools would be rated on the basis of reports from state inspectors and surveys of parents and students. The group is able to proclaim its commitment to the principle of accountability even as it opposes every effort to ensure that teachers are teaching or students are learning.

Another popular tack is the push to shrink class size. Notwithstanding the fact that class size has shrunk by nearly 50 percent since the early 1970s, status quo reformers can always count on the call to reduce class size to serve as an applause line. In fact, as we discussed in chapter 6, one would be hard put to find any industry that had ever increased its performance or efficiency by hiring more people to do the same amount of work. Hiring more teachers inevitably suppresses the pay of individual teachers, since each pay raise must be spread over more employees. Internationally, the evidence makes clear that nations either embrace a strategy of smaller classes and less productive, less professional teachers, or larger classes taught by more productive, more professional teachers; and that there are clear benefits to opting for the larger classes and more professional teachers. We are not going to dramatically improve teacher quality so long as we require a river of new teachers while slicing the salary pie into thinner and thinner slices. The answer is not pouring more adults into schools. It is using technology and more disciplined staffing to put students in small groups when useful, while focusing on building leaner staffs of outstanding, highly compensated faculty.

One of the most popular current reforms is the push for "small schools," schools that generally enroll 400 or fewer students.[15] The small-school movement has drawn particular support from the enormously wealthy Bill and Melinda Gates Foundation, which has poured hundreds of millions of dollars into advocating and supporting small schools. Small schools themselves are not a problem—they do make it easier to forge a cohesive culture and for teachers to bond with students. However, small schools are typically boutique schools that are effective because they are communities that both students and teachers have chosen, are run by acclaimed principals, are able to recruit elite teachers, enjoy exemptions from the staffing rules that hamstring most schools, and are able to pull together a few dozen handpicked faculty who are so passionate about their work that neither tough-minded accountability nor competition are needed to motivate them. Unfortunately, most small-school advocates do not indicate that they are aware of these unusual conditions. They too often wind up treating small size as the only variable distinguishing these schools from their larger counterparts.

As Robin Lake, associate director of the Center on Reinventing Public Education at the University of Washington, has eloquently observed, "Operators of small schools share good ideas about how to make their own schools work, but they regularly ignore the fact that they have escaped from a system that prevents others from doing the same thing. Lots of educators who decide to create small schools, often by negotiating special agreements with the local school district, do so because they don't have any confidence that they system can be changed in any real way. . . . But they act as if anyone could do what they have done. Their denial of their own special circumstances lets them ignore—and even oppose—the systemwide changes that must occur if their valuable ideas are to be widely replicated."[16]

A fourth reform advocated by the status quo reformers is simply to demand more of everything. In particular, the status quo crowd has enjoyed growing success with lawsuits that ask the courts to command state legislatures to spend more on schooling. A recent major victory from the "mo', mo', mo'" crowd came in New York during the summer of 2003, when the New York Supreme Court ruled that the New York City schools' 2001–2002 budget of more than $14,000 per pupil was not enough money to provide a minimally adequate education. The court's decision followed a drumbeat of sympathetic editorials, like that by *New York Times* columnist Bob Herbert, who cheered the "mo' money" crowd and agreed that "the heart of the problem" with New York City's schools was "the chronic lack of resources."[17]

The problem with many of these reforms is not that there is anything so *wrong* with them but that they distract us from what really matters. We all agree that schools should be pleasant and safe, that the opinions of students and parents matter, that teachers should be respected and supported, that schools should have adequate resources, and so on. For all the huffing and puffing, no one really disagrees on any of this. However, the truth is that we do not have unlimited resources to spare, schools don't fully use what they already have, and all of these minor adjustments won't do much good until we get the big problems straightened out. The status quo proposals go from distracting to harmful when educators and public officials say, "Let's hold off on that radical stuff until we see the results of [the newest flavor in status quo reform]." There is a studied refusal to accept reality or to find ways to improve an imperfect world and a desire to wish away inconvenient reality.

The Commonsense Constituency

The American system isn't particularly good at solving problems like those that hobble schooling. Skeptical of rash decisions and aware of the value of compromise, the Founders crafted American government to brake impulsive or harsh action. Changing policy is a tedious, frustrating process in which supporters of the status quo enjoy immense advantages borne of the decades they have invested in building schools of education, professional organizations, and school reform. When actions involve forcing painful, wrenching change upon an organized, vocal, sympathetic group—like educators and their allies—the odds can appear daunting.

Civic leaders have typically entered into tacit alliances with the educationists and unions, happy to be allied with a popular cause and having little desire for messy conflicts. Local philanthropists and elected officials endorse bond issues and education spending while trusting the professional educators to dream up status quo proposals for the new resources. Many well-intentioned education officials view accountability and flexibility as unnecessarily controversial distractions. Why? These officials work within the existing system, with the foundations, associations, state officials, unions, and schools of education, and merely accept the comforting confines of the status quo. Like professional education reformers, they mistakenly imagine that the way we run schools today is the way that schools have to be run—never mind that these schools are demonstrably failing our children. They see surmountable hurdles—like collective bargaining agreements or state funding mechanisms—as "impossible" barriers to reform.

As a realist, the commonsense reformer is fully aware of the barriers to reform but is confident that those who know that our schools must do better can breach the barriers and bring about real change. The commonsense reformer knows that he has three powerful cards to play: the structure of the federal system, the good sense of the public, and the ability to mobilize three critical constituencies. First, our federal system grants states and localities a great deal of leeway to try new policies. Commonsense reformers need not win massive national battles; they can work with receptive communities in states and districts where the leadership and the public is ready for commonsense change. Each time commonsense reforms are adopted, in whole or in part, it will help demonstrate that such change is possible and will weaken the hand of those who fear change.

Second, the commonsense reformer surveys the American public and is reassured by the practiced ability of Americans to eventually push through rhetoric and ideology in favor of good sense. While status quo reformers are forced to demand ever more money and heckle the public when it is reluctant to boost taxes, insist that testing doesn't measure anything worthwhile, or tell us that it's impossible to distinguish good teachers from bad ones, commonsense reformers need only remind Americans that today we don't apply to our children's schools the simple common sense that we trust in our daily lives.

I began this chapter by quoting Harry S. Truman remarking on the good sense of the American people. The rest of his thought is worth noting here. Surveying his long public life, he predicted, "When somebody gets too far out of line ... the people take charge and put him out of business." He continued, "In the long run people with common sense always take over."[18]

There are three great constituencies that can lead the commonsense charge. They have too long remained sidelined by uncertainty or distracted by status quo blandishments. The business community has too long allowed itself to be steered by status quo experts and failed to provide the commonsense leadership it is uniquely positioned to provide. The civil rights community has focused on issues of access and resource equity while being too tolerant of schools that fail minority children. Parents occupy themselves with helping their own children and supporting the local school, not realizing they are acquiescing to a culture of mediocrity that undercuts their efforts and puts their children at risk. Each of these three constituencies is practical, skeptical, and knows from hard experience and personal involvement that what matters are results. They recognize that failure is not an abstract or theoretical concept and cannot be excused or atoned for with good intentions or high-minded ideologies.

The fact is that neither educators nor the status quo constituencies are going to endorse commonsense reform. This doesn't make them villainous, despite the vitriol that some critics hurl at the teacher unions or at schools of education. It simply makes them human. It reflects their desire to insulate themselves from the uncertain and potentially painful. Granting the humanity of their opposition, however, does not mean accepting policies that maintain a culture of mediocrity in our schools. It is time for those who suffer most for this foolishness and who are able to see its flaws most clearly to rise up and be counted.

Why Business Must Lead

Business leaders bring two things to the table: first, they are the ones who will hire our graduates; second, they understand performance. As one school board member in the Brazosport, Texas, school district commented to the superintendent, just before the district launched itself on the path to dramatic improvement, "If we made excuses in our business like you guys make in your business, we'd be flat broke and out of business each year. You need to stop making excuses and find a way to teach these children."[19] That is exactly right.

Business leaders have a personal interest in the performance of our graduates, are familiar with what it takes to make organizations work, and appreciate the bracing discipline of accountability and competition. They know what it is like to run scared every day and to find the cost of incompetence so high that it puts their livelihood at stake. They know how hard it is to change routines but how important it is to do so. Business leaders, as business leaders and not as cheerleaders or community figures, are well-equipped to help tackle the challenges schools face.

I am constantly amazed by the number of tough-minded business executives who have fallen prey to the promises and pieties of the status quo reformers. Leaders who demand bottom line results from their own employees accept excuses and banalities from school reformers that they would find laughable in their own firms. Status quo reformers are simply wrong when they argue that teaching and learning are so unlike anything else that commonsense judgments about what will attract or motivate good employees, produce results, or constitute effective management do not apply. Commonsense principles are indeed the same in schooling as most anywhere else, and business leaders who abide by these principles every day in their own work should expect no less in the world of schooling.

The problem is that businesses get engaged in education out of a desire to be good corporate citizens and the last thing they want such efforts to do is provoke controversy. So they allow their internal grantmakers to partner with the status quo reformers, who are after all, full of warmth, good intentions, and promise. Fearful of being attacked as "anti-education," business leaders quietly defer to the reigning "experts" and write the checks to fund their ambitious programs.

Why have corporate leaders failed to see through the airy talk of status quo reformers and insist on commonsense reform? In the marketplace, ideas and individuals that stand the test of time have proven their merit against an impersonal benchmark. No such discipline has existed in education. Experts have succeeded at selling notions like whole language, multiple intelligences, and site-based management without any evidence that they actually serve children. When status quo reformers perched in prestigious universities or atop community partnerships have pooh-poohed commonsense reform, business leaders have too often undeservedly interpreted this as sage advice.

In other areas, like taxation and regulation and trade, business leaders are admirably tough-minded. They support reformers based on self-interested, tough-minded analysis. They regard tinkerers and vague utopians as a nuisance and neither defer to nor fund them. It is time they brought that same mind-set to education.

One irony is that business and civic leaders have long supported status quo reformers who take their spiritual direction from educators and professors disdainful of the American system and contemptuous of American business. Some leading status quo reformers have long suggested that American education is in the clutches of voracious executives who view the schools as breeding grounds for factory workers. Alfie Kohn, a best-selling education author, has declared, "There may be some sort of shadowy business conspiracy at work to turn schools into factories, but this seems unlikely if only because no such conspiracy is necessary to produce the desired results. ... To an extraordinary degree, business's wish becomes education's command."[20]

Arizona State University professor Alex Molnar, director of the institution's nationally hailed Commercialism in Education research unit, has said of corporate-sponsored educational programs: "[Some] may be less grotesque or appalling than others, but they all add up to the same thing: a river of exploitation that is running through the classrooms."[21] Author and anti-accountability crusader Susan Ohanian has referred to participants in the National Alliance of Business-Conference Board meeting on "The New Era of Education Reform" as "these thugs ... [who] are conspicuously silent about the child abuse that concerns resisters" and attacked U.S. Secretary of Education Rod Paige, a former superintendent of the year in Houston, as "crass," "stupid," and "demented."[22] The bulk of the status quo reformers are less openly vituperative, but they read the Kohns and Ohanians with delight and have made them celebrities in education circles.

Those status quo reformers who magnanimously grant that business leaders have a role in school reform want them to know their place and to understand that responsible behavior dictates that they take care not to advocate commonsense change. As Tony Wagner, professor at Harvard University Graduate School of Education has advised, "The problem is that business leaders often sound as though they know more about how to 'run the business of education' than educators do. ... The first thing business leaders—like politicians—must do is stop giving the impression that they have all the answers. Then they, too, must enter into a dialogue with educators to better understand the major issues in education. ...."[23] So there.

Business leaders must lose their hesitance. Of course, for their efforts they can expect to be pilloried by the leading lights of status quo reform. After all, in the strange cosmology of the status quo reformers, groups like the Business Roundtable and the U.S. Chamber of Commerce are regarded as threatening, shadowy cabals bent on promoting "high-stakes testing and accountability in the service of global economic competitiveness."[24] However, rather than seek to make common cause with those who regard the very principles of accountability and efficiency as morally dubious, business leaders should push to hold schools to the same commonsense discipline that makes America's economy a marvel of resilience and creativity.

Civil Rights Organizations

The nation's most troubled schools are those that serve poor minority children in the urban centers. These are the school systems where the culture of competence is no more than a distant dream, where the occasional successes of heroic educators are scattered sparks in a gloomy night.

There is a natural alliance between the civil rights community and commonsense reformers. Both are frustrated with schools that are inflexible, inefficient, and resistant to demands for improvement. Both are tired of half-hearted "reforms" that permit educators to shrug off responsibility for student learning, make it hard to remove ineffective teachers, do nothing to retain or reward good teachers, and fail to help schools tap the energy and entrepreneurial skills available in our cities.

For decades, in an alliance forged during the civil rights struggles of the 1960s, the African American community has stood alongside teacher unions, education schools, and professional education associations in a Democratic coalition. Blaming school mediocrity on insufficient spending, poverty, or racism allowed black leaders to lobby shoulder-to-shoulder for more spending and programs—but at the price of avoiding embarrassing questions about why the schools serving minority children are so often the site of such profound failure. The civil rights leadership has held their allies blameless by tracing nearly all their community's ills to racial discrimination and poverty, but this has required that they tacitly turn a blind eye to problems brought on by ineffective bureaucracies, uninspired public employees, and a culture of incompetence.

The status quo reformers have strong material incentives to oppose accountability, managerial flexibility, performance-based pay, the overhaul of teacher licensure, or competition because such changes threaten their personal interests. As a result, they have a reason to make excuses for current performance and oversell modest concessions. Black and Latino leaders are under no such compunction. African Americans are consistently more critical of school performance than is the general population. While a majority of the general population rates their local public schools as good or excellent, most black adults routinely rate schools as fair or poor. Within the black population, the gravest doubts about public schools emerge among those aged 26–35, the post-desegregation generation that lacks the affective attachment of their elders to the public system. Less than a third of blacks believe that their schools are improving, and younger blacks and low-income blacks are especially likely to report that they are getting worse.[25] In 2002, 56 percent of African American parents gave their public schools a "C" grade or lower.[26]

The old generation of civil rights leadership secured "access" to schooling. The challenge for the new generation is to ensure that their childrens' schools are effective ones. Although fed up with mediocre urban schools, African Americans are reluctant to abandon their traditional allies to align with conservative school voucher proponents of suspect motives. As one member of the NAACP leadership in Milwaukee remarked to me, "These Republican types, the ones in business and the suburbs, never used to care about black children. Now they do? I don't buy it. They're after something." The civil rights leadership needs a reform strategy that serves children without placing undue faith in the good intentions of conservative reformers. Commonsense reform fits the bill.

The fact that bad educators cannot be fired or good ones rewarded, that educators have not been held accountable for student learning, that entrepreneurship has been stifled and inefficiency tolerated—these are all the products of policies and contractual agreements sought by the allies of black America. A new generation of black and Latino youth has come of age in an era when avenues of success are open to them but where those who wish to return to their communities to aid the next generation often find the door barricaded by regulation, red tape, and lethargic bureaucracies.

Parents

Parents and their children enjoy the fruits of commonsense reform and bear the costs of the status quo. Parents who work at jobs where their performance is evaluated every six months or every year understand what responsibility entails and are well-suited to recognize when their children are being ill-served. However, parents are too often unorganized. When organized, they are prone to defer to those status quo "experts" who have complicated explanations for why commonsense solutions won't help to improve schools. It is time for the intimidation to stop. Making commonsense reform a reality requires parents to play a more prominent role in changing the education system, through active involvement in their local schools and through supporting those candidates, whether for local, state, or national office, who have a vision of commonsense reform.

That parents are rarely organized is not all that surprising. They lead busy lives, the systemic problems besetting public education are complex, and any given individual can easily believe that his or her efforts are unlikely to make any difference. After all, parents do not have unions and other organized groups to press for their interests. Those parents with the economic resources to make a choice do have power, whether in choosing to move into or out of a given district, or by sending their children to private schools. But absent a system that rewards schools and districts for such choices, the effect of atomized decisions on living location or private schooling is to leave the least advantaged portions of our population stuck with dismal schools and little opportunity for their children to succeed.

Parents are also far more reticent than they ought to be when it comes to advocating commonsense reform. Too often, when told that teacher performance can't be systematically evaluated or that we shouldn't pay educators on the quality of their work, parents scratch their head but then set aside their doubts and assent to the presumed wisdom of the educational professionals. This is a mistake. In much of life, old-fashioned horse sense is the most reliable guide. When stockbrokers told clients to buy overpriced technology stocks during the internet boom, those investors who trusted the "experts" rather than their own good sense were the ones who got burned. When your doctor advises you that she doesn't believe in laboratory results, you don't have to be a medical expert to suspect something is wrong. When education "experts" tell us that we shouldn't worry too much about whether students pass reading tests or that the performance of teachers cannot be judged, we should treat their warnings with similar skepticism. When someone tells you to trust them rather than your common sense, you are almost always well-served by taking a long, hard look. Even if you are not an expert, or, especially if you're not, you should look askance at those experts who would have you believe that simple truths don't hold in their domain.

In pushing for reform, parents must distinguish between those who set policy and those who implement programs. Elected public officials are positioned to set *policy*, but are poorly situated to design or push particular *programs*. Policy is the big-picture stuff—it says what a public agency is supposed to do, whom it will serve, how its performance will be measured, and what the consequences are of success or failure. Government is pretty good at laying down broad outlines for public enterprises—after all, no one else can. What are schools expected to do? What are the requirements for firing or hiring? How are children to be assigned to schools? How will success be recognized and rewarded, and how will ineffectiveness be identified and addressed? Only our elected officials have the authority to set these kinds of rules for our public schools.

Programs, on the other hand, are where educators determine what curriculum or pedagogy to use, how to manage a school, or how to choose whom to hire. Rule-bound bureaucrats are poorly equipped for these decisions. These calls should be left to locally attuned educators and school overseers, who must then be held accountable for the quality of the work they do.

What, exactly, should business leaders, civil rights leaders, and parents do to promote commonsense reform? If business leaders are to do more than convene commissions or write checks, if civil rights leaders are to adopt a new seriousness about educational opportunity, if parents are to become educational advocates, what should be their agenda? They should start with the following six demands:

1. Schools should be sure to first address the essentials by ensuring that every single student is, at an absolute minimum, mastering the gatekeeping skills of reading, writing, mathematics, and develops a basic familiarity with science and history.
2. States should adopt accountability systems that measure the performance of schools and districts on gatekeeper skills and hold school and district leaders accountable for the performance of their charges.
3. States should promote aggressive charter school or voucher policies that will permit new providers to open their doors and foster meaningful competition.
4. States should provide readily accessible report cards that document the relative performance of each school and district and should encourage nonprofit and for-profit groups that seek to disseminate this information.
5. District officials should reward teachers and administrators for excellence, taking on challenging assignments, possessing critical skills, and for taking on responsibilities that exceed their traditional role.

6. Districts should decentralize, rethink their practices, and invest thought-fully in information technology so that educators are better able to devote their energy and expertise to serving students.

A Look Ahead . . .

In *A Streetcar Named Desire*, Tennessee Williams's Southern belle Blanche Dubois famously purred, "I've always relied upon the kindness of strangers." This strategy didn't turn out so well even for the gorgeous Blanche. It's an even worse deal for our children, especially the neediest and most vulnerable among them. It is through our schools that a democratic nation invites its newest generation into the society, prepares them to assume the rights and responsibilities of citizenship, and equips them to pursue their chosen path. A responsibility of that magnitude requires more than happy thoughts. Kindness and charity are fine things, but we owe our young an education that consists of more than protestations of compassion.

Politically, commonsense reform can be a bitter pill for reformers to swallow. Conservative reformers have too often shied away from some harsh truths—that school choice does not automatically produce competition or flexibility, that federal accountability can impose rules but not excellence. They have often spent more time bashing the teacher unions or schools of education than promoting sensible remedies. Meanwhile, liberals have refused to stand up to the teacher unions, the schools of education, and the utopians demanding more money and more time. They have been unwilling or unable to call for the kind of tough-minded accountability, focus on performance, and relaxation of stifling regulations that can make commonsense reform work.

In the name of compassion, status quo reformers have fought commonsense measures while tinkering and dreaming of a grandiose new social order. While the status quo reformers claim to speak for the unfortunate, the children who suffer the most for their foolishness are those most in need. Commonsense reformers must avoid the temptation to solicit the blessing of "compassionate" status quo reformers and be willing to declare it a hollow compassion that sacrifices children on the altar of good intentions.

As would-be commonsense reformers have tackled individual issues like accountability or choice or teacher quality, they have too often done so by embracing only the rhetoric of commonsense change or by pursuing measures in a disjointed fashion that ignored necessary safeguards. In fact, many of the political and technical problems that have plagued efforts to promote accountability or school choice or alternative teacher licensure exist precisely because reformers are trying to address one piece of a dysfunctional system without reconfiguring the system itself. The answer is not this adjustment or that reform, but creating an entire system of schooling that will demand and embrace a culture of competence.

Would-be commonsense reformers are too often apologetic for advocating tough-minded measures, challenging romanticized depictions of teachers, or using words like "efficiency." The truth is that tough-minded commonsense reformers have nothing to apologize for. Well-meaning efforts to make competition, accountability, and workforce reform more appealing have produced toothless measures that leave the culture of incompetence unscathed. Commonsense reformers cannot allow themselves to be enticed by airy promises of partnership with the status quo reformers; they must focus on tipping the world so that the experts and educators are oriented by a culture of competence. It is precisely at that moment that a new, fruitful collaboration of the commonsense and the status quo reformers will become possible.

It is time that we step back and look forward. It is only when the public sees past the facile appeals of the status quo reformers and recognizes their fundamental lack of seriousness that we will make progress on providing all our children a brighter future. It is not until the politicians see the public's resolve that they will be willing to take on the status quo crowd. In a world as complex and diverse as ours, it is easy for simple truths to get lost. Simple truths like responsibility, accountability, merit, and opportunity. Real school reform must begin by resurfacing those truths.

Notes

CHAPTER 1

1. Paul Peterson, "Little Gain in Student Achievement," *Our Schools and Our Future*, ed. Paul Peterson (Palo Alto, CA: Hoover Institution Press, 2003).
2. Jay P. Greene and Greg Forster, "Public High School Graduation and College Readiness Rates in the United States," *Education Working Paper* 3 (September 2003). Center for Civic Innovation, Manhattan Institute.
3. Ibid.
4. National Center for Education Statistics, *The Nation's Report Card* (Washington, D.C.: U.S. Department of Education, 2003).
5. Ibid.
6. National Center for Education Statistics, 2003, available at: http://nces.ed.gov/nationsreportcard/reading/results2002/districtachieve.asp.
7. Jean Johnson and Ann Duffett, *Where Are We Now? 12 Things You Need to Know about Public Opinion and Public Schools* (New York: Public Agenda, 2003), pp. 22–23.
8. Namjikim Steinemann, Edward B. Fiske and Victoria Sackett, "Asia in the Schools: Preparing Young Americans for Today's Interconnected World," *A Report by the National Commission in Asia in the Schools* (New York: Asia Society, 2001).
9. National Center for Education Statistics, *The Nation's Report Card* (Washington, D.C.: U.S. Department of Education, 2001).
10. Monty Neill, "Leaving Children Behind," *Phi Delta Kappan* 85, no. 3 (2003): 225–228, p. 226.
11. Marilyn Cochran-Smith, "Sometimes It's Not About the Money," *Journal of Teacher Education* 54, no. 5 (2003): 371–375, p. 374.
12. Michael Fullan, *Change Forces: Probing the Depths of Educational Reform* (New York: Falmer Press, 1993), p. 6.
13. In Houston, Texas, between January 2001 and January 2003, the district sought to remove teachers for admittedly "viewing morbid, lewd, and objectionable pictures on a classroom computer," for being taped "punching a female student three times," and for admitting to the "use and possession of drugs on campus." In each case, it took the district nine or more months to proceed through the

termination process. See report prepared by the Office of Business Services, *Sample Timelines for Various Cases* (Houston, TX: Houston Independent School District, 2003).

14. Fullan, *Change Forces*, p. 5.

15. Thomas J. Peters and Robert Waterman, *In Search of Excellence* (New York: Warner Books, 1982), p. 72.

16. David C. Berliner and Bruce J. Biddle, *The Manufactured Crisis: Myths, Fraud, and the Attack on America's Public Schools* (Cambridge, MA: Perseus Books, 1995), p. 348.

17. Carl Vuono quoted in Bob Woodward, *The Commanders* (New York: Pocket Books, 1991), pp. 129–130.

18. The classic depiction of how teachers and students reach accommodations in which all can readily agree to float along in a pleasant, if largely ineffective, routine is still Theodore Sizer's *Horace's Compromise: The Dilemma of an American High School* (Boston: Houghton Mifflin, 1984).

19. Louise Stoll and Kate Myers, introduction to *No Quick Fixes: Perspectives on Schools in Difficulty* (Philadelphia: Falmer Press, 1998), pp. 1–14, p. 2.

20. Jeff Archer, "N.Y.C. Administrators' Contract Lacks Major Changes," *Education Week*, April 30, 2003, p. 5.

21. M. Gail Jones, Brett D. Jones, and Tracy Y. Hargrove, *The Unintended Consequences of High-Stakes Testing* (Lanham, MD: Rowman & Littlefield, 2003), p. 5.

22. Ibid.

23. Vincent Ferrandino and Gerald Tirozzi, "Principals' Perspective: The Sad State of the States," *Education Week*, March 5, 2003, paid advertisement.

24. Reg Weaver, keynote address to the NEA, New Orleans, LA, July 3, 2003.

25. David W. Murray, "Waiting for Utopia," *Education Next* 2, no. 2 (2002): 73–78.

26. Jean Anyon, *Ghetto Schooling: A Political Economy of Urban Educational Reform* (New York: Teachers College Press, 1997), p. 13.

27. David Berliner, "Averages That Hide the True Extremes," *Washington Post*, Outlook section, January 28, 2001.

28. Cochran-Smith, "Sometimes It's Not About the Money," p. 374.

29. Jonathan Kozol, *Savage Inequalities: Children in America's Schools* (New York: Crown Publishers, 1991), p. 205.

30. Craig D. Jerald, *Dispelling the Myth Revisited* (Washington, D.C.: Education Trust, 2001).

31. Samuel Casey Carter, *No Excuses: Lessons from 21 High-Performing, High-Poverty Schools* (Washington, D.C.: Heritage Foundation Press, 2000).

32. Willam G. Howell and Paul E. Peterson, *The Education Gap: Vouchers and Urban Schools* (Washington, D.C.: Brookings Institution Press), p. 59.

33. There is an extensive and sophisticated tradition of research on parochial schools. See, for instance, Anthony S. Bryk, Valerie E. Lee, and Peter B. Holland, *Catholic Schools and the Common Good* (Cambridge, MA: Harvard University

Press, 1993). Also see Derek Neal, "What Have We Learned About the Benefits of Private Schooling?" *Economic Policy Review* 4, no. 1 (1998): 79–86.

34. Gerald Bracey, *What You Should Know about the War against America's Public Schools* (Boston: Allyn and Bacon, 2003), pp. 33–34.

35. Peter Schrag, *Final Test: The Battle for Adequacy in America's Schools* (New York: New Press, 2003).

36. "Expenditure on Educational Institutions per Student (2000)," *Education at a Glance: OECD Indicators 2003*, Table B1.1, p. 197. The specific figures for the various countries were (primary and secondary): Germany $4,198 and $6,826, France $4,486 and $7,636, Japan $5,507 and $6,266, United Kingdom $3,877 and $5,991, Sweden $6,336 and $6,339, Belgium $4,310 and $6,889, Finland $4,317 and $6,094, and South Korea $3,155 and $4,069.

37. Myron Lieberman and Charlene Haar, *Public Education as a Business: Real Costs and Accountability* (Lanham, MD: Scarecrow Press, 2003), p. 45.

38. The New York and Los Angeles figures are from William G. Ouchi, *Making Schools Work: A Revolutionary Plan to Get Your Children the Education They Need* (New York: Simon and Schuster, 2003), p. 10.

39. Buckeye Institute for Public Policy Solutions, *Public Choices, Private Costs: An Analysis of Spending and Achievement in Ohio Public Schools* (Columbus, OH: Buckeye Institute for Public Policy Solutions, 1998).

40. Caroline Hoxby, "What Has Changed and What Has Not," *Our Schools and Our Future*, ed. Paul E. Peterson (Palo Alto, CA: Hoover Institution Press, 2003), pp. 73–110.

41. Jon Fullerton, "Mounting Debt," *Education Next* 4, no. 1 (2004): 11–19.

42. Data available from the National Center for Education Statistics, *Digest of Education Statistics, 2002* (Washington, D.C.: U.S. Department of Education, 2003).

43. Erick A. Hanushek and Steven G. Rivkin, "Understanding the Twentieth-Century Growth in U.S. School Spending," *Journal of Human Resources* 32, no. 1 (1997): 35–68.

44. National Center for Education Statistics, *Digest of Education Statistics, 2000* (Washington, D.C.: U.S. Department of Education, 2001), Table 80.

45. Ouchi, *Making Schools Work*, p. 10.

46. Hoxby, "What Has Changed," p. 107.

47. National Center for Education Statistics, *Digest of Education Statistics, 2001* (Washington, D.C.: U.S. Department of Education, 2002), Table 82.

48. Dale Russakoff and Linda Perlstein, "States Cutting School Funding," *Washington Post*, March 15, 2003, p. A1.

49. Ibid.

50. Steve Farkas, Jean Johnson, and Ann Duffett, *Rolling Up Their Sleeves: Superintendents and Principals Talk About What's Needed to Fix Public Schools* (Washington, D.C.: Public Agenda, 2003), p. 11.

51. Alan Richard and David J. Hoff, "Schools Trim Fiscal Fat, and Then Some," *Education Week*, September 24, 2003, p. 1.

52. Ibid.

53. Jacqueline L. Salmon, "American Red Cross to Cut 231 Jobs," *Washington Post*, June 6, 2003, p. A10.

54. Scott Smallwood, "TIAA-CREF Cuts 500 Jobs," *Chronicle of Higher Education*, October 3, 2003, p. A27.

55. Paul Farhi, "Public TV Learns to Do Without," *Washington Post*, September 15, 2003, p. C1.

56. Jamilah Evelyn, "Tuition Is Up 11.5% at Community Colleges," *Chronicle of Higher Education*, September 26, 2003, p. A43.

57. Stephanie Armour, "Outlook for Pay Raises: 'Bleak,'" *USA Today*, September 23, 2003, p. 1A.

58. Chester E. Finn, "Budget Woes and Whines," *American Experiment Quarterly* 6, no. 2 (Summer 2003): 90–92, p. 92.

59. Ouchi, *Making Schools Work*, p. 10.

60. Lawrence W. Lezotte, *Correlates of Effective Schools: The First and Second Generation* (Okemos, MI: Effective Schools Products, Ltd., 1991).

61. New American Schools, *Exploring Comprehensive School Reform* (Arlington, VA: New American Schools, 2001).

62. National Center for Education Statistics, *Teaching Mathematics in Seven Countries: Results from the TIMMS 1999 Video Study* (Washington, D.C.: U.S. Department of Education, 2003).

63. For one of the most perceptive discussions of why it is so hard to replicate individual successes, see Richard Elmore, "Getting to Scale with Good Educational Practice," *Harvard Education Review* 66 (1996): 1–26.

CHAPTER 2

1. Michael Apple, "Foreword," in Linda McNeil, *The Contradictions of School Reform: Educational Costs of Standardized Testing* (New York: Routledge, 2000), p. xvii.

2. Tony Wagner, *Making the Grade: Reinventing America's Schools* (New York: RoutledgeFalmer, 2003), p. 142.

3. Claudia Meek, "Classroom Crisis: It's About Time," *Phi Delta Kappan* 84, no. 8 (April 2003): 592–595.

4. For a colorful portrayal of the opposition to accountability, see Richard P. Phelps, *Kill the Messenger: The War on Standardized Testing* (Somerset, NJ: Transaction Publishers, 2003).

5. Mickey VanDerwerker, "Succeeding on Tests Isn't Accountability," *Education Week*, February 26, 2003, p. 29.

6. David W. Murray, "Waiting for Utopia," *Education Next* 2, no. 2 (2002): 73–78, p. 74.

7. Susan Ohanian, "Capitalism, Calculus, and Conscience," *Phi Delta Kappan* 8, no. 10 (June 2003): 736–747, p. 738.

8. Ibid, p. 747.

9. Paul Freire, *Pedagogy of the Oppressed* (New York: Seabury Press, 1970).

10. Jean Johnson and Ann Duffett with Jackie Vine and Leslie Moye, *Where We Are Now* (New York: Public Agenda, 1999), pp. 13–14.

11. John Gehring, "Mass. Chief Steers Steady Course Through Conflicts," *Education Week*, March 5, 2003, p. 18.

12. M. Gail Jones, Brett D. Jones, and Tracy Y. Hargrove, *The Unintended Consequences of High-Stakes Testing* (Lanham, MD: Rowan & Littlefield, 2003), p. 24.

13. Andy Baumgartner quoted in Peter Temes, *Against School Reform (and in Praise of Great Teaching)* (Chicago: Ivan, December 2002), p. 202.

14. Terry Moe, *Schools, Vouchers, and the American Public* (Washington, D.C.: Brookings Institution Press, 2001).

15. Joseph Pedulla, Lisa Abrams, George Madaus, Michael Russell, Miguel Ramos, and Jing Miao, *Perceived Effects of State-Mandated Testing Programs on Teaching and Learning* (Boston: National Board on Educational Testing and Public Policy at Boston College, 2003).

16. Ludger Woessman, "International Evidence of Accountability," in *No Child Left Behind? The Politics and Practice of School Accountability*, ed. Paul E. Peterson and Martin R. West (Washington, D.C.: Brookings Institution Press, 2003).

17. Margaret E. Raymond and Eric A. Hanushek, "High-Stakes Research," *Education Next* 3, no. 3 (2003): 48–55.

18. Martin Carnoy and Susanna Loeb, "Does External Accountability Affect Student Outcomes? A Cross-State Analysis," *Educational Evaluation and Policy Analysis* 24, no. 4 (2002): 305–331.

19. For a deconstruction of the best-known example of such work, see Raymond and Hanushek, "High-Stakes Research."

20. See the collection of papers in their edited volume, *Raising Standards or Raising Barriers? Inequality and High-Stakes Testing in Public Education*, ed. Gary Orfield and Mindy L. Kornhaber (New York: Century Foundation, 2001).

21. Californians for Justice, *First Things First: Why We Must Stop Punishing Students and Fix California's Schools* (Oakland, CA: Californians for Justice, 2003), p. 27.

22. See, for example, John H. Bishop, Ferran Mane, Michael Bishop, and Joan Moriarty, "The Role of End-of-Course Exams and Minimum Competency Exams in Standards-Based Reforms," in *Brookings Papers on Education Policy 2001*, ed. Diane Ravitch (Washington, D.C.: Brookings Institution Press, 2001).

23. Jean Johnson and Ann Duffett, *Reality Check 2002* (New York: Public Agenda, 2002).

24. Alfie Kohn, *The Case Against Standardized Testing* (Portsmouth, NH: Heineman, 2000), pp. 20, 38–39.

25. Kim Marshall, "A Principal Looks Back," *Phi Delta Kappan* 85, no. 2 (October 2003): 104–113.

26. Amber Winkler, "Division in the Ranks: Standardized Testing Lines Drawn Between New and Veteran Teachers," *Phi Delta Kappan* 84, no. 3 (November 2002): 219–225.

27. Frederick M. Hess, "Reform, Resistance . . . Retreat? The Predictable Policies of Accountability in Virginia," in *Brooking Papers on Educational Policy 2002*, ed. Diane Ravitch (Washington, D.C.: Brookings Institution Press, 2002).

28. Thomas J. Kane and Douglas O. Staiger, "Volatility in School Test Scores: Implications for Test-based Accountability Systems," in *Brooking Papers on Educational Policy 2002*, ed. Diane Ravitch (Washington, D.C.: Brookings Institution Press, 2002). Also see Jane Hannaway, "Accountability, Assessment, and Performance Issues: We've Come a Long Way, or Have We?" in *American Educational Governance on Trial: Change and Challenges*, ed. William L. Boyd and Debra Miretzky (Chicago: University of Chicago Press, 2003).

29. A useful discussion of the kinds of data that school districts should collect is provided by a study of five exemplary school districts conducted by the Learning First Alliance, *Beyond Islands of Excellence* (Washington, D.C.: Learning First Alliance, 2003), pp. 19–22.

30. For a more extended discussion, see Frederick M. Hess, "The Case for Being Mean," *Educational Leadership* 61, no. 3 (November 2003): 22–26.

31. Michael D. Rettig, Laurie L. McCullough, Karen Santos, and Chuck Watson, "A Blueprint for Increasing Student Achievement," *Educational Leadership* 61, no. 3 (November 2003): 71–76, p. 73.

32. Linda Darling-Hammond, "What's at Stake in High Stakes Testing?" *The Brown University Child and Adolescent Behavior Letter*, January 2002.

33. Stela B. Holcombe, "High Stakes: School Leaders Weigh in on Testing, Reform, and the Goal of Educating Every American Child," *Ed.* 46, no. 1 (2002): 20.

34. David Driscoll quoted in Gehring, "Mass. Chief Steers Steady Course," p. 18.

35. McNeil, *The Contradictions of School Reform*, p. 203.

36. Alex Berenson, *The Number: How the Drive for Quarterly Earnings Corrupted Wall Street and Corporate America* (New York: Random House, 2003).

37. Alan Richard, "GAO Says Cost for State Tests All in How Questions Asked," *Education Week*, May 21, 2003, p. 19.

38. Caroline Hoxby, "The Cost of Accountability," in *School Accountability*, ed. Williamson Evers and Herbert Walberg (Palo Alto, CA: Hoover Institution Press, 2002).

39. Brian A. Jacob and Stephen D. Levitt, "To Catch a Thief," *Education Next* 4, no.1 (2004): 69–75, p. 75.

40. Audrey L. Amrein and David C. Berliner, "High-Stakes Testing, Uncertainty, and Student Learning," *Education Policy Analysis Archives* 10, no. 18 (2002): electronic journal available at http://epaa.asu.edu/epaa/.

41. For more extensive discussion, see Frederick M. Hess, "Refining or Retreating? High-Stakes Accountability in the States," in *No Child Left Behind? The Politics*

and Practice of School Accountability, ed. Paul E. Peterson and Martin R. West (Washington, D.C.: Brookings Institution Press, 2003).

42. Web communication.

43. See David B. Tyack and William Tobin, "The Grammar of Schooling: Why Has It Been So Hard to Change," *American Educational Research Journal* 31 (1994): 453–479.

44. Al Shanker quoted in Kati Haycock, "The Elephant in the Living Room." Paper prepared for Brookings Papers on Education Conference "The Teachers We Need" held at the Brookings Institution, Washington, D.C., May 21–22, 2003, p. 27.

CHAPTER 3

1. John Chubb and Terry Moe, *Politics, Markets, and America's Schools* (Washington, D.C.: Brookings Institution Press, 1990).

2. For a careful analysis of the data on choice-based reform and a summary of the case for the benefits of providing school choice, see, William G. Howell and Paul E. Peterson, *The Education Gap: Vouchers and Urban Schools* (Washington, D.C.: Brookings Institution Press, 2002). For a critique of the Howell and Peterson analysis, see Alan Krueger and Pei Zhu, "Another Look at the New York City School Voucher Experiment." Presented at the annual conference of the American Association for Policy Analysis and Management, Washington, D.C., November 5, 2003.

3. For an extensive discussion of how competition works in education, see chapters 1–3 of Frederick M. Hess, *Revolution at the Margins* (Washington, D.C.: Brookings Institution Press, 2002).

4. Frederick M. Hess and Patrick McGuinn, "Muffled by the Din: The Competitive Non-Effects of the Cleveland Voucher Program," *Teachers College Record* 104, no. 4 (2002): 727–764.

5. National Working Commission on Choice in K-12 Education, *School Choice: Doing It the Right Way Makes a Difference* (Washington, D.C.: Brookings Institution Press, 2003), p. 3.

6. Caroline M. Hoxby, "If Families Matter Most," in *A Primer on America's Schools*, ed. Tery M. Moe (Stanford, CA: Hoover Institution Press, 2001), p. 105.

7. Dale McDonald, *United States Catholic Elementary and Secondary School Statistics 1999–2000* (Washington, D.C.: National Catholic Educational Association, 2000). Also see National Center for Education Statistics, *Digest of Education Statistics, 2001* (Washington, D.C.: U.S. Department of Education, 2002).

8. See Anthony Bryk, Peter Holland, and Valerie Lee, *Catholic Schooling and the Common Good* (Cambridge, MA: Harvard University Press, 1993). Also see Derek Neal, "What Have We Learned About the Benefits of Private Schooling?" *Federal Reserve Bank of New York* 4, no. 1 (1998): 79–86.

9. National Center for Education Statistics, *Homeschooling in the United States, 1999* (Washington, D.C.: U.S. Department of Education, 2001).

10. National Center for Education Statistics, *Public School Student, Staff, and Graduate Counts by State, School Year 2001–02* (Washington, D.C.: U.S. Department of Education, May 2003). Available at http://nces.ed.gov/pubs2003/snf_report03/#1.

11. For a comprehensive overview of the status of charter schooling and school vouchers across the United States, see Krista Kafer, *School Choice 2003* (Washington, D.C.: Heritage Foundation Press, 2003).

12. Perhaps the best single overview of charter schooling today is provided in *The Charter School Landscape*, ed. Sandra Vergari (Pittsburgh: University of Pittsburgh Press, 2002).

13. National Governor's Conference quoted in Joseph Viteritti, *Choosing Equality* (Washington, D.C.: Brookings Institution Press, 2000).

14. David Osborne, "Healthy Competition," *New Republic*, October 4, 1999, pp. 31–33.

15. John Merrifield, *The School Choice Wars* (Lanham, MD: Scarecrow Press, 2001), p. 35.

16. Steve Farkas, Jean Johnson, and Anthony Foleno with Ann Duffett and Patrick Foley, *On Thin Ice* (New York: Public Agenda, 1999), p. 19.

17. Frederick M. Hess, "The Work Ahead," *Education Next* 1, no. 4 (Winter 2001): 14–19.

18. See Caroline M. Hoxby, "School Choice and School Productivity (Or, Could School Choice Be a Tide That Lifts All Boats?)," NBER Working Paper Number 8873 (Cambridge, MA: National Bureau of Economic Research, 2002).

19. Frederick M. Hess, Robert Maranto and Scott Milliman, "Little Districts in Big Trouble: How Four Arizona School Systems Responded to Charter Competition," *Teachers College Record* 103, no. 6 (2001): 1102–1124.

20. Chester E. Finn, Bruno V. Manno, and Gregg Vanourek, *Charter Schools in Action: Renewing Public Education* (Princeton, NJ: Princeton University Press, 2000), p. 152.

21. National Working Commission on Choice in K-12 Education, *School Choice: Doing It the Right Way*, p. 25.

22. For a review of the evidence from several studies, see Paul E. Peterson, "Choice in American Education," in *A Primer on America's Schools*, ed. Terry M. Moe (Stanford, CA: Hoover Institution, 2001).

23. Terry Moe, *Schools, Vouchers, and the American Public* (Washington, D.C.: Brookings Institution Press, 2001), p. 62.

24. Hess, *Revolution at the Margins*, pp. 30–52.

25. For an excellent overview of what we currently know about families and how they use information in making educational choices, see Mark Schneider, "Information and Choice in Educational Privatization," in *Privatizing Education*, ed. Henry M. Levin (Boulder, CO: Westview, 2001).

26. Mark Schneider, Paul Teske, and Melissa Marshall, *Choosing Schools: Consumer Choice and the Quality of American Schools* (Princeton, NJ: Princeton University Press, 2000), p. 268.

27. Quentin Quade, *Financing Education* (New Brunswick, NJ: Transaction Publishers, 1996), p. 158.

28. Louann Bierlein Palmer and Rebecca Gau, *Charter School Authorizing: Are States Making the Grade?* (Washington, D.C.: Fordham Institute Press, 2003).

29. Paul Hill, "Charter School Districts," *Backgrounder* (Progressive Policy Institute), May 16, 2001.

30. Bruce Manno, "Yellow Flag," *Education Next* 3, no. 1 (Winter 2003): 16–22.

31. Moe, *Schools, Vouchers, and the American Public.*

32. Michael Engel, *The Struggle for Control of Public Education: Market Ideology vs. Democratic Values* (Philadelphia, PA: Temple University Press, 2000).

33. Amy Stuart Wells, "The Sociology of School Choice: Why Some Win and Others Lose in the Educational Marketplace," in Edith Rassell and Richard Rothstein, *School Choice: Examining the Evidence* (Washington, D.C.: Economic Policy Institute, 1993).

34. Schneider, *Choosing Schools.*

35. Jay P. Greene, "Civic Values in Public and Private Schools," in *Learning from School Choice*, ed. Paul Peterson and Bryan Hassel (Washington, D.C.: Brookings Institution Press, 1998).

36. Lee Anderson, Nancy Adelman, Kara Finnigan, Lynyonne Cotton, Mary Beth Donnelly, and Tiffany Price, *A Decade of Public Charter Schools, Evaluation of the Public Charter Schools Program: 2000–2001 Evaluation Report* (Washington, D.C.: SRI International, 2002).

37. Paul T. Hill with Kacey Guin, "Baselines for Assessment of Choice Programs," in *Choice With Equity*, ed. Paul T. Hill (Stanford, CA: Hoover Institution, 2002), p. 48.

38. Patrick J. Wolf, "School Choice and Civic Values: A Review of the Evidence." Paper delivered at the annual meeting of the American Political Science Association, Boston, August 2002.

39. George Whalin quoted in Margaret Pressler, "Buy, Bye," *Washington Post*, March 23, 2003, p. H5.

40. Eric Hanushek, *Making Schools Work: Improving Performance and Controlling Costs* (Washington, D.C.: Brookings Institution Press, 1994), p. 114.

41. Tom Loveless, *Brown Center Annual Report on American Education* (Washington, D.C.: Brookings Institution Press, 2003).

42. Mary Graham, *Information as Risk Regulation: Lessons from Experience* (Cambridge, MA: Institute for Government Innovation, 2001).

43. Edward B. Fiske and Helen F. Ladd, *When Schools Compete: A Cautionary Tale* (Washington, D.C.: Brookings Institution Press, 2001).

44. Peter Brimelow, *The Worm in the Apple* (New York: HarperCollins, 2003), p. 144. Also see Andrew J. Coulson, *Market Education: The Unknown History* (New Brunswick, NJ: Transaction, 1999), p. 391.

45. One of the most helpful discussions of this issue is provided by Jeffrey Henig, *Rethinking School Choice* (Princeton, NJ: Princeton University Press, 1994).

CHAPTER 4

1. Vivian Troen and Katherine C. Boles, *Who's Teaching Your Children?* (New Haven, CT: Yale University Press, 2003), p. 5.

2. Dan Goldhaber, "The Mystery of Good Teaching," *Education Next* 2, no. 1 (2002): 50–55.

3. Caroline Hoxby, "What Has Changed and What Has Not," *Our Schools and Our Future*, ed. Paul Peterson (Stanford, CA: Hoover Institution Press, 2003), pp. 73–110, p. 107.

4. Ruth Mitchell and Patte Barth, "Not Good Enough: A Content Analysis of Teacher Licensing Examinations," *Thinking K-12* 3, no. 1 (Washinton, D.C.: Education Trust, 1999).

5. Richard Cohen, "Houston's Disappearing Dropouts," *Washington Post*, September 4, 2003, p. A21.

6. F. Howard Nelson, Rachel Drown, and Jewell C. Gould, *Survey & Analysis of Teacher Salary Trends 2001* (Washington, D.C.: American Federation of Teachers, 2002).

7. No Author Identified, "Prime Numbers," *Chronicle of Higher Education*, September 26, 2003, p. A9.

8. Richard Vedder, "Comparable Worth," *Education Next* 3, no. 3 (2003): 14–19, p. 16.

9. Calculation uses figures from Vedder, "Comparable Worth," p. 16, and from Michael Podgursky, "Fringe Benefits," *Education Next* 3, no. 3 (2003): 71–76, p. 72 (Fig. 1).

10. Podgursky, "Fringe Benefits," pp. 71–76, p. 72.

11. Vedder, "Comparable Worth," pp. 14–19, p. 16.

12. Ibid, pp. 14–19.

13. National Center for Education Statistics, *Schools and Staffing Survey, 1999–2000. Overview of the Data for Public, Private, Public Charter, and Bureau of Indian Affairs Elementary and Secondary Schools* (Washington, D.C.: U.S. Department of Education, 2002). Available at http://nces.ed.gov/pubs2002/2002313.pdf.

14. Mike Podgursky, "Improving Academic Performance in U.S. Public Schools: Why Teacher Licensing is (Almost) Irrelevant." Paper prepared for conference "A Qualified Teacher in Every Classroom" held at the American Enterprise Institute, Washington, D.C., October 23–24, 2003, p. 41.

15. H. Carl McCall quoted in Peter Schrag, *Final Test: The Battle for Adequacy in America's Schools* (New York: New Press, 2003), p. 202.

16. Susan Moore Johnson, *Teachers at Work* (New York: Basic Books, 1990).

17. Carolyn Kelley, Allan Odden, Anthony Milanowski, and Herbert Heneman III, *The Motivation Effects of School-Based Performance Awards* (Philadelphia, PA: Consortium for Policy Research in Education, 2000).

18. David Steiner, "Preparing Teachers: Are American Schools of Education Up to the Task?" Paper prepared for conference "A Qualified Teacher in Every Classroom" held at the American Enterprise Institute, Washington, D.C., October 23–24, 2003, pp. 33–34.

19. David Leal, "Assessing Traditional Teacher Preparation: Evidence from a Survey of Graduate and Undergraduate Programs." Paper prepared for conference "A Qualified Teacher in Every Classroom" held at the American Enterprise Institute, Washington, D.C., October 23–24, 2003.

20. Goldhaber, "The Mystery of Good Teaching," pp. 50–55.

21. Michael B. Allen, *Eight Questions on Teacher Preparation: What Does the Research Say?* (Denver, CO: Education Commission of the States, 2003).

22. For instance, a 2000 study by Public Agenda found that one of the two main reasons that college graduates opted for a field other than teaching was that they didn't want to have to return to school to take education courses. See Steve Farkas, Jean Johnson, and Anthony Foleno, *A Sense of Calling: Who Teaches and Why* (New York: Public Agenda, 2000).

23. Jay Mathews, "How Urban Schools Keep Good Teachers at Bay," *Washington Post*, October 28, 2003, p. A12.

24. Jessica Levin and Meredith Quinn, *Missed Opportunities: How We Keep High-Quality Teachers Out of Urban Classrooms* (New York: New Teacher Project, 2003).

25. Edward Liu, "New Teachers' Experiences of Hiring: Preliminary Findings from a Four-State Study." Paper presented at the annual meeting of the American Educational Research Association, April 2003, Chicago, p. 19.

26. Ibid, p. 20.

27. Al Gore, *Reinventing Human Resource Management, an Accompanying Report of the National Performance Review* (Washington, D.C.: Office of the Vice President, 1993), p. 7.

28. Levin, *Missed Opportunities*.

29. Mathews, "How Urban Schools," p. A12.

30. Jay Mathews, "Pursuing Happiness, Through Hard Work," *Washington Post*, October 14, 2003, p. A13.

31. Paul J. Phillips, President of the Quincy Education Association in Quincy, MA in a letter to *Education Week*, "To Teachers, Pay Is Not a Competitive Concept," *Education Week*, October 15, 2003, p. 39.

32. Lynette Tanaka, "Editorial," *NEA Today*, May 1996, p. 31.

33. Howard Nelson, oral remarks at American Enterprise Institute forum entitled "Are Teachers Paid Too Little . . . or Too Much?" May 20, 2003.

34. Al Shanker quoted in Kati Haycock, "The Elephant in the Living Room." Paper prepared for Brookings Papers on Education Conference "The Teachers We Need" held at the Brookings Institution, Washington, D.C., May 21–22, 2003, p. 27.

35. Steve Farkas, Jean Johnson, and Ann Duffett, *Stand by Me: What Teachers Really Think about Unions, Merit Pay and Other Professional Matters* (New York: Public Agenda, 2003), p. 24.

36. See Caroline Hoxby, "Changing the Profession," *Education Matters* 1, no. 1 (Spring 2001): 57–63.

37. Eric A. Hanushek, John F. Kain, and Steven G. Rivkin, "The Revolving Door," *Education Next* 4, no. 1 (2004): 76–82.

38. Michael Podgursky, *The Single Salary Schedule for Teachers in K-12 Public Schools* (Houston, TX: Center for Reform of School Systems, 2002).

39. "Perceived Difficulty of Hiring Qualified Teachers in Various Study Areas (2001)," *Education at a Glance: OECD Indicators, 2003*, Table D7.3, p. 402.

40. Michael Podgursky, "Personnel Policy in Traditional Public, Charter, and Private Schools," *NCSC Review* 1, no. 1 (2003): 10–13.

41. Lynn Olson, "The Great Divide," *Education Week Quality Counts 2003*, January 9, 2003, p. 10.

42. Farkas, *Stand By Me*, p. 24.

43. Ibid, p. 25.

44. See Bryan Hassel, *Better Pay for Better Teaching* (Washington, D.C.: Progressive Policy Institute, 2002).

45. Russell Miller quoted in Steve Bates, "(Top) Pay for (Best) Performance," *HR Magazine* 48, no. 1 (January 2003): 30–38, p. 37.

46. National Commission on the Public Service, *Urgent Business for America: Revitalizing the Federal Government for the Twenty-First Century* (Washington, D.C.: National Commission on the Public Service, 2003). Available at http://www.brook.edu/gs/cps/volcker/reportfinal.pdf.

47. See Allan Odden, Eileen Kellor, Herbert Heneman, and Anthony Milanowski, *School Based Performance Award Programs: Design and Administration Issues Synthesized from Eight Programs* (Madison, WI: Consortium for Policy Research in Education, 1999). Also see Bradford R. White and Herbert G. Heneman III, *A Case Study of Proposition 301 and Performance-Based Pay in Arizona* (Madison, WI: Consortium for Policy Research in Education, 2002). Both available at http://www.wcer.wisc.edu/cpre/papers.

48. Eric Hanushek and others, *Making Schools Work: Improving Performance and Controlling Costs* (Washington, D.C.: Brookings Institution Press, 1994). For instance, Palm Beach County offered $10,000 to veteran teachers who would transfer to low-performing schools, and fewer than ten of the ninety targeted teachers moved. To be effective, inducements intended to get teachers to leave familiar, comfortable environments for low-performing schools need to be large,

sustained, part of a coherent package, and augmented by commonsense reforms that makes it easier for every school to replicate the focus and collegial culture of high-performing schools.

49. President of the Wilson Group Consultants quoted in Bates, "(Top) Pay," p. 32.
50. Robert Heneman quoted in Bates, "(Top) Pay," p. 32.
51. Julie Blair, "New Pension Plans Provide Educators with Options, Risks," *Education Week*, April 3, 2002, p. 1.
52. Sandra Ruppert, *Improving Pension Portability for K-12 Teachers* (Denver, CO: State Higher Education Executive Officers, 2001).
53. U.S. Department of Labor (Pension and Welfare Benefits Administration).
54. Steve Farkas, Jean Johnson, and Ann Duffett, *Rolling Up Their Sleeves: Superintendents and Principals Talk About What's Needed to Fix Public Schools* (Washington, D.C.: Public Agenda, 2003), p. 31.
55. Peter Brimelow, *The Worm in the Apple* (New York: HarperCollins, 2003), p. 41.
56. Farkas, *Rolling Up Their Sleeves*, p. 35.
57. Podgursky, "Personnel Policy in Traditional Public, Charter, and Private Schools," 10–13.
58. Frederick M. Hess, *Revolution at the Margins* (Washington, D.C.: Brookings Institution Press, 2002), p. 81.
59. Robin Wilson, "Contracts Replace the Tenure Track for a Growing Number of Professors," *Chronicle of Higher Education*, June 12, 1998, p. A12.
60. Farkas, *Stand by Me*, p. 21.
61. Ibid.
62. Ibid, p. 240.
63. Ibid, p. 21.
64. Ibid.
65. National Commission on Teaching and America's Future, *No Dream Denied: A Pledge to America's Children* (New York: National Commission on Teaching and America's Future, 2003).
66. Jack Welch, *Jack: Straight from the Gut* (New York: Warner Books, 2001), p. 158.
67. Farkas, *Rolling Up Their Sleeves*, p. 21.
68. Farkas, *Rolling Up Their Sleeves*, p. 16.
69. Linda Darling-Hammond, "The Challenge of Staffing Our Schools," *Educational Leadership* 58, no. 8 (May 2001): 12–17, p. 16.
70. Dan Goldhaber, David Perry, and Emily Anthony, *NBPTS Certification: Who Applies and What Factors Are Associated With Success?* (Washington, D.C.: Urban Institute Press, 2003).
71. James Nehring, "Certifiably Strange," *Teacher Magazine* 13, no. 1 (August 2001): 49–51.
72. Goldhaber, *NBPTS Certification*.
73. For a systematic and scholarly indictment of the NBPTS's standards and the manner in which they are implemented, see Danielle Dunne Wilcox, "The National Board for Professional Teaching Standards: Can It Live Up to Its

Promise?" in *Better Teachers, Better Schools*, ed. Marci Kanstoroom and Chester E. Finn (Washington, D.C.: Thomas B. Fordham Foundation, 1999). For evidence on the fact that NBPTS teachers don't perform any better than others, see Michael Podgursky, "Defrocking the National Board," *Education Matters* 1, no. 2 (Summer 2001): 79–82.

74. Podgursky, "Personnel Policy in Traditional Public, Charter, and Private Schools," 10–13.

CHAPTER 5

1. See Jeff Archer, "Budget Errors Leave Schools Feeling Pinch," *Education Week*, January 8, 2003, pp. 1, 11. Also see Meredith May and Seth Rosenfeld, "Bankrupt Dreams," *San Francisco Chronicle*, February 9, 2003, p. A1. Also see Philip Matier and Andrew Ross, "Chaconas' $389,000 Farewell Gift," *The San Francisco Chronicle*, June 4, 2003, p. A19.

2. Justin Blum, "D.C. School Payroll Far Exceeds Its Budget," *Washington Post*, March 26, 2003, p. B1.

3. Liz Bowie and Tanika White, "710 City School Employees Get Notice of Jan. 1 Layoffs," *Baltimore Sun*, November 26, 2003, p. A1.

4. Karla Scoon Reid, "Budget Woes Forcing Districts to Close Schools," *Education Week*, April 16, 2003, p. 5.

5. Ibid.

6. Steve Farkas, Jean Johnson, and Ann Duffett, *Rolling Up Their Sleeves: Superintendents and Principals Talk About What's Needed to Fix Public Schools* (Washington, D.C.: Public Agenda, 2003), p. 38.

7. Jon Fullerton, "Mounting Debt," *Education Next* 4, no. 1 (2004): 11–19.

8. Frederick M. Hess, *School Boards at the Dawn of the Twenty-first Century: Conditions and Challenges of District Governance* (Alexandria, VA: National School Boards Association, 2002).

9. Howard Fuller, with Christine Campbell, Mary Beth Celio, James Harvey, John Immerwahr, and Abigail Winger, *An Impossible Job? The View from the Urban Superintendent's Chair* (Seattle, WA: Center on Reinventing Public Education, 2003).

10. Paul T. Hill, *School Boards: Focus on School Performance, Not Money and Patronage* (Washington, D.C.: Progressive Policy Institute Press, 2003).

11. Susan M. Gates, Jeanne S. Ringel, and Lucrecia Santibanez, *Who Is Leading Our Schools? An Overview of Administrators and Their Careers* (Santa Monica, CA: RAND Corporation, 2003).

12. Bradley Portin, Paul Schneider, Michael DeArmond, and Lauren Gudlach, *Making Sense of Leading Schools: A Study of the School Principalship* (Seattle, WA: Center on Reinventing Public Education, 2003).

13. Marc S. Tucker and Judy B. Codding, "Preparing Principals in the Age of Accountability," in *The Principal Challenge*, ed. Marc S. Tucker and Judy B.

Codding (San Francisco: Jossey-Bass, 2002), p. 5. A revealing example on the question of what preoccupies administrators: A quick check of the NASSP e-mail exchange for principals on September 12, 2002 (the day after the first anniversary of the September 11, 2001, terrorist attacks on the World Trade Center towers) found that the leading topic of discussion was "tardy and parking policies."

14. Diana G. Pounder and Randall J. Merrill, "Job Desirability of the High School Principalship: A Job Choice Theory Perspective," *Education Administration Quarterly* 37, no. 1 (2001): 27–57.

15. Farkas, *Rolling Up Their Sleeves*, p. 38.

16. Jeff Archer, "Private Managers Stir Up St. Louis Schools," *Education Week,* September 3, 2003, p. 1.

17. Jean Johnson and Ann Duffett, *"I'm Calling My Lawyer": How Litigation, Due Process and Other Regulatory Requirements Are Affecting Public Education* (New York: Public Agenda, 2003), p. 11.

18. Marc Fisher, "Pass/Fail," *Washington Post Magazine*, April 6, 2003, p. 44.

19. Johnson, *"I'm Calling My Lawyer,"* p. 8.

20. Farkas, *Rolling Up Their Sleeves*, p. 40.

21. Ibid., p. 39.

22. Steve Farkas, Jean Johnson, and Ann Duffett, *Trying to Stay Ahead of the Game: Superintendents and Principals Talk about School Leadership* (Washington, D.C.: Public Agenda, 2001).

23. Paul Houston, "Superintendents for the 21st Century: It's Not Just a Job, It's a Calling," *Phi Delta Kappan* 82, no. 6 (2001): 428–433.

24. In 1999–2000, 34.1 percent of the nation's principals had been a coach or athletic director. See National Center for Education Statistics, *Schools and Staffing Survey 1999–2000, Public School Principal Survey* (Washington, D.C.: U.S. Department of Education).

25. Figures provided courtesy of the Broad Foundation, KIPP, and New Leaders for New Schools.

26. Thomas Sergiovanni, *Leadership for the Schoolhouse* (San Francisco: Jossey-Bass, 1996), p. xiv.

27. See Frederick M. Hess, *A License to Lead* (Washington, D.C.: Progressive Policy Institute Press, 2003).

28. See Tucker and Codding, "Preparing Principals," p. 13.

29. Vicki N. Petzko, Donald C. Clark, Jerry W. Valentine, Donald G. Hackmann, John R. Nori, and Stephen E. Lucas, "Leaders and Leadership in Middle Level Schools," *NASSP Bulletin* 86, no. 631 (June 2002): 3–15.

30. James W. Guthrie and Ted Sanders, "Who will lead the public schools?" *The New York Times*, January 7, 2001, pp. A4, 46.

31. For practical guidance in assessing educational leaders, see Douglas B. Reeves, *Assessing Educational Leaders: Evaluating Performance for Improved Individual and Organizational Results* (Thousand Oaks, CA: Corwin Press, 2003).

32. For a good discussion of how organizations can approach the need for new measures of performance, see chapter 4, "Inventing New Measures," in Marc J. Epstein and Bill Birchard, *Counting What Counts: Turning Corporate Accountability to Competitive Advantage* (Reading, MA: Perseus Books, 1999).

33. Alicia R. Williams, "Principals' Salaries, 2002–03," *NAESP* 82, no. 5 (2003): 42–44. And Educational Research Service, *Salaries and Wages Paid Professional and Support Personnel in Public Schools, 2002–2003* (Arlington, VA: Educational Research Service, 2003).

34. Jeff Archer, "Challenges Will Help Decide Principals' Pay," *Education Week*, March 26, 2003, p. 3.

35. Fullerton, "Mounting Debt," 11–19.

36. Farkas, *Rolling Up Their Sleeves*, p. 32.

37. The groups included the American Association of School Administrators, National Association of Secondary School Principals, and the National Association of Elementary School Principals.

38. Kate Beem, "Testing Superintendents," *School Administrator*, Web Edition, February 2002.

39. Education Testing Service, *The School Leadership Series Tests at a Glance*. Preparation materials available online at ftp://ftp.ets.org/pub/tandl/SLSTAAG. pdf, p. 14. As even Martha McCarthy, Chancellor Professor of education leadership at Indiana University and a staunch defender of education administration programs and licensure, has noted, "It is difficult to envision that responding to a set of vignettes—no matter how skillfully crafted—can confirm that administrative licensure candidates exhibit the desired skills, knowledge, and values for effective school leaders." Martha McCarthy, "Challenges Facing Education Leadership Programs: Our Future is Now," *Newsletter of the Teaching in Education Administration Special Interest Group of the American Education Research Association* 8, no. 1 (2001): 1.

40. The group included the usual vested players, including the American Association of Colleges for Teacher Education, the Association for Supervision and Curriculum Development, the American Association of School Administration, the University Council for Educational Administration, the National Association of School Boards, and the National Council of Professors of Education Administration.

41. For a discussion of how this has played out in the case of teacher preparation, see Sandra Vergari and Frederick M. Hess, "A Vigilant Sentry?: The National Council for Accreditation of Teacher Education," *Education Next* 2, no. 3 (2002): 48–57.

42. Rakesh Khurana, *Searching for a Corporate Savior: The Irrational Quest for Charismatic CEOs* (Princeton, NJ: Princeton University Press, 2002).

CHAPTER 6

1. David Osborne and Ted Gaebler, *Reinventing Government: How the Entrepreneurial Spirit Is Transforming the Public Sector* (New York: Plume, 1993), p. 146.

2. Michael Lewis, *Moneyball: The Art of Winning an Unfair Game* (New York: W.W. Norton, 2003).

3. Jim Collins, *Good to Great: Why Some Companies Make the Leap... and Others Don't* (New York: HarperCollins, 2001).

4. Lisa A. Petrides and Thad R. Nodine, *Knowledge Management in Education: Defining the Landscape* (Half Moon Bay, CA: Institute for the Study of Knowledge Management in Education, 2003), p. 11.

5. Del Jones and Barbara Hansen, "Companies Do More with Less," *USA Today*, August 13, 2003, B1.

6. Lydia G. Segal, *Battling Corruption in America's Public Schools* (Boston, MA: Northeastern University Press, 2004).

7. Henry Giroux, "Schools for Sale," in *Education, Inc.: Turning Learning into a Business*, ed. Alfie Kohn and Patrick Shannon (Portsmouth, NH: Heinemann, 2001), p. 106.

8. See chapter 2 in William G. Ouchi, *Making Schools Work: A Revolutionary Plan to Get Your Children the Education They Need* (New York: Simon & Schuster, 2003).

9. James P. Womack, Daniel T. Jones, and Daniel Roos, *The Machine that Changed the World: The Story of Lean Production* (New York: Harper Perennial, 1991), p. 99.

10. Ouchi, *Making Schools Work*, p. 15.

11. Quoted in Ouchi, *Making Schools Work*, p. 35.

12. David C. Anderson, "Crime Control by the Numbers," *Ford Foundation Report* (Winter 2001). See also William K. Rashbaum, "Crime-Fighting by Computer: Scope Widens," *New York Times*, March 24, 2002, p. A43.

13. Raymond Dussault, "Maps and Management: Comstat Evolves," *Government Technology*, April 2000.

14. John Marzulli, "Cops Tackle Road Perils: Computer Helping to Identify Hotspots," *New York Times*, July 19, 1998, p. 4.

15. Elliott Levine, "The Data Trek," *American School Board Journal* 190, no. 9 (2003): 46–48.

16. Quoted in Wendy Togneri and Stephen E. Anderson, *Beyond Islands of Excellence: What Districts Can Do to Improve Instruction and Achievement in all Schools* (Washington, D.C.: Learning First Alliance, 2003), p. 39.

17. Lynn Olson, "Schools Discovering Riches in Data," *Education Week*, June 12, 2002, p. 1.

18. Eric A. Hanushek, *Making Schools Work* (Washington, D.C.: Brookings Institution Press, 1994), p. 113.

19. Nelson D. Schwartz, "Bent but Unbowed," *Fortune*, July 22, 2002, p. 118.

20. Brett Nelson, "An All-New Cast," *Forbes*, April 16, 2001, p. 318.

21. Peter Marsh, "Nucor Finally Comes in from the Cold," *Financial Times (London ed.)*, July 10, 2002, p. 27.

22. Steve Overbeck, "Mini-Mills, Motivated Workers Put Nucor Atop the Steel Heap," *Salt Lake Tribune*, February 21, 1999, p. E1.

23. Schwartz, "Bent but Unbowed," p. 118.

24. Marianne D. Hurst, "California District Awarded Urban Education Prize," *Education Week*, October 1, 2003, p. 5.

25. Togneri, "Beyond Islands of Excellence."

26. Stacy Mitchell, "Jack and the Giant School," *New Rules Journal* 2, no. 1 (Summer 2000).

27. John M. Berry, "Efficiency of U.S. Workers Up Sharply," *Washington Post*, February 7, 2003, p. E1.

28. Stephen Barr, "As Automation Eliminates Jobs, Postal Service Wants to Offer Early Retirement," *Washington Post*, January 30, 2003, p. B2.

29. National Center for Education Statistics, *Digest of Education Statistics, 2001* (Washington, D.C.: U.S. Department of Education, 2002), Table 82.

30. Department of Defense figures were taken from *Active Duty Military Personnel by Rank/Grade* (Washington, D.C.: U.S. Department of Defense, September 30, 2003). Attorney figures were taken from the American Bar Association, *National Lawyer Population by State* (Washington, D.C.: American Bar Association, 2003).

31. Martin R. West and Ludger Woessmann, "Crowd Control," *Education Next* 3, no. 3 (2003): 56–62, p. 62.

32. North Central Regional Educational Laboratory, *Using What We Know: A Review of the Research on Implementing Class-Size Reduction Initiatives for State and Local Policymakers*, ed. Sabrina W. M. Laine and James G. Ward (Oak Brook, IL: North Central Regional Educational Laboratory, 2000). Report available at http://www.ncrel.org/policy/pubs/pdfs/weknow.pdf.

33. Alan Richard, "Rural Routes," *Education Week*, October 8, 2003, p. 21.

34. *Chronicle of Higher Education* online, September 19, 2003, p. A30.

35. Austin superintendent quoted in Richard J. Murnane and Frank Levy, "Evidence from Fifteen Schools in Austin, Texas," in *Does Money Matter? The Effect of School Resources on Student Achievement and Adult Success*, ed. Gary Burtless (Washington, D.C.: Brookings Institution Press, 1996), pp. 93–96, p. 94.

36. William G. Ouchi, "Academic Freedom," *Education Next* 4, no. 1 (2004): 21–25.

37. Jay Mathews, "Rule Aids Students but Drains Some Schools," *Washington Post*, June 10, 2003, p. A8.

38. Cuban, *Oversold and Underused*.

39. Susan E. Ansell and Jennifer Park, "Tracking Tech Trends," *Education Week*, May 8, 2003: 43–49, p. 45.

40. Caroline Hoxby, "What Has Changed and What Has Not," in *Our Schools and Our Futures*, ed. Paul E. Peterson (Palo Alto, CA: Hoover Press, 2003).

41. Todd Oppenheimer, *The Flickering Mind* (New York: Random House, 2003).

42. Diane Curtis, "A Computer for Every Lap," *Edutopia* (Spring 2003): 4–5.

43. For good accounts of the disappointing results of education technology to date, see Oppenheimer, *The Flickering Mind*. Also see Larry Cuban, *Oversold and Underused: Computers in the Classroom* (Cambridge, MA: Harvard University Press, 2003).

44. Associated Press, "Strapped School Districts Contracting Out for Services," July 11, 2003. Accessed on July 18, 2003, at CNN.com/Education.

45. William D. Eggers, *Overcoming Obstacles to Technology-Enabled Transformation* (Cambridge, MA: Institute for Government Innovation at John F. Kennedy School of Government, 2003), p. 16.

CHAPTER 7

1. Richard Rothstein, *The Way We Were? The Myths and Realities of America's Student Achievement* (New York: Century Foundation Press, 1998), p. 111.

2. Jonathan Kozol, *Savage Inequalities: Children in America's Schools* (New York: Crown Publishers, 1991), p. 233.

3. Marilyn Cochran-Smith, "Sometimes It's Not About the Money," *Journal of Teacher Education* 54, no. 5 (2003): 371–375, pp. 372–373.

4. Sonia Nieto, *What Keeps Teachers Going?* (New York: Teachers College Press, 2003), p. 5.

5. David Tyack and Larry Cuban, *Tinkering Toward Utopia: A Century of Public School Reform* (Cambridge, MA: Harvard University Press, 1995). Also see Diane Ravitch, *Left Back: A Century of Battles Over School Reform* (New York: Touchstone Books, 2001).

6. Bret Schundler quoted in Peter Schrag, *Final Test: The Battle for Adequacy in America's Schools* (New York: New Press, 2003), p. 123.

7. Casey J. Lartigue, *School Choice in the District of Columbia* (Washington, D.C.: Cato Institute Press, 2003).

8. Californians for Justice, *First Things First: Why We Must Stop Punishing Students and Fix California's Schools* (Oakland, CA: Californians for Justice, 2003), p. 5.

9. Michael Apple in the foreword to Linda McNeil, *The Contradictions of School Reform: Educational Costs of Standardized Testing* (New York: Routledge, 2000), pp. xvi–xvii.

10. Clayton Christensen, *The Innovator's Dilemma: When New Technologies Cause Great Firms to Fail* (Boston: Harvard Business School Press, 1997). Also see Clayton Christensen and Michael Ravnor, *The Innovator's Solution: Creating and Sustaining Successful Growth* (Boston: Harvard Business School Press, 2003); Jim Collins, *Good to Great: Why Some Companies Make the Leap . . . and Others*

Don't (New York: HarperCollins, 2001); Jim Collins and Jerry I. Porras, *Built to Last: Successful Habits of Visionary Companies* (New York: HarperBusiness, 2002); Daniel Goleman, *Emotional Intelligence* (New York: Bantam, reprint edition 1997); and James Champy, *X-Engineering the Corporation: Reinventing Your Business in the Digital Age* (New York: Warner Books, 2003).

11. Abigail Thernstrom and Stephen Thernstrom, *No Excuses: Closing the Racial Gap in Learning* (New York: Simon and Schuster, 2003), p. 251.

12. Matthew Miller, "Rethinking and Relearning about How to Teach Teachers," *Orlando Sentinel*, June 25, 2000, p. G1.

13. Brendan Halpin, *Losing My Faculties* (New York: Villard, 2003), p. 6.

14. Deborah Meier, *The Power of Their Ideas* (Boston: Beacon Press, 1995), p. 23.

15. For the best overview of the small-schools movement and a portrayal of some outstanding small schools, see Thomas Toch, *High Schools on a Human Scale* (Boston: Beacon Press, 2003).

16. Robin Lake, "Marginal Impact," *Education Next* 3, no. 3 (2003): 83–86.

17. Bob Herbert, "In Search of Magic," op-ed, *New York Times*, March 21, 2002, p. A37.

18. Merele Miller, *Plain Speaking: An Oral Biography of Harry S. Truman* (New York: Berkley Publishing, 1973), p. 453.

19. Patricia Davenport and Gerald Anderson, *Closing the Achievement Gap: No Excuses* (Houston, TX: American Productivity and Quality Center, 2003), p. 19.

20. Alfie Kohn, "Introduction: The Five Hundred Pound Gorilla," in *Education Inc.: Turning Learning Into a Business*, ed. Alfie Kohn and Patrick Shannon (Portsmouth, NH: Heinemann, 2002), pp. 5–6.

21. Alex Molnar quoted in Caroline E. Mayer, "A Growing Market Strategy: Get 'Em While They're Young," *Washington Post*, June 3, 2003, p. A1.

22. Susan Ohanian, "Capitalism, Calculus, and Conscience," *Phi Delta Kappan* 84, no. 10 (June 2003): 736–747, p. 746.

23. Tony Wagner, *Making the Grade: Reinventing America's Schools* (New York: RoutledgeFalmer, 2002), p. 125.

24. Steven L. Strauss, "An Open Letter to Reid Lyon," *Educational Researcher* 30, no. 5 (June/July 2001): 26–33, p. 31.

25. Joint Center for Political and Economic Studies, *1998 National Opinion Poll: Education* (Washington, D.C.: Joint Center for Political and Economic Studies, 1998). Available at http://jointcenter.org/databank/NOP/reports/1999_educ_report.htm.

26. Black American's Political Action Committee, *2002 National Opinion Poll* (Washington, D.C.: Black American's Political Action Committee, 2002). Available at http://www.bampac.org/opinion_polls.asp.

Index